BEST NEWSPAPER WRITING 2001

WINNERS: THE AMERICAN SOCIETY OF NEWSPAPER EDITORS COMPETITION

Featuring
Community Service Photojournalism Award
and New Companion CD-ROM

EDITED BY KEITH WOODS

The Poynter Institute
and
Bonus Books, Inc.

03 02 01 00 99   5 4 3 2 1

International Standard Book Number: 1-56625-166-4
International Standard Serial Number: 0195-895X

The Poynter Institute for Media Studies
801 Third Street South
St. Petersburg, Florida 33701

Bonus Books, Inc.
160 East Illinois Street
Chicago, Illinois 60611

Book design and production by Billie M. Keirstead,
Director of Publications, The Poynter Institute

Cover illustration by Jeff Papa of Phillip Gary Design,
St. Petersburg, Florida.

Photos for the cover illustration were provided by the Associated
Press and are used with permission. Photo credits: AP photographers
Mary Ann Chastain (Confederate flag), stringer Alan Diaz (Elián
González), Srdjan Ilic (Yugoslavia), Beth A. Keiser (Diallo protest),
John Riley (Navy bombing protest), and stringer Jeff Zelevinsky
(Seton Hall dormitory fire). Photos in the Community Service Pho-
tojournalism section were provided by the photographers. Photos of
winners and finalists were provided by their news organizations.

Printed in the United States of America

For Helen Malin,
who first stoked the creative embers
of the writer burning inside.

Looking for a pro
in convergence

As a kid reporter-photographer for my hometown Ohio paper, I weighed 97 pounds and carried a third as much in gear—a Crown Graphic camera with a huge flash attachment, a battery not much smaller than the one in your Buick, a bag full of 4-by-5 film holders, and a steno pad to take notes.

I was convergence. Forty-five years ago.

It was a kick to be reporter and photographer, and affirming. With all that professional camera gear, no one could dismiss easily the claim of a high school kid to be a real newspaper employee. At nearby Lake Erie beaches, young women would pose "for the paper" and would provide names and phone numbers "for the captions." And there was one memorable night when, through exceedingly dumb luck, by climbing to the top of a grain elevator next to a soybean processing factory that was on fire, I got a spectacular photo that *The Painesville Telegraph* played across all eight columns of Page One.

My career as a photojournalist was brief. When I landed a job at a metro newspaper after college, they wouldn't let me take photos anymore; the Newspaper Guild would've raised a stink. Chances are, the editors understood that while I might have had a chance to become a writer, I never was likely to excel as a shooter. Over time, I came to value this specialization and to understand that the roles were sufficiently different, and it would be exceptional to be good at both.

I'm tickled to have the chance in this edition of *Best Newspaper Writing* to pay homage to real photojournalists, to congratulate the American Society of Newspaper Editors and particularly outgoing president Rich Oppel for calling attention to the essential link between photojournalism and community, and to say a word or two about the latest fad in corporate journalism—convergence.

The name of this book is *Best Newspaper Writing*. We realize the inclusion of photographs challenges the title.

Keith Woods, the new editor of these volumes, is managing our internal debate about future alternative titles. Should it be *Best Newspaper Journalism*? *Best Newspaper Storytelling*? *Best Newspaper Writing with Mighty Fine Photography*? Some suggestions, as we fine wordsmiths say, suck. We've settled, for now, on the slightly gawky approach of a subtitle on this edition's cover. It tells you that remarkable photojournalism is now being honored.

The subtitle doesn't necessarily tell you what some of us have concluded: that fine photojournalism *is* writing; that it is a visual way to tell a story. I've had the pleasure of working over the years with shooters who conceived their work not as illustrative but as investigative. The late George Tames of *The New York Times* was one of the best reporters in Washington, often uncovering news he alone witnessed by being in the room when it happened. At *The Philadelphia Inquirer*, it was Ron Tarver, the photographer, not David Zucchino, the reporter, who initiated their brilliant series showing how everyday lives of decent families were diminished by the drug bazaar all around them in a North Philly neighborhood called "The Badlands." And Ron's colleague, April Saul, consistently produces photo essays that persuasively document systemic problems in our society.

Poynter is honored, in short, to join ASNE in recognizing that memorable photojournalism belongs in a volume of admirable writing, especially so in a period in which the push toward greater profit in newspaper corporations threatens to dilute journalism in the name of efficiency.

A few years ago, news companies avidly underwent "re-engineering." Then they fostered "agents of change." For a time, the slogan was "synergy." Now it is "convergence." Like the preceding movements, the incentive behind convergence is economic—to maximize profit by consolidating duties, staffs, even whole news organizations such as AOL/Time-Warner/CNN/Turner/Baby Blues. There are some places where this is being done with an eye toward enhancing the journalism, toward telling stories more creatively across varied media, toward giving audiences the same high quality news coverage by broadcast, cable, computer, or print. These places are few. More evident are those in which convergence amounts to looking for new ways to reduce the most costly component of newsgathering: the people who do this work.

There are good reasons to explore convergence. I personally doubt that they include combining into one the roles of broadcaster, still photographer, reporter, writer, and editor. To the American newspaper editors who saw virtue in celebrating photography and writing, and who thus encouraged continued specialization in these separate aspects of fine storytelling, thanks. So far as *Best Newspaper Writing 2001* is concerned, convergence means honoring both forms in one volume.

Cheers,
Jim Naughton, President
The Poynter Institute

* * *

The role of an awards judge is an opportunity to be affirmed by the quality of journalism being performed outside our customary glimpse and a daunting obligation to honor work that both reflects and encourages excellence. Here are the members of the ASNE Writing Awards Committee who selected the 2001 honorees:

Andrew N. Alexander, Cox Newspapers, Washington
Richard Aregood, *The Star-Ledger*, Newark, N.J.
Martin Baron, *The Miami Herald*
Leonard Downie Jr., *The Washington Post*
G. Maria Henson, *Austin American-Statesman*
Clark Hoyt, Knight Ridder, Washington
David A. Laventhol, *Columbia Journalism Review*
Joseph Lelyveld, *The New York Times*
Walker Lundy, *St. Paul Pioneer Press*
Gregory L. Moore, *The Boston Globe*
Richard A. Oppel, *Austin American-Statesman*
Michael Parks, University of Southern California,
     Los Angeles
Robert Rivard, *San Antonio Express-News*
Sandra Mims Rowe, *The Oregonian*, Portland
Edward L. Seaton, *The Manhattan* (Kansas) *Mercury*
Cynthia A. Tucker, *The Atlanta Constitution*
N. Don Wycliff, *Chicago Tribune*

The photojournalism awards were chosen by the committee on recommendations from this panel:

Craig Gemoules, *The Tampa Tribune*
Kenny Irby, *The Poynter Institute*
Carolyn Lee, *The New York Times*
Zach Ryall, *Austin American-Statesman*
Cynthia Tucker, *The Atlanta Constitution*
N. Don Wycliff, *Chicago Tribune*

Acknowledgments

The amazing sequence of events that so quickly brought together the work, reflections, and teaching wisdom of the journalists in this book could not have been done so well or so quickly without the help and guidance of a number of people. First in that sequence was the American Society of Newspaper Editors, led by president Rich Oppel of the *Austin American-Statesman*, executive director Scott Bosley, and *The Atlanta Constitution*'s Cynthia Tucker, who chaired the writing awards committee. The committee chose the winners and finalists in two intense days of judging.

Everything that happened from there was guided by Poynter's publications director, Billie M. Keirstead, whose experience putting together 20 of the 22 previous editions of *Best Newspaper Writing* made the editing of this book seem much easier than it was. I also had the assistance and moral support of three previous editors of these volumes—Roy Peter Clark, Karen Dunlap, and Christopher Scanlan, along with faculty colleagues Aly Colón and Kenny Irby. They interviewed winners and wrote the Writers' and Photographers' Workshop sections at the end of each collection of stories. David Shedden assembled the bibliography that is an important regular feature.

Helping to edit their work was copy editor Vicki Krueger and proofreaders Patty Cox and Kathleen Tobin. Design intern Jen Ogborn and producer/designer Larry Larsen of Poynter's publications department put together the first CD-ROM to accompany a book in this series. Program assistant Jeannie Nissenbaum provided administrative assistance. Joyce Barrett, Priscilla Ely, and Marty Gregor of the Poynter staff also assisted in the book's production.

All of this is done to celebrate the wonderful stories and photos, insightful interviews, and thoughtful "Lessons Learned" provided by the journalists honored here. Their compelling work and generous support of this book's goals bring honor to the Distinguished Writing Awards, the Jesse Laventhol Prizes, and the Community Service Photojournalism Award.

Contents

Writers discover the difference that unites

Grocer An Van Do died violently in the swell of a deadly New Orleans crime wave in 1988. He was a Vietnamese immigrant whose sacrifice and tireless work only deepened the tragedy in a city littered with dead innocents. When he was gunned down in his modest Uptown store, I was sent to write his story.

The story I told focused on Do's life as a husband and provider. It was about what his pastor called "The Vietnamese Way." It was about his family's faith and his 15-year-old son's burden of early manhood. It was about a poor neighborhood in crisis. It was about 1,000 words long, and it was riddled with holes.

They weren't the sort of omissions easily caught, even by good editors. The names and times and dates were all there, and all the facts checked out. What was missing was something deeper and less tangible: understanding. The day I walked into Do's living room was the first time I'd talked to someone Vietnamese since saying hello to an assembly-line seamstress while working in a clothing factory a decade earlier.

I didn't know enough about the "Vietnamese Way" to ask a good question. I didn't know much about the neighborhood beyond what you get from a police report. And it was a bad time to play catch-up. So I stood there, marveling at the Catholic altar Do's family constructed in his honor, left to rely too heavily upon the words of a teen-ager struggling to translate his family's grief.

I wish I had had this volume of *Best Newspaper Writing* to guide me then. Celebrated in these pages, along with stinging commentary, sharp deadline reporting, and provocative editorial writing, are outstanding examples of how journalists have climbed into the worlds of people markedly different from themselves and produced storytelling that rings of authenticity and understanding. In their work is a blueprint for covering the "other" in words and photographs.

Like all winning journalism, the stories between

these covers all make generous use of the tools of excellence. Leonard Pitts of *The Miami Herald* and Stephen Henderson of the Baltimore *Sun* show how passion and creativity can enrich commentary and breathe rhetorical life into opinion columns and editorials. Steven Erlanger of *The New York Times* blends historical context with clean, simple sentences to state the case for why Slobodan Milosevic fell from power. The team at the Newark, N.J., *Star-Ledger* brought readers to the scene of a horrific college dormitory fire.

The Sacramento Bee's Stephen Magagnini used quotes and details with precision and purpose to tell the complex story of Hmong immigrants facing a cultural implosion. Pulitzer Prize-winner Tom Hallman Jr. of *The Oregonian* took readers on a roller-coaster ride with the narrative arc, surprising, enthralling, and rewarding them with the tale of a remarkable boy with an uncommon condition.

Pittsburgh Post-Gazette photojournalist John Beale, the first winner of the American Society of Newspaper Editors Community Service Photojournalism Award, captured the emotion, devotion, and earthly eccentricities of Pittsburgh's faith communities.

I'm sure that seeing their work and reading their thoughts would have made me use more active verbs, paint better scenes, choose stronger quotes, search for more meaningful details. Good writing can do that. I would also have been wary of the tendency reporters have to write in sweeping generalities about foreign countries, so I would have learned something about Do's village—the name, for example.

Writing with excellence about people who are different, however that difference is defined, demands precisely the same skills as all good writing. What's different is that reporters have to work against the unconscious, unexamined, and rationalized stereotypes that masquerade as knowledge. It requires that they rise above fears of human difference so they can tell a story that is not merely voyeuristic, but unveils the universal truths within that difference.

Hallman had to look beyond the vascular deformity engulfing young Sam Lightner's face to find a story about teen-agers and fitting in. Beale had to see past the peculiarities of Amish farmers and orthodox Jews to show readers in Pittsburgh how belief in a higher power united them. Writing about a Hmong culture with traditions most Westerners would find strange, Magagnini still told the universal story of families, generation gaps, and the longing for a nobler past.

That would be one of the lessons I might have taken from this book 13 years ago: Talk about what makes people different, but put it in the context of what makes them the same. I imagine that when An Van Do's pastor talked about the "Vietnamese Way," I might have learned more about what he meant and how it related to the American Way.

There were a few other lessons for me here:

■ **Bring knowledge with you.** Spend time off deadline learning about the people in your community. Know as much about their history, customs, and beliefs as you can before you have to write about them. That way your reporting and writing are not at the mercy of those whose knowledge and points of view may be limited.

■ **Find guides.** John Beale moved around Pittsburgh's diverse faith community by going hand-to-hand, asking each person he met to introduce him to another. It's a time-honored journalistic technique rendered all the more important when the reporter crosses into an arena where people are suspicious of journalists. The pastor in my story was a good guide, connected as he was to the mostly Catholic Vietnamese community of eastern New Orleans.

■ **Go somewhere to listen.** Non-deadline finalist Charlie LeDuff of *The New York Times* found a street corner where Latino immigrants waited to be picked up for itinerant work assignments. From that "listening post," he was able to find stories that helped readers know about the lives of those men, their families, their homelands, and the people who would be their new countrymen.

■ **Beware of sweeping characterizations.** They are often clichés, too general to be totally true, and reliant upon shared stereotypes. The winning work in this book keeps characterizations specific and reflects the deep knowledge of the writers. In my story, I used the words "crime-ridden" and "desperation" to describe the neighborhood surrounding Do's grocery store. I had not walked those streets nearly enough to know what I was talking about.

■ **Write *from* the people, not *about* them.** Strive to tell your story the way your subject might tell it. Hallman writes about Sam Lightner, in many ways, from the perspective of a 14-year-old boy. Steve Magagnini understood Hmong values well enough to write in an authoritative, matter-of-fact way. He treats the unique Hmong traditions with the same weight as Hmong might treat them, rising above the weird-culture treatment such groups often get from journalists.

Travel through the stories in this book and you'll find those lessons and countless more. The ideas and tips are timeless, simple, and they work whether you're covering the fall of a despot, the implosion of a culture, or the death of a New Orleans grocer. Having seen their work and heard their stories, I know I could have made one story better 13 years ago. Use this book to produce a better story today.

ABOUT THIS BOOK

Through recorded conversations and e-mails, members of the Poynter faculty produced the interviews that follow the stories honored in this book. For the sake of clarity, flow, and brevity, some of the answers are compressed and some questions have been edited or added.

Keith Woods
June 2001

Best Newspaper Writing 2001

Tom Hallman Jr.
Non-Deadline Writing

Tom Hallman Jr. is a senior reporter for *The Oregonian* where he specializes in narrative feature stories. He began his journalism career there as a copy boy "ripping the wire for the copy desk, making the lunch run for the city desk editors, and changing ribbons on electric IBM typewriters." A Portland native, he graduated from Drake University in 1977. He worked as a copy editor for Hearst Magazines Special Publications in New York City, and as a reporter at *The Hermiston Herald* in Hermiston, Ore., and the *Tri-City Herald* in Kennewick, Wash., before returning to *The Oregonian* in 1980.

In Portland, he spent a decade as a crime reporter: the best possible beat, he says, for his brand of in-depth stories that explore and illuminate the human condition. Hallman's storytelling gifts have won numerous awards and acclaim from readers and his fellow writers. In addition to the Livingston Award, he has been a Pulitzer finalist once for beat reporting and twice for feature writing, an ASNE finalist for non-deadline reporting, and the ASNE's non-deadline winner in 1997. "The Boy Behind the Mask" took numerous awards for feature writing, including the Ernie Pyle Award for Human Interest Reporting, the Society of Professional Journalists' national feature writing award, and the Pulitzer Prize for feature writing.

Tom Hallman is one of the most thoughtful practitioners of the art and craft of the newspaper narrative. "The Boy Behind the Mask," his stunning four-part series about the pivotal moments in the life of a boy with a deformed face, puts his storytelling talents on full display. It reflects his passion for immersion reporting that is tenacious yet empathetic, his dedication to critical and creative thinking about everything from theme and structure to the tiniest detail, and his belief in the benefits of a reporter-editor relationship based on mutual respect for each other and the story. With dramatic scenes as his building blocks, he constructs a narrative that is a tale of medical suspense, and a moving character study of a remarkable boy and the constellation of family and friends who care for him.

—Christopher Scanlan

The boy behind the mask: Pt. 1

SEPTEMBER 30, 2000

At a certain age, nothing is more important than fitting in.

The boy sits on the living room sofa, lost in his thoughts and stroking the family cat with his fragile hands. His younger brother and sister sit on the floor, chattering and playing cards. But Sam is overcome by an urge to be alone. He lifts the cat off his lap, ignoring a plaintive meow, and silently stands, tottering unsteadily as his thin frame rises in the afternoon light.

He threads his way toward the kitchen, where his mother bends over the sink, washing vegetables for supper. Most 14-year-old boys whirl through a room, slapping door jambs and dodging around furniture like imaginary halfbacks. But this boy, a 5-foot, 83-pound waif, has learned never to draw attention to himself. He moves like smoke.

He stops in the door frame leading to the kitchen and melts into the late-afternoon shadows.

He watches his mother, humming as she runs water over lettuce. The boy clears his throat and says he's not hungry. His mother sighs

---

How we wrote the story

To report "The Boy Behind the Mask," Tom Hallman Jr. spent hundreds of hours, over more than 10 months, poring over medical records, reading Lightner family journals, hanging out at the Lightner house, attending school with Sam, interviewing Sam's friends, and twice traveling across the country with the family. He saw virtually every important development with his own eyes and heard every key conversation with his own ears.

As a result, relatively few scenes in "The Boy Behind the Mask," are reconstructed, and those are the result of careful interviews with all key participants. Every such scene contains attribution to the memories of the participants.

No dialogue appears within quotation marks unless Hallman heard a conversation himself.

—Jack Hart
Managing Editor
The Oregonian

with worry and turns, not bothering to turn off the water or to dry her hands. The boy knows she's studying him, running her eyes over his bony arms and the way he wearily props himself against the door frame. She's been watching him like this since he left the hospital a few months before.

"I'm full," he says.

She bends her head toward him, about to speak. He cuts her off.

"Really, Mom. I'm full."

"OK, Sam," she says quietly.

The boy slips behind his mother and steps into a pool of light.

A huge mass of flesh balloons out from the left side of his face. His left ear, purple and misshapen, bulges from the side of his head. His chin juts forward. The main body of tissue, laced with blue veins, swells in a dome that runs from sideburn level to chin. The mass draws his left eye into a slit, warps his mouth into a small, inverted half moon. It looks as though someone has slapped three pounds of wet clay onto his face, where it clings, burying the boy inside.

But Sam, the boy behind the mask, peers out from the right eye. It is clear, perfectly formed and a deep, penetrating brown.

You find yourself instantly drawn into that eye, pulled past the deformity and into the world of a completely normal 14-year-old. It is a window into the world where Sam lives. You can imagine yourself on the other side of it. You can see yourself in that eye, the child you once were.

The third of Sam's face surrounding his normal eye reinforces the impression. His healthy, close-cropped hair is a luxuriant brown, shaped carefully in a style any serious young man might wear. It's trimmed neatly behind a delicate, well-formed ear. His right cheek glows with the blushing good health that the rest of his face has obscured.

The boy passes out of the kitchen, stepping into the staircase that leads to the second floor. A ragged burst of air escapes from the hole in his throat—a tracheotomy funnels air directly into his lungs, bypassing the swollen tissue that blocks the usual airways. He walks along the worn hallway and turns into his room, the one with the toy license plate on the door. It reads "Sam."

The Northeast Portland house, wood-framed with a wide front porch and fading cream-colored paint, is like thousands of others on Portland's gentrifying eastside. Real estate prices have soared, but the Lightners still need new carpets in every room and could use new appliances. Although she'd rather stay home with the children, Debbie Lightner works part time as a bank teller. The paycheck helps, but she really took the job for the health insurance.

From upstairs, Sam hears 12-year-old Emily and 9-year-old Nathan laughing. The kitchen, though, is silent. The boy figures his mother and father are talking about him and this night. For months Feb. 3, 2000, has been circled on the family calendar that hangs on a kitchen wall.

He grabs a small foam basketball and throws up an arcing shot that soars across the room and hits a poster tacked to the far wall.

His mother made the poster by assembling family photographs and then laminating them. In the middle is a questionnaire Sam filled out when he was 8. He had been asked to list his three wishes. He wanted $1 million and a dog. On the third line, he doodled three question marks—in those oblivious days of childhood, he couldn't think of anything else he needed.

Finally, his mother calls out. His teeth are brushed, his face washed. He runs his left hand through his brown hair, parting it to the right.

He must imagine what he looks like. There's no mirror to examine his face.

In this boy's room, there's never been a mirror.

* * *

"Ready for this, Sam?" asks David Lightner, a weathered jewelry designer who saves money by riding a motorcycle 25 miles to work. Sam nods his head and replies with a garbled sound, wheezing and breathless, the sound of an old man who has smoked too long and too hard.

"OK," his father replies. "Let's go."

His sister and brother watch from the window as Sam and his parents walk to a Honda Accord that has

140,000 hard miles on the odometer. The boy gets in the back seat, and the Honda backs down the driveway.

Just a few blocks from home, Sam senses someone looking at him. After a lifetime of stares, he can feel the glances.

The Accord is stopped at a light, waiting to turn west onto Northeast Sandy Boulevard, when a woman walking a poodle catches sight of him. She makes no pretense of being polite, of averting her eyes. When the light changes, the woman swivels her head as if watching a train leave a station.

Grant High School's open house attracts more than 1,500 students and parents. Even though they've come early, the Lightners must search for a parking place. Sam's father circles the streets until he finds one nearly 15 blocks from the school.

The family steps out onto the sidewalk and walks through the dark neighborhood. As Sam passes under a streetlight, a dark-green Range Rover full of teen-age boys turns onto the street. A kid wearing a baseball cap points at the boy. The car slows. The windows fill with faces, staring and pointing.

Sam walks on.

Soon, the streets fill with teen-agers on their way to Grant. Sam recognizes a girl who goes to his school, Gregory Heights Middle School. Sam has a secret crush on her. She has brown hair, wavy, and a smile that makes his hands sweat and his heart race when he sees her in class.

"Hi, Sam," she says.

He nods.

"Hi," he says.

The boy's parents fall behind, allowing their son and the girl to walk side by side. She does most of the talking.

He's spent a lifetime trying to make himself understood, and he's found alternatives to the words that are so hard for him to shape. He uses his good eye and hand gestures to get his point across.

Two blocks from Grant, kids jam the streets. The wavy-haired girl subtly, discreetly, falls behind. When the boy slows to match her step, she hurries ahead. Sam lets her go and walks alone.

Grant, a great rectangular block of brick, looms in the distance. Every light in the place is on. Tonight, there are no shadows.

He arrives at the north door and stands on the steps, looking in through the windowpanes. Clusters of girls hug and laugh. Boys huddle under a sign announcing a basketball game.

Sam grabs the door handle, hesitates for the briefest of moments and pulls the door open. He steps inside.

He walks into noise and laughter and chaos, into the urgency that is all about being 14 years old.

Into a place where nothing is worse than being different.

* * *

Years later she still wonders if it was something she missed, some sign that things weren't right. But it wasn't until her seventh month that Debbie Lightner learned something had gone terribly awry.

She struggled to sit up on the examination table. The baby, her doctor said, was larger than it should be. Debbie watched him wheel up a machine to measure the fetus. She felt his hands on her stomach.

Something's wrong, the doctor said again.

He told Debbie he would call ahead to the hospital and schedule an ultrasound. He laughed and told Debbie he just wanted to be sure she wasn't having twins.

The next morning, at the ultrasound lab, the technician got right to work.

He immediately ruled out twins.

Then, a few minutes into the test, the technician fell silent. He repeatedly pressed a button to take pictures of the images on the monitor. After 30 minutes, he turned off the machine, left the room and returned with his boss. The two studied the photographs.

They led the Lightners down the hall to a prenatal specialist. Their unborn child, he said, appeared to have a birth defect. The ultrasound indicated that the child's brain was floating outside the body.

He had to be blunt. This child will die.

Some parents, he said, would choose to terminate.

No, Debbie remembers telling him. She and her husband were adamant that they would not kill this baby.

On Sunday, Oct. 6, 1985, six weeks before she was

due, Debbie went into labor at home. David drove her to the hospital, and the staff rushed her to the delivery room for an emergency Caesarean.

She heard a baby cry. A boy. The boy they'd decided to name Sam.

She passed out.

When she came to, she asked to hold her child.

No, her husband said. The boy was in intensive care. He needed surgery.

David handed his wife two Polaroids a nurse had taken. A bulging growth covered the left side of the baby's face and the area under his neck.

What is it? Debbie asked.

I don't know, David said. But he's alive.

When the Lightners arrived at the neonatal ICU, they were led to an isolette, a covered crib that regulates temperature and oxygen flow. A nurse had written "I am Sam; Sam I am"—a line from *Green Eggs and Ham* by Dr. Seuss—and taped it to the contraption.

Wires from a heart monitor snaked across the baby's tiny chest. He was fragile, a nurse said, and the parents couldn't hold him.

The mass fascinated Debbie, and she asked if she could touch her son.

The nurse lifted the cover of the isolette, and Debbie reached down with a finger. The mass was soft. It jiggled. Debbie thought it looked like Jell-O.

The nurse closed the cover.

Debbie and her husband returned to her room, and she climbed into bed. She picked up one of the pictures her husband had given her and covered the mass with her fingers to see what her son should have looked like. He had brown hair and eyes.

She wept.

* * *

Tim Campbell, a pediatric surgeon known for tackling tough cases, walked into the ICU and peered into the isolette. The boy had a vascular anomaly. They were rare enough, but what this tiny infant had was even rarer. The anomaly was a living mass of blood vessels. And it had invaded the left side of Sam's face, replacing what should have been there with a terrible tangle of lymphatic and capillary cells.

The malformation extended from his ear to his chin. Campbell knew there was no way to simply slice it off, as if it were a wart, because it had burrowed its way deep inside Sam's tissue. Doctors knew little about such anomalies except that they were made up of fluid-filled cysts and clots that varied in size from microscopic to as big as a fingertip.

Campbell gently pulled the baby's mouth open. The mass swelled up from below and wormed its way into his tongue, threatening to block his air passage. He could barely breathe, and only immediate action would save him. He asked a nurse to direct him to the Lightner room.

Campbell introduced himself, explaining the surgery. He didn't mince words.

I'm going to be in there a long time, the Lightners remember him saying. It's risky. He's little, and he's premature.

Campbell operated for six hours and removed 1 pound, 10 ounces of tissue from under Sam's neck. He operated a second time to remove bulk above his left ear and to ease his breathing with a tracheotomy tube. But there was no way, he told the Lightners, that he could safely remove the mass on Sam's face.

Campbell had sliced away a quarter of the infant's weight. Baby Sam, who weighed 5 pounds after the surgeries, spent three months recovering in the hospital.

* * *

He was 3 when he first realized he was different. His father remembers Sam running up and down a hallway when he stopped in midstride and stared at his image in a full-length mirror. He touched the left side of his face, almost as if to prove to himself that he was in fact that boy in the mirror.

He cried.

His parents had been expecting this day. His father bent over and took Sam by the hand. He led him to a bedroom off the hall. Debbie joined them. David lifted Sam onto the bed. And then his parents told the little boy the complicated facts of his life.

Except for the deformity, Sam was normal in every way. But everyone outside Sam's circle of family and friends would have a hard time seeing beyond the mass of tissue on his face.

And so it was.

A little girl grabbed her mother's hand when Debbie pushed Sam, in a stroller, onto an elevator. The girl stared at the little boy, pointed at him and then loudly told her mother to "look at the ugly baby."

Bystanders often assumed Sam was retarded. A woman asked Debbie what drugs she had taken during her pregnancy. Strangers said they'd pray for the boy. Others just shook their heads and turned away.

His parents went to another surgeon to see if he could reduce the mass. He removed some tissue from behind Sam's left ear but encountered heavy bleeding and closed up. Even then, the incisions wouldn't heal. Sam bled for six weeks.

When the Lightners realized their son would have to live with his face, they refused to hide him from the world. They took him to the mall, to the beach, to restaurants. In Northeast Portland, where the Lightner family lived, people talked about seeing a strange-looking boy. "That boy," they called him.

The Lightners enrolled Sam in the neighborhood school. Sam, his breathing labored, caused a stir during registration. Teachers worried about having the boy in their classes.

But he was an excellent student. He made friends, joined the Cub Scouts and played on a baseball team. He tried basketball for a year, but he fell easily because his head was so heavy.

When Sam turned 12, he told his parents that he wanted to change his face. They took him to Dr. Alan Seyfer, an OHSU professor who chaired the medical school's department of plastic and reconstructive surgery. What Seyfer saw made him leery.

The mass was near vital nerves and blood vessels that surgery could destroy, leaving Sam with a paralyzed face. Hundreds of vessels ran through the deformed tissue, and every incision would cause terrible bleeding. Sam could bleed to death on the operating table.

Nonetheless, Seyfer, who spent 11 years as a Walter Reed Army Hospital surgeon, wanted to help. And so he scheduled Sam for surgery in June 1998. A month before he asked a friend, the chairman of the plastic-surgery department at Johns Hopkins Hospital in Baltimore, to join him.

A week before the surgery, Seyfer and his partner examined Sam one last time. They peered down his throat so they could study the mass without having to make an incision.

They didn't like the view.

That afternoon, Seyfer met with Sam and his parents and said he had made an agonizing decision. The surgery was too risky. In good faith, he could not operate.

The news crushed Sam. He realized he had always held out hope that a surgeon would pull him out of the horrible spotlight that targeted him every time he went out in public. But no. He was trapped.

* * *

Sam Lightner pedaled his bike as hard as he could, but his family zoomed ahead. His legs ached, and he panted for breath. Even his younger brother could ride his bike farther and longer.

Most days during this spring 1999 vacation, Sam wanted to just lie in bed and watch television.

And when he spoke, his family kept asking him to repeat himself. No one—the desk clerk at Central Oregon's Sunriver Lodge, the woman in the gift shop—could understand him. He garbled his speech, as if he were speaking with a mouthful of food.

But he wasn't eating. At dinner, he sat with his family, listening, picking at his food, waiting to go lie down on the sofa. Over his protests, his mother took him into the bathroom and weighed him.

Five pounds, she said. He'd lost five pounds. But a later visit to his pediatrician turned up nothing.

Sam woke up one morning in pain. He touched his face and found it tender. The mass was growing. His mother gave him Advil, but the mass continued to swell. Within a week, he couldn't swallow the pill. He stuck his finger in his throat. His tongue felt bigger. By the end of the week, Sam cried continually.

A doctor removed a lump where Sam's shoulder met his neck, thinking the lump was pressing against a nerve. But the pain continued.

On Sunday, Aug. 8, 1999, Sam came downstairs from his bedroom. He found his mother outside, sitting on the front porch. He walked out and sat next to her, crying. His speech slurred, and he had to repeat himself. The pain, he managed to tell her, had spread across the entire left side of his face.

The next morning, at the hospital, nurses poked and probed his face. He sat still while strange machines whirled about his head. And then he waited while specialists reviewed the X-rays and CAT scans. They found nothing.

Sam refused to go home. Someone, he pleaded, had to help him.

Doctors admitted him and ran more tests. Four days later, on Aug. 13, the mass awakened.

Pain racked Sam's body. He tried to call for help but couldn't speak. With his fingers, he reached up. His swollen tongue stuck several inches out of his mouth. He punched the button beside his pillow to call for help.

He wrote in a notebook to communicate with nurses and doctors, a notebook his mother would later store away with the other memorabilia of Sam's medical journey.

"I have no idea why. Since I was a baby. I was born with this.

"When I cough hard, little capillaries burst and a little blood comes out.

"Don't touch.

"Please, it hurts."

He held out his arm so nurses could give him morphine. They fed him through a tube.

Then the door to his room opened, and a new doctor walked in. The man asked Sam if he knew him. Sam shook his head.

I'm Tim Campbell, the doctor said.

He'd been making routine rounds when he spotted Sam's name on the patient board. Campbell hadn't seen the boy since he'd operated on him nearly 14 years before, the day after he was born.

Dr. Campbell thumbed through the reports at the nurses' station. He checked Sam's chart. The boy weighed 65 pounds—he was wasting away.

Campbell pulled up a chair.

How do you feel?

Sam wrote in his notebook: "Anything to stop the headaches."

Anything else?

"I really don't think this is going to work out."

The doctors are trying.

"Please try your hardest."

Hang in there, Sambo.

"I'm in pain. It was really bad this morning."

Campbell made a note to order more morphine.

"I hurt."

And methadone.

"I'm tired."

Try to sleep.

"Will it kill me?"

The boy behind the mask: Pt. 2

OCTOBER 2, 2000

*Acceptance sometimes comes in the struggle
to achieve it.*

Dr. Tim Campbell looked down into Sam Lightner's
face. The boy, he remembers thinking, was giving up.
Unless something dramatic happened, he would die.

The 14-year-old lay motionless in his bed at Portland's Legacy Emanuel Children's Hospital. His bloat-
ed face spilled across most of the pillow. His tongue
protruded grotesquely from his mouth, and the swelling
on the left side of his face wrenched one eye completely
out of position. In late summer of 1999, the deformity
he'd carried since birth had suddenly grown to life-
threatening size, choking off his airway and esophagus.

Sam, Campbell remembers thinking in blunt medical
slang, was "circling the drain." He'd seen the same look
in children battling terminal cancer. At a certain point,
they accepted their fate and surrendered to death.

The doctor hurried back to his office, rummaged
through his desk drawers and pulled out a slim blue
book, a list of every pediatric surgeon in North America.
He flipped through the pages.

Campbell paused when he reached the résumé of Dr.
Judah Folkman, a cancer researcher he'd met 30 years
earlier when they were both young surgeons. Folkman's
research team had controlled tumors in mice by stifling
the growth of the blood vessels that supplied them,
causing a national stir and overwrought speculation that
a cancer cure was at hand.

Folkman planned to test his technique on humans for
the first time in May 1999. Campbell considered the
fact that a wild excess of blood vessels had created
Sam's deformity. Maybe, he thought, Folkman's strategy would work on the boy.

But Folkman, besieged by more than a thousand desperate cancer patients a week, is fiercely protective of his
time. He grants no interviews. A secretary screens all calls.

Campbell punched in the telephone number listed in the blue book, hoping Folkman might grant a favor to an old friend. The secretary put him on hold. Then Folkman came on the line.

His response was discouraging. Sam's malformation was fully formed, and his method worked only on growing tumors. But Folkman suggested Campbell call a pediatric surgeon who worked for him as a research fellow. Campbell scribbled out a name: Jennifer Marler.

She was a member of the Boston's Children's Hospital Vascular Anomalies Team, which treated malformations just like Sam's. Pleas for help deluge that team, too, and the surgeons can respond to only a fraction. But when Campbell reached her, Folkman's name provided instant access.

Marler suggested that Campbell take some photographs of Sam and send them along with the boy's medical file. Campbell should address the package to her to make sure it didn't get lost in the slush pile.

The best she could offer was that she'd take a look.

* * *

Sam Lightner turned his head and stared straight into the camera while Campbell photographed his face. After Campbell left the hospital room, a psychiatrist walked in, pulled up a chair and began asking questions. Sam scribbled his answers in the notebook he used to communicate.

Then Sam asked a question.

"Why is this happening?"

The psychiatrist had no answer. Instead, he asked another question. Tell me how you feel about life, Sam remembers him saying. Is life unfair?

How stupid, Sam thought. His tongue was sticking three inches out of his mouth. He couldn't eat. His left eye bulged abnormally, reacting to pressure that seemed to build each hour. An IV drip line ran into his arm and pumped him full of drugs: morphine, methadone, Celebrex and nortriptyline—a combination of painkillers, anti-inflammatories and antidepressants. None of them helped. No one could tell him what was wrong.

Is life unfair?

"Sometimes."

And then the swelling receded. Doctors couldn't

explain why, but the sudden eruption died down as mysteriously as it had come to life. On Sept. 2, 1999—after a monthlong hospital stay—Sam went home.

But everything was different. Physically, Sam was a shell. He had lost 17 pounds and was down to 63 pounds. He could not speak. And the battle with the malformation had scarred him. His mother remembers a listless child who wouldn't stir from bed.

* * *

On Nov. 15, 1999, doctors determined Sam was healthy enough to get back into his old routine. When he returned to Gregory Heights Middle School, however, something had changed. All the talk in the hallways was about high school—girls, dances, sports. Being popular.

Life as Sam Lightner knew it was ending. All his classmates were obsessed with how they looked and how they fit in. But for Sam, the issues every young teen faces were magnified a thousandfold. He was moving out of the cocoon of familiarity that kept him among family and longtime classmates, who could see past the disfiguring mass he carried on his face. He was moving into a world of judgmental teen-agers and he would carry with him a terrible handicap, a face drastically shortchanged of its ability to reach others with a subtle expression, a slightly raised eyebrow, a flicker on the edge of his mouth. He was being cast among strangers who would turn away from his alien features so fast that they would miss the boy behind the mask.

Like all teens, Sam's perception of how others saw him would determine how he saw himself.

And when strangers looked at Sam, they first fixated on the left side of his face, a swollen mass that looked like a pumpkin left in the fields after Halloween. His left ear was even more abnormal, a purple mass the size and shape of a pound of raw ground beef. His jaw, twisted. His teeth, crooked. His tongue, shoved to the side. His left eye, nearly swollen shut.

When he walked to school each morning, he stopped at the crosswalk on Northeast Sandy Boulevard and watched passengers in cars and buses stare at him. When he walked through the neighborhood, he heard laughter and comments.

Once, a neighbor boy led his friends over to Sam's

house and knocked on the front door so the others could see Sam's face.

* * *

In late August, a thick envelope arrived in Dr. Jennifer Marler's office. She noticed it was from a Dr. Tim Campbell, an unfamiliar name, and tossed it aside. At the end of the day, after a brutal round of surgery, clinics and lab research, she was about to head home to her husband and three children when she spotted the envelope.

She dropped into her chair, grabbed it, ripped it open along one end and dumped the contents onto her desk. She started with the medical report:

Patient has lymphaticovenous malformation of the left side of face and neck. Condition was diagnosed prenatally. Involvement of the airway necessitated a tracheotomy. Difficulty swallowing necessitated a gastronomy tube. Malformation has grown to the point of orbitaldystopia. In all other areas of life, though, the patient has developed normally.

She remembered—the Portland boy.

She searched through the paperwork and found several photos. She picked one up and held it between her fingers. The photograph haunted Marler.

The boy lay in a hospital bed, staring at the camera with pleading eyes. He looked like one of the children featured in ads aimed at raising money to help poor kids overseas.

Marler scanned the reports. The kid was on a morphine drip, diagnosed as clinically depressed.

Marler was 38 and had been a doctor for 11 years. Outside of a textbook, she had never come across such a profound facial deformity. He was the saddest-looking child she'd ever seen.

And she had seen many. A score of photographs hang on her office wall, the faces of children who have set the course of Jennifer Marler's life. Some of the images show children she successfully operated on, relieving them of the deformities that robbed them of their futures. Others tell sadder stories, reminding her of children who died from their abnormalities or who took the risk of surgery and didn't survive.

Marler picked up the telephone and spoke with the

nurse who scheduled weekly team conferences for the Vascular Anomalies Team. During the meeting, doctors discuss cases and decide whether they want to tackle them. The nurse said the next chance to present a case would be Sept. 22, 1999, just three weeks away.

She decided she'd present Sam Lightner's case and argue that he be brought to Boston. First, though, she had to get the facts down cold. She picked up the telephone again, called her husband, apologized and told him to have dinner without her. She talked to her three young daughters and told them Mommy had something important to do.

* * *

The team met Wednesday evenings in the surgical library. Members, fellows and residents gathered around a 15-foot-long oak table, nibbling cookies and sipping soft drinks.

Everyone found a seat, the lights dimmed and the patients' images appeared, one by one, on an overhead screen. The team members flipped through paperwork, scanning each patient's medical history. They spoke in short, clipped sentences, rife with medical jargon, challenging one another, looking for potential problems that might rule out surgery.

Marler remembers studying the paper in front of her. Nineteen children were up for consideration. Fewer than half would be chosen.

The team moved quickly: The agenda included an 8-month-old girl from Argentina. A 3-year-old girl from Italy. A 9-year-old boy from Minnesota.

Sam Lightner was next. His picture—the one Dr. Tim Campbell had taken—flashed on the screen.

Who is he? someone asked.

Marler recalls choosing her words carefully. She wanted to make sure the team knew something of the boy's life. He was in pain, she says she told them. Without hope. The disfigurement severe.

Although the center takes some of the most difficult cases in the world, Marler knew Sam Lightner presented major problems.

Behind her, she heard papers rustle as the team read his medical history. They quickly zeroed in on those risks. They hesitated. Before making any decision, the team members wanted more information.

Next case.

Marler scheduled Sam for the Nov. 3, 1999, meeting. Again the answer was no.

At the Nov. 10 meeting, she tried again, focusing not on the entire team, but on Dr. John Mulliken, the surgeon who directs the Vascular Anomalies Team and a researcher who's trying to figure out the causes of defects such as Sam's. Mulliken lectures at hospitals around the world and co-founded the International Society for the Study of Vascular Anomalies. He's written 185 scientific articles, 40 book chapters and two complete books.

The way Marler saw it, a team of doctors would have to operate on Sam. And Marler wanted to be on the team.

At this meeting, she spent an unusual 30 minutes arguing her case, knowing this was her last chance. She studied Mulliken, an impatient man, as he reviewed the files. She knew what he was thinking—the horrendous bleeding, and the tangle of nerves in the mass. If Mulliken damaged one, the boy might lose the ability to speak, to close his left eye or to smile.

She appealed to Mulliken's pride and compassion. No other surgeons, Marler remembers telling him, believe they can fix this.

She watched Mulliken, Sam's last hope.

The projector's motor hummed. Sam Lightner's face peered out into the room. Mulliken looked up at that face.

Bring him to Boston, he said.

* * *

On April 7, 2000, Sam Lightner and his parents walked three blocks from their Boston hotel to Children's Hospital. The Lightners silently rode an elevator to the third floor, where a smiling receptionist waved them over and took the Lightner file. Sam found a seat and flipped through a stack of magazines. He caught the eye of a woman sitting across from him. She turned away. Sam saw her whisper something to a woman sitting next to her before both turned back to stare.

"Samuel Lightner," the receptionist called.

A woman led them down a hallway to an examination room. Sam climbed onto the table. A few minutes later, the Lightners heard a soft knock.

She stood 5 feet 7 inches tall and wore a white doctor's smock over a long black skirt with matching black hose and shoes. Her brown hair was cut in a pageboy. "I'm Dr. Marler," she said.

She sat down on a doctor's stool, tugged on her glasses and fiddled with a string of pearls that lay across her white and blue-striped blouse. "I'm so glad to meet you," she told Sam. A flush spread up his neck.

Debbie Lightner dug through her purse and handed Marler a picture taken shortly after Sam's premature birth. Marler stared at the image of the tiny infant. "Boy," she said, "you were a little peanut."

The Lightners explained Sam's medical history—the emergency surgery right after his birth, the ear surgery that led to six weeks of persistent bleeding and the reluctance of other surgeons to even attempt cutting away the main mass of tissue. Marler took notes, interrupting occasionally to ask a question or to look at additional photos.

"I think you're in the right place," she continued. "Dr. Mulliken is both a craniofacial surgeon and a specialist in vascular anomalies. That makes him the right man for the job." She swiveled to face the examination table.

"So let's take a look, Sam." She patted his knee. He smiled.

"What grade are you in now?"

"Eighth," he said, in his raspy voice.

Marler ran her fingers across the mass, sizing it up. She sighed.

Sam's father cleared his throat. "He's going into the ninth grade," David Lightner said. "He wants the size of his head made smaller. He's a little bit more concerned about his appearance now."

Marler patted Sam on the shoulder. "I can understand that, Sam," she said. "I'll bring in Dr. Mulliken and our cast of thousands. On this one, we're going to need everyone's opinion."

She walked out, closing the door after her.

"You've been waiting for this a long time, haven't you, Sam?" Debbie Lightner asked her son.

"Nervous?" his father asked.

"I'm just hoping."

The door opened, and Marler walked back in, followed by six doctors who formed a semicircle around Sam. A man wearing a bow tie with blue and red polka dots stepped forward.

"Hi, Sam. I'm Dr. Mulliken. Nice to see you."

He perched on the examination table next to Sam. He took the boy's head in his hands as if holding a basketball and moved it gently, running his fingers from one side of the face to the other. He frowned. All the blue veins showing through Sam's waxen skin worried him.

"Oh, boy," he said. "There's a lot of venous component there. This is an incredible overgrowth."

He released Sam's head and climbed off the examination table. He stepped back two feet and crossed his arms, looking like a sculptor studying a block of granite. He moved to the left. The semicircle moved with him. Back to the right. The other doctors shuffled into place.

Mulliken ran his hands over his face. He groaned.

Marler jumped in. "I think he has very good facial nerve function."

"Smile, Sam," Mulliken commanded.

He sighed again. "OK," Mulliken said. "Let's write down some things."

That was what Marler had waited eight months to hear. She smiled, sat on a stool and opened her notebook, ready to send off instructions on what Mulliken needed to know about the inside of Sam Lightner's head.

"I want Reza to look down the trach and see what's going on there," Mulliken said, asking one of his colleagues to peer down Sam's airway. "Send him to AP for a Panorex. Find a CP and get pictures downstairs. We're going to have to decide what's going on in terms of flow, and if there's anything we can do to make it easier." He looked at Marler.

"Got all that?"

"Right," Marler said.

Mulliken boosted himself back onto the exam table. He scooted up next to Sam as if he were the boy's grandfather. He put his hand on Sam's knee.

"What bothers you the most?" he asked. "If you had

one thing you wanted, what would that be?"

Sam shrugged. He stared at his hands, folded in his lap.

"Should I give you some choices?" Mulliken asked. "Some multiple choices?"

Sam responded with a barely perceptible nod.

"Our goal will be to make you look as symmetrical as possible, to balance out your face," he said. "A Picasso is a great painting, but no one wants to walk around with one for a face. We have many things to talk about: Making your ear smaller, the tongue movement, the eye. The neck's pretty good."

He put his arm around Sam's shoulder. "What do you want, Sam?" he asked quietly, as if the room were empty except for the two of them.

Sam bowed his head and stared at his hands.

"Well, you're really down to the choice of two things," Mulliken said. "We can focus on the face or the ear, but we can't do both at the same time. If we get the face smaller, the ear will look bigger. Frankly, I just don't know. The face is tough, very tough. Lord, I just can't imagine..."

Sam raised his head. He looked deeply into Mulliken's face with his one good eye. "I want to fit in," he said in his raspy whisper. "I want to look better."

Mulliken nodded, his features softening. He pulled the boy a little closer. "I can understand, Sam."

David Lightner, standing against the back wall, pushed his way through the semicircle until he faced Mulliken, who dropped his arm from Sam's shoulders and faced the father. "His goal?" Lightner said. "Well, Sam's 14 years old. Like you put it, he'd like a more symmetrical face. I'm ambivalent. I understand the risk of the whole thing. But this is something Sam wants. We're supporting him."

"OK, Dad," Mulliken said. Then he swiveled on the table and faced the doctors.

"I think it will be reasonable to focus on this huge area on the side of his face," Mulliken said. "It's no-man's land, and it will be hard to work in that area. The problem's going to be finding the facial nerve branches and separating them from the malformation. They look exactly alike."

Mulliken slid off the table and paced. He shook his

head, as if he were having an argument with himself. "The bleeding. Boy! When you are dealing with a pure lymphatic tissue malformation, bleeding is just an annoyance. But if you have these venous components, which he has, it's more than a problem."

He smiled. "But Sam, I'm going to try."

The goal, Mulliken told the room, was to get the mass on the side of Sam's face down to the bone. If Mulliken could eliminate the mass, Sam could return to the hospital for more surgery to reshape the bone. That surgery would be much easier.

"Another operation?" Debbie Lightner asked. "The insurance company's going to really love us."

Mulliken broke through the semicircle and stopped in front of her. "Listen," he said, "you show that insurance company photographs of this boy and there won't be a dry eye in the house."

The Lightners looked at each other.

Mulliken moved aside so they could look at Sam.

"Sam?" his father asked.

Sam nodded, more firmly this time.

Mulliken moved back to his patient. "This is going to be tough. We're in for a rough time in the operating room. It's going to be a microscopic dissection, and we're going to need a team."

He looked around the room. "Dr. Marler, me and one or two others."

He stepped back once more to look at Sam. "His face is going to be swollen for a long time," Mulliken said. "By the time he goes to school, though, he should look considerably better. Push me to the wall, and I'd like to think we could make it 50 percent better."

"Sam," he asked, "is this something you really want?" Sam nodded. Mulliken patted the boy on the shoulder.

"Let's schedule for July," he told Marler.

Sam's father cleared his throat. "From seeing him in person, is this something you want to do?"

Mulliken frowned. "Well..."

"I'm being blunt," David said. "We have to know."

Mulliken sat on the exam table again. "I don't know if 'want' is quite the right word," he said quietly. "I think that we can do it."

He ran his hands over his face. "I know we can do it," he said. "I wish I could make him perfect. All plastic surgeons search for perfection, just like Michelangelo. I can't give him perfection."

He hoped he could remove a large amount of tissue from the side of Sam's face. But he also knew the underlying bone would remain seriously misshapen. When the world looked at Sam after the first surgery, it would still see an extraordinary deformity. But removing the tissue was the necessary first step to dealing with the bone.

"Dad, I'm bothered that he has to live with this mass," Mulliken said. "Everyone should have the right to look human."

* * *

The giddiness the Lightners felt vanished almost as soon as the jet roared down the runway at Logan International Airport and headed west, back to Portland, back to reality. Once home, David and Debbie went back to work, and Sam returned to eighth grade.

Sam's mother took Sam to register at Grant High School. An administrator walked in, noticed the Lightners sitting outside the counselors' office and stopped. They remember him introducing himself and shaking Sam's hand. He turned away from the boy, as if Sam were deaf. He told Debbie that Grant had a great special-education class for mentally retarded students.

Her son, he said, would love it.

* * *

The telephone rang in the Lightner home. Dr. Jennifer Marler told Debbie Lightner that surgery was scheduled for July 6. Having a date, something to put on the calendar, made it real. And frightening.

After dinner, the Lightners called their children together. Sam sat at one end of the dining-room table, his father at the other. In between were Debbie, Emily, 12, and Nathan, 9. The family cat, Alice, jumped onto the table.

David Lightner played with a pencil, turning it end over end. "I wanted to discuss how this is going to affect us," he said. "We're up in the air about whether we should do it. Mommy talked with Dr. Marler for quite a while. There are dangers, but Dr. Marler said if Sam was her child, Dr. Mulliken would be the man."

David fiddled with a magazine. "There are some things that could happen," he said. "We have to be honest about that."

"Like what?" Nathan asked.

"If some of the nerves are damaged, Sam's face could droop," his mother said. "He'd be paralyzed on that side."

"You mean he wouldn't feel it?" Emily asked.

"Right."

No one looked at Sam.

"He might bleed a lot during surgery," his mother said. "They think they can control it, but you never know. I think Dad just wanted to have it all out on the table for everyone to talk about one last time."

David Lightner shifted in his chair.

"Now that we're 3,000 miles away," he said, "it puts a different spin on it. It's more complicated sitting here."

Debbie touched Sam's arm. "Sam, do you still want to do this?"

Sam nodded.

"I want to hear it."

"Yes," Sam said, firmly.

"It's your decision," his father said. "That's the deal. If I felt something was wrong, I'd intervene. I don't sense that. But I have to be honest, it scares me a little bit."

"Me, too," Nathan said.

"Me, too," Emily said.

"I worry about the potential damage to him," said David. "As it stands, he's Sam. He is who he is."

"He'll look different," Emily said. "Sam is Sam."

"He is who he is," said David. "We don't think anything's wrong with him."

David leaned forward, arms on the table, and stared across at his son. "Any doubts, Sam?" he asked. "If you say 'no,' we call and cancel right now, date or no date."

"I'm a little nervous," Sam said. "But I like the doctors."

"Well, it scares me," his father said. "It's the unknown. Here we have the situation that Sam deals with. It's the known. It's not ideal for him because of his face.

His face freaks people out. But it's a known property. And it's a little bit scary to risk everything because the world doesn't accept his face."

"Dad, I'm sure," Sam said. "Look what happened at Grant."

His father bowed his head.

"That's what people think about him," Debbie said. "They think he's mentally defective."

Sam leaned forward and mustered all his strength.

"I want to do this," he said.

David placed both hands on the table.

"We are fearfully and wonderfully made," he told his family. "And very fragile."

He sighed.

"All right," he said. "It's a go."

The boy behind the mask: Pt. 3

OCTOBER 3, 2000

The risks we take can tell us who we are.

A nurse appears in the doorway. It's time to go, she says. Sam Lightner takes a deep breath and nods feebly. He lifts himself, his hands trembling slightly on the arms of the chair, and walks across the small pre-op waiting room to give his parents a hug.

"We love you, sweetie," says his mother. She pulls him close and kisses him softly on his left cheek, right on the mass that the waiting team of doctors will target. Sam looks at his mother through his right eye—the only truly normal feature on his face. He blinks it once. A wink.

"Have a nice sleep," says his father as he gives his son a hearty pat on his shoulder.

The nurse touches the 14-year-old on the arm and leads him down the hallway. His gown hangs loosely on his 83 pounds, exposing his spindly legs. In another room, nurses help him onto an operating table. He lies down, and a nurse inserts an IV line into an arm. Then she injects drugs to make him drowsy. When his eyes flutter, he's wheeled into Operating Room 16.

It is Thursday, July 6, 2000, just three months since Sam and his parents visited Boston to find out if this elite surgical team, the only one in the world with any chance of correcting his deformity, would take his case.

The room is about the size of a two-car garage with a 15-foot ceiling. It's chilled to 64 degrees, which cuts down on the growth of germs and keeps the doctors comfortable as they work. Two massive operating lights, each with four bulbs, hang over the table. Everything but the white walls—the drapes that cover the patient and the operating table, the surgical scrubs and the shoe covers—is light blue.

"You're just falling asleep now, Sam," says a nurse as she strokes his hair. "Just falling asleep, Sam."

His eyes close.

An anesthesiologist takes her place behind the bank of machines that will control the boy's body during the operation. She switches a knob, and the sound of a pump fills the room. It is a steady beat—one swoosh every two seconds—and fills Sam's lungs with air, breathing for the unconscious boy.

The circulating nurse, responsible for everything that comes in and out of the room, sorts through a cluttered desk to find Sam's medical history. In these final quiet moments, she sits on a corner stool and flips through a folder the size of a small telephone book, reading about this small boy's long journey. The nurse puts the file down and walks to the operating table. An intravenous line pumps Sam's body full of saline, a way of making up blood volume as it's depleted by the bleeding that is sure to follow.

The swinging door to the scrub room opens with a bang, and Dr. Jennifer Marler enters Operating Room 16. Her arms drip with water. The circulating nurse hands her a sterilized towel.

Marler, a 38-year-old mother of three, lobbied to bring Sam here to Boston, to Children's Hospital, the nation's largest pediatric medical center. In late 1999, Marler presented and pressed Sam's case before the hospital's Vascular Anomalies Team. The team members balked—the surgery was tremendously risky. But eventually Marler won them over.

The goal is to cut away a mass on the left side of the boy's face. If all goes well, that will set the stage for a later operation on the misshapen bones in his face. But first, surgeons must cut their way down to the facial bone.

A nurse helps Marler into her surgical gown and a set of gloves. She moves to the operating table. She runs her hands across Sam's face, gently, almost caressing the boy, not as a doctor but as a mother.

"We'll take good care of you, Sam."

She leans over his body and begins suturing his eyelids. She does not want his eyes to open during surgery—the swirl of scalpels, needles and surgical gowns around his face could scratch a cornea.

Word about Sam and the impending operation has filtered through the building, Harvard Medical School's primary pediatric teaching hospital. The staff is curious about something that pushes the boundaries of medical practice.

A nurse from Operating Room 17 pops in. "Wow," she says. "How old is he?"

"Fourteen," says Marler.

"Where's he from?"

"Oregon."

"Does he go to school?"

"He does," says Marler. "He's very personable."

As Marler begins preparing Sam's face, the scrub doors swing open, and Dr. John Mulliken, the surgeon who will lead the team, strides silently into the room. He stops to study Sam's three-dimensional CAT scans, which hang from a lighted viewing board. He has never encountered so complex a case.

He holds out his hands. A nurse helps him into his gown and gloves. He walks to the operating table and looks at his patient. "Good preparation," he tells Marler. "Good preparation."

Surgery is Mulliken's life. He works weekends. He hasn't had a vacation in years. He's never married and has no children. He dotes on his dog, Girlie, and his cat, Felicia. A cabinet in the operating room carries 19 photographs of the two pets.

During surgery Mulliken can be gruff, and some of the rotating nurses have complained to the administration that he barked at them when they didn't move quickly enough or when they handed him instruments he didn't consider clean. But for this operation, Mulliken has assembled a team of people who have worked with him for years. They all have thick skins.

He reaches down and grabs Sam's head with both hands. "His head's just so big," he mutters. "It just rolls around."

He turns to a nurse. "I can't have it rolling," he says. "Stop it."

The nurse scurries through the room, searching in cabinets until she finds something that looks like a doughnut the size of a dinner plate. Sam's head fits in the hole. Mulliken tries moving the head. It doesn't budge. "Good," he says.

The swinging doors open again. Dr. Gary Rogers

joins Mulliken at the head of the operating table. The blue surgical scrubs cover their bodies. The caps fit snugly over their heads. Masks hide their mouths and noses. Each wears special black glasses outfitted with surgical microscopes that will allow them to peer deep into the boy lying in front of them.

Mulliken ignores his teammates. He walks around Sam's head, studying it from all angles. Knowing this would be a difficult operation, he had scheduled a warm-up earlier in the morning: repairing a cleft palate in an infant. His hands are limber and steady.

The surgical nurse makes the final adjustments to tool-lined trays beside her. The circulating room nurse awaits her first order. Mulliken, Rogers and Marler adjust the microscopes over their eyes. Mulliken points to a spot near Sam's left ear. That, he says, is where he wants to make the first cut.

"Everyone agree?"

Marler and Rogers bend over Sam. "Yes," they say in unison.

Mulliken takes a deep breath. "OK," he says.

He holds out his right hand and asks for a scalpel. He grasps it firmly. "This is going to be a bear," he says. "Let's do it."

The scalpel parts the skin, and the flesh gives way to the blade.

Then the blood begins to flow.

* * *

The first drop of blood lands on the floor, and Mulliken calls for suctioning. Marler uses a tool attached to a clear plastic tube. In seconds, it resembles a piece of red licorice that snakes across Sam's body, down the floor and to a holding tank where the boy's blood collects.

Rogers holds back the skin, allowing Mulliken to proceed. After 15 minutes, the lead surgeon has opened up a 3-inch incision. The bleeding hasn't slowed.

He calls for a syringe. Marler injects more drugs designed to speed clotting into Sam's neck, hoping they will slow the bleeding.

The team waits. The blood flows freely.

The team confers. Mulliken could close up now, suture the incision and end the operation. When the

Lightner family traveled to Boston three months earlier to meet Mulliken and Marler, Mulliken made it clear that this surgery was risky. The only other time Mulliken tackled a case this serious, he made an incision, encountered massive bleeding and closed.

If he continues, he and his team will have to work furiously, trying to stay one step ahead of massive bleeding while they peel back the skin. And even if they expose the mass, they might never find the nerves that branch out into the tissue. If they cut a nerve, they could paralyze the left side of Sam's face.

The tissue mass is a jumble of skin, tissue, nerves, lymphatic vessels, veins and arteries. A Nerf ball filled with blood and fluid. Mulliken has no road map. If he plunges ahead, it will be like replumbing a house with the water turned on.

Operating Room 16 awaits his decision.

He leans over Sam's body. "Let's do it," he finally says.

The circulating nurse jumps from her chair and hustles to a phone. She punches in the four-digit number to the hospital's blood bank. Six units of blood are now in a cooler in Operating Room 16. The nurse tells the bank to set aside an additional six. Even if all goes well, Sam will bleed so much during the operation that she will have to replace his entire blood supply.

She glances to a plastic bag holding a unit of blood that drips from an IV line into Sam's right arm. The bag is half-empty.

Mulliken lengthens the incision. The bag drains.

Mulliken, Marler and Rogers operate quickly, the suctioning line thick with the boy's blood. Each time the scalpel moves, it slices a blood vessel. They go through 50 surgical towels and countless sponges, soaking up blood so they can see where they are.

Mulliken calls for the Bovie, a machine that electrically cauterizes blood vessels. In a normal body, the machine stops bleeding, and the surgery is almost bloodless. Marler leans over Sam's body and grasps the Bovie, a device that looks like a dental drill, in her right hand.

There is the sound of sizzling, as if grease has been dropped onto a grill. A plume of smoke rises from

Sam's face. But the bleeding continues.

A nurse walks behind the surgical team and hangs a third bag of blood on the IV line. "Jesus Christ," Mulliken mutters.

The team begins to pull back the skin. They can see the edge of the mass. "Easy," Mulliken tells Marler. "Easy."

The side of the boy's face oozes blood. Drops splatter the floor. A red stain spreads through the surgical drape as if someone had spilled a glass of wine on a white tablecloth. Nurses call for another 10 towels. Within minutes, they are soaked through, and the nurses dump them into a bucket.

The insides of Marler's shoes are soaked with Sam's blood. She asks for a new pair of wool socks.

Mulliken sees only one option: They're going to have to stitch each blood vessel closed. He calls for needles.

While Marler continues cutting, Rogers uses the Bovie, and Mulliken starts stitching. The surgical nurse goes through packet after packet of stitches and tells the circulating room nurse she needs more.

Mulliken's fingers tire, and Marler takes over. Then Rogers. The bleeding slows to a trickle. The team has tied more than 200 stitches.

Slowly, they pull Sam's skin back and cover it with a towel to keep it moist.

The mass is exposed.

Mulliken looks to a board in the far corner of Operating Room 16. Sam has gone through three units of blood. And the team hasn't even reached the heart of the operation. He steps away from the table. He tells Marler and Rogers to clean up the area surrounding the mass. He's going to take a break.

The phone rings, and the circulating nurse answers it. "We're No. 1 again," she calls out to the room.

For the past 10 years, *U.S. News & World Report* magazine has ranked Children's Hospital best in the country. It's won the award again.

"Your friend says you had a bet with him," she tells Mulliken. "He says you owe him a dinner. He wants lobster."

Mulliken strolls toward the door. "Yeah, yeah, yeah," he says, disappearing through the swinging doors.

* * *

Surgical coverings hide Sam's body and most of his face, leaving only the tissue mass exposed under the glare of the surgical lights. It looks like a piece of raw prime rib.

Even to someone as experienced as Mulliken, the mass is a mystery. X-rays don't show soft tissue. So there's no way of knowing how invasive the mass is or what it's wrapped around. A single nerve leaves the brain and divides into five branches that spread out to control the side of the face. But the mass could rest on top of nerves, or it could spread under them. Or the nerves could snake right through it.

The boy has few enough pathways to connect him with the rest of the world. If Mulliken guesses wrong and cuts a nerve, Sam loses an important part of what he has left—the ability to blink his eye, to crinkle his forehead or to smile.

News of what's going on in Operating Room 16 has spread throughout the third floor. Residents and other doctors wander in to look at the CAT scans hanging on the wall. They stand back and stare at the mass, bloody and glistening in the high-powered lights.

"Unbelievable," says a visiting doctor.

He turns to the circulating nurse. "How old is he?"

"Fourteen," she says. "And he's really nice."

The doctor looks at scans, which make Sam look like a cyborg in a science-fiction movie.

"Isn't that the saddest thing you've ever seen?" he asks. "It's heartbreaking. This kid must have a tough life. That's no way to live."

On the way out of the room, he passes Mulliken, who re-enters Operating Room 16 with a shout. "Children's Hospital is tops," he says. "We're No. 1." Even through his surgical mask it's clear he is frowning.

"I was hoping we would be second or third," he announces. "That way we won't be so damn complacent around here."

He checks with Marler. The blood has slowed to a trickle.

His job now will be to hunt for the nerve branches and to cut away the mass of tissue. The team will use an electric probe. If they touch a nerve, a portion of Sam's face will twitch.

Out of habit the circulating nurse pulls down a thick anatomy book. She turns to the page that details the facial nerves and leaves it open on a table so the team can refer to it. But it will do them no good. In this section of Sam's body, nothing is where it should be.

The team works under microscopes. Looking for the nerve will be like hunting for a white rope encased in white concrete.

Test. Cut. Test. Cut.

They begin removing bits of the mass. The bleeding begins again.

An hour passes, and Mulliken goes to the scrub room. He takes off his gown and gloves, and returns to flop in a chair away from the operating table. The pressure is intense, physically and mentally, and the team plans on working shifts—when one surgeon tires another will take the scalpel. Mulliken leans back and rests his head on a cabinet. He closes his eyes. After 15 minutes, he stirs.

"How's it going," he calls to Marler.

"The nerve must be surrounded by scars from his previous surgery," she says.

"Don't relax," he tells her. He knows the biggest danger is in getting sloppy and cutting something that appears to be tissue but may in fact be the edge of a hidden nerve.

"Jennifer, are you looking?"

"There's nothing," she tells him.

He leaves the room to scrub and to check on his cleft-palate patient. He returns 30 minutes later. About four and a half hours have passed since the surgery began.

"How you guys doing?" he yells when he enters Operating Room 16. The silence is ominous. After getting in his gown and gloves, he moves to Marler's side. He looks over her shoulder.

"Is this the same case?" he jokes.

"Hey," she admonishes him with a chuckle.

"You found it yet?"

"We think we found the region."

"I know the region," he says. "I want the nerve. Where is it?"

He takes over, and Marler strips off her gown. She is

going to take a shower, get something to eat and call her family and tell them she won't be home until late that night.

Test. Cut. Test. Cut.

A nurse walks behind the surgical team and hooks up a fourth unit of blood to Sam's IV line. Marler returns 20 minutes after leaving and finds Mulliken frustrated and worried. They haven't found any branches of the main nerve, and the operation is entering its fifth hour.

And the kid is bleeding. He thinks of Dr. Alan Seyfer, the Portland surgeon who nearly attempted a similar operation on Sam when the boy was 12, and then decided the risks were simply too great.

"Seyfer was right," Mulliken grumbles. "Seyfer was right."

He mops up more blood and turns to see that the fourth unit is nearly gone. "This was a mistake to take this case," he says. "I don't think we can help this boy."

Mulliken tells his team there are two choices: Increase the risk of destroying part of the nerve by cutting even faster. Or close up.

"I've been here before," he says. "I think we should close up."

Marler turns to him. "Let's keep going."

Mulliken moves to the side. "Jennifer," he snaps, "you take over. You wanted to bring him here; you look for the nerve."

Marler takes the probe, and 90 more minutes pass. The team has gone through more than 200 sponges and towels soaking up Sam's blood. The holding tank where the suction line empties sloshes red.

"I think I got it," Marler shouts.

"This is in a portion of scar tissue like you have never seen," she tells Mulliken, who gives her an encouraging nudge.

She applies the electric probe again, and a muscle twitches. "You got it?" Mulliken asks.

"I got it," says Marler. "It's all encapsulated. I can't distinguish the nerve from the scar tissue. And it's deeper than it should be. I'm afraid to dissect any farther."

Mulliken trades places with her. He peers into the side of Sam's face and holds out his right hand. A nurse hands him a scalpel. He leans over, inches from the mass. He touches it with the tip of his scalpel.

"Well, I can't budge it from the scar tissue," he says. "It is literally entangled in it."

Marler uses the probe. Sam's forehead moves.

"Every time I dissect, I'm worried," Marler says. She and Mulliken turn away from Sam and look intently at each other.

"It's bad," he says. He peers back into the mass, which is oozing blood. He stands up.

"We've come this far," he says. "We've got to get it out."

Rogers assists with suctioning and controlling the bleeding so Mulliken can see where the nerve might lie.

"Let's stimulate around what we think is the edge, Mulliken says.

Test. Nothing. Test. Nothing. Test. Reaction.

Mulliken cuts. "It should be under here," he says. "Jesus."

He sighs. "I would go right here," he says.

Mulliken, Marler and Rogers, instruments in each hand, all focus on a spot in the mass the size of a quarter. "I think I found a branch above," Mulliken says.

The fourth bag of blood is nearly gone.

Mulliken turns to Marler and asks for the probe. He tries to work his way back up the tiny nerve he's located, searching for the main branch.

He applies the probe again, but the room is silent.

"Come on, people," he snaps. "Talk to me."

"Yes," says Marler. "His forehead moved."

Mulliken tries again. They are more than six hours into the operation.

"Bingo," says Mulliken.

* * *

The team moves out from the nerve they've located, hunting for other branches. "We have to see it, to get around it," Mulliken says. "The nerve is going right through this mass."

Marler turns to him. "Just imagine what it's going to be like getting there," she says. "What are we going to do?" Mulliken says nothing.

"Could we get the malformation off and then go back and do a nerve graft?" she asks.

"No," he says. "We can't even find all the nerves.

Jesus Christ," he says. "We've been here nearly seven hours, and we can't even get to the nerves."

Rogers strips off his gown and leaves the room for a break. Mulliken and Marler bend over Sam. Suddenly, blood spurts onto Marler's blue gown. The scalpel has nicked a branch of the carotid artery.

"Bleeder," Mulliken yells, calling for clamps and sutures to stanch the spurting blood. The surgical nurse doesn't move fast enough for him. "Come on," he shouts. "Come on."

He works frantically. "We got a real bleeder here," Mulliken yells. "Oh, Jesus."

The fourth bag of blood is gone. A nurse scurries to hang a fifth, which drains as though it has a hole in it. A sixth bag begins to empty just as fast.

The blood loss could send Sam Lightner into cardiac arrest. He is close to death.

Mulliken leans into Sam's body, violently shifting the head, stitching and then reaching out to grab another instrument and stitching again. The bleeding slows.

Rogers returns. "What's up?" he asks.

"We get into the carotid branch of the vessel, and you walk off?" Mulliken says.

Rogers, mystified, looks at Marler.

"We're fine," she says. "We're fine."

* * *

The hallway outside Operating Room 16 empties. It's 10:30 p.m., and janitors are already cleaning the surrounding rooms, readying them for the next day's cases. In all of Children's Hospital, only one surgery continues—the one in Operating Room 16.

The members of the team have to get reoriented. They suction off the blood and begin testing, looking for nerves again. Mulliken probes. "Let's get going here," he says. "We're losing time."

He asks the surgical nurse for a tool covered with green dye and maps the nerve branches right on the exposed tissue. The team can cut anything in between the green lines. When they reach the edge, they must test, getting as close to the nerve as possible. They think they've found all the nerves, but they won't be sure until Sam regains consciousness and actually tries to move.

They begin cutting.

Small pieces, the size of a toenail clipping. Then much larger, some of them the size of a marble. "Say," Mulliken says. "You know that we're the No. 1 hospital in the country?" He chuckles.

Nurses and doctors laugh.

"You know what we are doing now?" he asks. "We're rolling, rolling, rolling." He sings lines from the theme to the old television show *Rawhide*. And hacks away at the mass.

"You ever see anything like this?" one nurse asks another.

Marler dissects the area under Sam's chin. "That should go," she says as she pulls out a large chunk. "Let's go the extra mile."

Mulliken pulls the flap of skin back over Sam's face. "He looks a lot better," he says.

He folds the flap back down. "Folks," he says, "We're down to the bone."

* * *

Sam's blood has completely lost the ability to clot, and the nurse rushes to replenish it with a seventh bag. "He's bleeding from every little hole," Mulliken says. "Jesus Christ, things are starting to blow up. We're getting out of here."

He stands to speak to the room. "Close," he says.

Rogers and Marler stitch Sam's skin flap back to the side of his face. "That chin of his is going to look awesome," Marler says.

"Not a bad way to start high school," says Mulliken. He steps away from the table, taking off his gloves, gown and mask. He sits at a table and fills out forms. He glances at a wall clock to note the time.

It is midnight. The surgery has lasted nearly 13 hours.

He files the paperwork and walks out the door and down the empty hallways. Through another set of doors and then into the bowels of the hospital. In the waiting room, he finds Sam's parents asleep on separate sofas.

He clears his throat. They stir.

"Everything is fine," he tells the Lightners. "All is well."

"How difficult was it?" David asks.

Mulliken sits on a chair and runs his hands across his face.

"This was very difficult," Mulliken says. "The most difficult surgery I've ever performed. At times we were very discouraged, and it wasn't easy. But no one ever wanted to give up."

He yawns. "All is well," he says, rubbing the back of his neck. "The next step will be fixing the mandible bone, probably next summer. That won't be a problem."

The Lightners turn to each other. They hold hands.

"You know, doctor, when I talk with you, I realize how Sam's face really looked," David says, his voice breaking. "To me, to us, he's always been just Sam. I guess we got used to it. To us, he's just a kid with a big old head."

Mulliken nods.

"The family doesn't see it," he says. "It's the rest of the world, all of us, the strangers who can't see beyond the face. That's the sad part."

The Lightners stand. They move toward Mulliken but hesitate, not sure of what to do or what to say.

"Thank you," says Debbie Lightner. She runs her hand across her eyes.

Mulliken smiles. "You're welcome," he says.

Then he turns and disappears through the door.

The boy behind the mask: Pt. 4

OCTOBER 4, 2000

"I am Sam; Sam I am."

The doors to Operating Room 16 opened with a bang, and two intensive-care nurses pushed Sam Lightner's gurney into the hallway, maneuvered it to their left and toward an elevator.

Behind them, a nurse tossed bloody sponges and towels into a bucket on the floor. Another nurse put the final touches on official reports, glancing at the wall clock to note that the boy was leaving the room just after 12:30 a.m. on July 7, 2000. Thirteen hours had passed since a highly specialized team of world-class surgeons had begun Sam's operation on the morning of July 6.

A thick bandage—brilliant white except for a streak of red left by the blood still oozing through sutures on his neck—encased Sam's head. An IV line pumped drugs and painkillers into his body. He was heavily sedated, not expected to stir for at least the next 36 hours.

Dr. Jennifer Marler, one of Sam's three surgeons, pulled off her surgical gown and gloves. In her blue surgical scrubs, she hurried after the gurney and pushed her way into the elevator. She wanted to be next to Sam when he arrived in the Intensive Care Unit.

The elevator doors opened, and nurses wheeled Sam into a private room. Quickly they plugged lines running from his body into a bank of monitors. They adjusted the screens, and Marler motioned to the nurses. They followed her to the nurse's station.

She opened Sam's file and pulled out a color photograph taken in April, when Sam had first been evaluated at Boston's Children's Hospital. Sam, Marler explained, was a 14-year-old from Portland, Ore. He'd been born with a venous malformation—a bulging mass of blood vessels and tissue—on the left side of his face. And this, she said, is what he had looked like. She dropped the photograph on the counter. The nurses murmured.

Marler left the file on the counter and walked back

into Sam's room. The frail boy's body barely filled the bed. His head had swelled to the size of a basketball, completely cloaking his features. Never, Marler told nurses checking on Sam, had she seen a head that big. Make sure it was always supported, she told them. If it somehow dropped off the bed, the weight could cause a spinal injury.

Marler wondered what Sam would look like when the swelling went down in a month. The goal had been to remove the tissue mass, setting the stage for a future surgery on the underlying bone. This first stage of his facial reconstruction might make Sam look 50 percent better, the surgeons figured.

But 50 percent improvement on a facial deformity such as Sam's—the worst Marler had ever seen—still left a lot of work undone. And Sam was only 10 weeks from his first day at Portland's Grant High School, a day when he would walk into a mob of judgmental adolescents who'd never seen him before.

Marler remembers standing over the boy's bed and wondering: Was 50 percent enough?

* * *

On Saturday, July 8, Sam Lightner stirred. His mother, hovering over him, called his name. He briefly opened his eyes before slipping back to sleep. Sam, unable to speak, was supposed to communicate with a small computer. Four responses—"I hurt," "I need to go to the bathroom," "yes" and "no"—had been pre-programmed. Sam had only to lift a finger and push one button to answer.

Debbie Lighter asked Sam how he felt.

Sam slowly raised a finger and punched button No. 1.

The pain, nurses told his mother, would be severe for at least three weeks. Even after he left the hospital, he would need painkillers.

That afternoon Marler showed up at the hospital. It was her day off, but she wanted to check on Sam. She recalls reminding herself, as she made her way to the ICU, to look confident, to hide her worry from the Lightners.

The surgery had been the most difficult operation of the lead surgeon's career and one that had tested the entire team's resolve. Sam's anatomy was abnormal, the malformation just a jumble of tissue, blood vessels and nerves. Because X-rays don't show soft tissue, the nerves lay concealed in the surrounding mass. Damaging a key nerve would have paralyzed the left side of Sam's face. If that had happened, Sam would have lost the ability to blink his eye, to crinkle his forehead or to smile.

She checked in at the nurse's station, received an update on Sam and then walked to his room.

She remembers the Lightners standing by the bed, looking at their son. A line from a ventilator—the machine was still breathing for Sam—was hooked into his tracheotomy, the hole in his throat that bypassed the tissue mass. The hole would remain until Sam completed all his surgeries.

Marler made small talk with the Lightners, wondering how she could check on Sam's nerves. She felt good about the branches leading to his eye and forehead. But what about the branch to his mouth? That area had been hellish in Operating Room 16. She had to know, but Sam seemed to be sound asleep.

She asked if Sam had been awake at all. Yes, said Debbie, he'd woken up enough to stir when she spoke.

Can you make him smile? asked Marler. I need to see if he can smile.

Debbie Lightner leaned over Sam's bed, moved her head closer to her son's. Marler inched in right behind. His mother called to Sam.

The only sound in the room was the steady whoosh from the ventilator.

Marler saw the boy's eyes flutter. Good sign. Try again, she told Debbie.

Sam, Debbie Lighter said, I need you to smile for me.

There was no response, and Debbie Lightner tried again. Sam, she said, smile.

Then, slowly, the outer edge of his mouth began to curl.

And Sam Lightner smiled.

* * *

Eight days after surgery, an internist walked into Sam's room. The time had come to remove the bandages.

The surgeons who had operated on Sam had told the Lightners to be realistic. The unveiling would be anticlimactic, even disappointing. Sam's face had taken a beating in the surgery. The buildup of internal fluids would make his face look more distorted than at any time in his life. For the next two months, he would wear an elastic mask each night to force his face into shape and to combat the swelling. The true results, they said, would be revealed in late September or early October.

Even so, Sam could hardly wait to see his new face. Later, he remembered the bandages coming off. The cool air on his face. The doctor backing away from the bed, and his mother moving in to help him.

He was unsteady, a colt learning to walk, and she guided him to the bathroom, to the mirror. The surgeons' message played in his head—don't get your hopes up. And then he looked at his reflection.

He focused first on the chin: It was rounder.

Then he examined the entire left side of his face: For the first time in more than a year, he could actually see his left ear, huge and distorted, because the tissue mass that had obscured the ear was gone.

Sam turned to his mother. He smiled, raised his hands to give her a thumbs-up sign. Then she led him back to bed.

Days later, doctors released Sam from the hospital, although they asked that he stay in Boston for several days so that he'd be close to the hospital if an infection set in. Painkillers made the days bearable; so he and his mother explored a museum and visited Fenway Park to see where the Boston Red Sox played.

Then, on July 19, the day before they were to fly home, he felt a lump on his chin.

He showed his mother. When she touched his chin, it hurt. She called the hospital. She was told to bring him right over.

She and Sam walked three blocks from their hotel, checked in and took a seat in the waiting room.

Dr. Jennifer Marler remembers that she was on her way to the laboratory when she spotted the Lightners sitting on a bench. She walked over and asked how they were doing. Debbie explained. Marler asked Sam how he felt. He couldn't speak. He shrugged his shoulders. He cried.

Marler told them to wait there. She walked over to

the receptionist, picked up the telephone, called the lab
and canceled her appointment—she had something
more important to take care of. She checked with the receptionist, found an empty examination room and col-
lected the Lightners.

Once in the room, she turned the lights low to calm
Sam. The mass under his chin, she explained, was not a
growth but a buildup of fluid.

He was fine.

What she needed to do, she explained, was to drain
the fluid. She administered a local anesthetic, and—
while she waited for it to take effect—studied this boy
who had dropped into her life 10 months before when
an envelope and a plea for help from Tim Campbell,
Sam's Portland doctor, arrived in her office.

Their relationship had begun with a simple photograph, one Campbell had taken as a way to show the
desperation of Sam's situation. That photo had haunted
Marler. It was the photo that led her to repeatedly petition
the reluctant team of elite surgeons who would ultimately
give in and bring Sam to Boston. It was that photo that
would ultimately change his life…and hers.

But on this day in July, she was thinking of a different
photo—the picture of a new Sam, a post-surgery Sam,
that would join the gallery of photos on her office wall.
There his face would appear among the 20 that most
touched her during her medical career, the children—
some dramatically transformed and some who failed to
survive—who had come to her for help. After all she'd
been through with this boy, one day Marler wanted to
hang a picture of Sam on that wall.

She touched his chin. He did not flinch. She reached
for a syringe to drain the fluid. She wanted to distract
him when the needle pierced his skin.

Sam, she remembers saying as she jabbed him, I
want you to promise to send me a photograph of you
when you get home.

She finished her work, and they all moved to the
door, ready to go their separate ways. Marler didn't
know what to say. And then she realized there was nothing to say. She spread her arms wide, pulling Sam close.
She hugged him tightly, and tears rolled down her
cheeks.

* * *

The Frontier Airlines jet touched down in Portland on July 20. Sam Lightner made his way up the aisle and into the crowded terminal. He saw his father, brother and sister carrying balloons reading: "Welcome Home." They all hugged Sam and told him he looked good.

The surgery was behind in more ways than one. The family's insurance company, negotiating directly with Children's Hospital, had reached final resolution on the cost of the surgery. The grand total was $75,000.

It was time to celebrate.

But Sam felt listless. The skin that had been peeled back during surgery, which had been so healthy in Boston, was pale and waxy. His mother remembers feeling his forehead on the flight and thinking he was running a slight fever.

On July 25, the Lightners took Sam to see Dr. Tim Campbell, the pediatric surgeon who had operated on him when he was a day old, the doctor who had sent the plea for help to Jennifer Marler.

Sam shuffled into the waiting room, barely able to pick up his feet. He found the first chair, fell into it and leaned against the wall. He closed his eyes and curled his legs under him. A bead of sweat glistened on his forehead.

The receptionist called his name. With effort, he pushed himself out of the chair and followed her down the hallway to the examination room. His parents trailed behind. He climbed onto the examination table and let his head sag forward. His mother walked over and ran her hands through his brown hair.

The door opened and Campbell, in his light-green surgical scrubs, strolled in carrying Sam's file.

"Sambo, you old dog," he said. "How are you?"

Sam slumped against the wall.

"He's not feeling well," Debbie Lightner said. "He had a fever of about 100 this morning. And he seems so tired. I don't know if it's from the trip home or what. But he just doesn't seem himself."

Campbell put the file down, washed his hands and walked over to the examination table. He leaned close to Sam.

"Sambo," he said gently, "let me take a look at you."

Sam raised his face.

"He looks a little swollen," he said, "but that's to be expected. Sam, how about lying down for me?" He ran his hands over Sam's face, checked the file and then walked over and touched Sam's forehead, feeling the tube the Boston surgeons had sutured under the boy's scalp. "I think it's time we take that drain tube out," he said.

"Now this might hurt a bit, Sam," Campbell said. "But it's going to be over quickly."

Sam tried to sit up, struggling, kicking his legs. "No," he moaned. "No."

His father held Sam's legs. His mother moved to grasp his arms. Even so, he struggled and wiggled. Campbell yanked twice and drew out a clear line. "OK, big boy," he said. "It's over."

Sam sat up, tears streaking his face.

"He's lost 10 pounds," Debbie Lightner said. "Some, I know, is from the surgery. But..."

Campbell asked if Sam was eating well, and when he heard that the boy's appetite had lagged, he sighed.

"I think I'm going to put Sam in the hospital," he said.

"No," croaked Sam. "No. Please."

Campbell patted Sam on the shoulder, kept his hand there and talked to Sam's parents. "I want him in there for a day or two," he said. "I want a blood culture, a blood count and I want him on IV antibiotics. I'm sure that blood count will be way off. I think he has an infection. We have too much invested here to take any risk."

Sam sobbed, appalled that—after all the painful days he'd spent bedridden in Boston—he was headed back to the hospital.

"I know he's not happy about it," Campbell said. "I know he wants to go home. But he can get real sick, real fast. Those germs could spread through his body and cut off his windpipe. It could be life-threatening."

Campbell patted Sam once on the shoulder. "I'm sorry, Sam," he said. "I really am. Don't give up, Sam. We'll lick this."

"At least we're home," David Lightner told his son.

"And it will only be a couple days," Debbie Lightner added.

An attendant pushed Sam's wheelchair across an

atrium and into the main hospital building. A nurse poked at the boy with a needle while Sam cried and thrashed. She finally connected with a vein and started antibiotics flowing.

Sam checked into a hospital room and spent the next two days watching TV and reading magazines.

The swelling went down. His temperature dropped. And he started slipping out of bed to stroll the hospital halls, dragging his IV setup along with him.

Two days later, as Campbell had promised, Sam checked out of the hospital and headed for the family home in Northeast Portland. When he got to the house, he looked in the bathroom mirror. With the swelling receding, the left side of his face was noticeably reduced. The bottom of his chin, once distended and pointed, was flat and smooth. Even his left eye, which the mass had pushed and distorted, seemed to be in a more normal position. His parents told him he looked great.

But…

When he scrutinized his face, looking at himself the way he knew strangers would, he realized that he didn't look dramatically different from before the surgery.

The skin on the left side of his face, even though relieved of the huge mass of tissue that had once supported it, still formed a dome over the deformed bone underneath it. His jaw remained out of alignment, and it still distorted his mouth and teeth. Removing the tissue mass had further exposed his left ear, large, spongy and misshapen.

The surgeons would turn to all those problems the following spring. But in a month, on Aug. 24, 2000, the freshmen will register at Grant High School.

* * *

The boy sits on the living-room sofa, lost in his thoughts. His parents are at work. His younger brother and sister are enjoying the last two weeks of summer vacation. He moves through the house, looking at the clock, waiting for his mother to come home and take him to Grant.

Today he will register, officially joining the class of 2004. His sister asks him a question, but he ignores her. He has too many things on his mind.

He walks up to his bedroom, the one with the toy

license plate on the door that reads "Sam."

He hasn't been back to Grant, Portland's largest high school, for an official event since the open house on Feb. 3, 2000. That night, he joined more than 1,500 students and parents. He was nervous then.

And now…

He stands and checks out his shirt. Brand-new—pulled from his closet for the first time just for this day. He's showered, and his hair is neatly combed. He walks downstairs and looks at himself in the mirror. He combs his hair again, carefully pressing the last stubborn strand into place.

He walks into the kitchen to make himself lunch. He opens the refrigerator door—glancing at the list of chores his parents expect him to do each day to earn his $5 weekly allowance. He's thrown the dirty clothes down the chute to the basement. He's cleaned the bathroom countertop and swept the floor. He's picked up the basement and vacuumed the upstairs hallway.

He pulls out a jar of peanut butter and a jar of jam and makes himself a sandwich. His mother walks in the door as he's finishing it up, and the phone rings. Three of Sam's Gregory Heights Middle School classmates have gathered at a neighbor's house and are calling to let him know they're ready for their ride. Sam's ready, too. He smoothes his shirt once more and reaches to touch his neck. But when he pulls his hand away, he sees blood on his finger.

Not today.

Not on this day.

Please.

"Mom."

He points to his neck. Blood oozes from one of his stitches. He dabs at it with a napkin.

"Mom!"

His mother searches for a Band-Aid.

"No one will see this," his mother says as she gently pushes the strip over the stitch. "Don't worry."

The two of them walk out the front door and climb into the family's old Honda, back down the driveway, turn through tree-lined streets and pull up in front of a wood-frame house. Three strapping young men jump down the steps, move like athletes toward the Lightner car and jump into the back seat. Sam sits next to his mother in front. At 76 pounds, he looks like a little brother along for the ride.

Just as it did on orientation night, traffic clogs the streets around Grant. So Debbie Lightner has to park five blocks away. Sam and his friends step onto the sidewalk and walk through the neighborhood.

On that February evening nearly seven months before, darkness cloaked the long walk, and Sam covered the distance almost invisible to everyone gathering at Grant. Today, the sun shines brightly on streets filled with students.

Sam touches the Band-Aid on his neck. He adjusts his shirt collar, trying to hide it, but nothing works.

He walks on, his pals towering over him. With Grant looming in the distance, all of them grow quiet. The group spreads out as the boys climb the front steps. They head for separate metal doors.

Sam pulls one of the doors open and steps into the front hall. Linoleum floors. Trophy cases. Metal lockers. Noise and laughter and chaos and all the urgency that is about being 14 years old.

Sam's friends disappear into the crowd, and he stands alone in the midst of the milling mob. An adult hollers instructions, and the students form a rough line that engulfs Sam where he stands. His friends pay no attention to him as they move up and down the line to talk with buddies they have not seen in months.

The line snakes toward the cafeteria, where the students will get their schedules and receive their student identification cards.

Parents show up to pay fees. More students arrive and join the line. The crowd clogs the hall, and someone announces that it will be hours before everyone is registered. Adult volunteers herd the students along, shouting instructions. A teacher brings out a fan to keep everyone cool.

Sam watches new students arrive and walk past him toward the end of the line. He turns to his left, toward a bank of lockers. From this angle, no one can see the left side of his face. Even the students who stand next to him seem unaware of his presence.

"Hey there."

Sam turns. A Grant administrator motions to him and then walks over.

"How you doing?" he asks as he sticks out his hand.

"Fine," says Sam, shaking hands while wondering who this man could possibly be.

The man raises his hand, starts to gesture toward Sam's face, then thinks better of it and lets his hand drop to his side.

"Say, you don't have to wait here in line," he says. "I mean..."

The words hang in the air.

"Let me take you down the back way," he says, rattling a set of keys. "I can get you in and out of here in a couple minutes. Otherwise, you're going to be here for a couple hours. No reason you should have to wait out here in front of everyone. I know how you must be feeling right now."

The man steps closer, putting his arm around Sam's shoulder.

"Let's go," he said. "You don't need this."

Sam weighs his options and makes a quick response that will be colored, as such things are, by everything that has come before. The years of living with his deformity. The decision to risk a life-threatening surgery. The choices he has made—to take a great chance and to confront life head on. "I am Sam," read the Dr. Seuss line the nurse posted over his isolette when he was born. "Sam I am."

He wriggles out from under the man's arm.

"No," he says.

"What?"

"I'll wait with the rest of the students," Sam says.

"But you don't have to."

"I'll wait," Sam says firmly. "This is where I belong."

* * *

The line moves, and Sam watches the administrator walk away. There is no turning back. Sam is carried, step by shuffling step, toward the cafeteria. He descends a flight of steps, walks through a set of double metal doors and pauses, looking out at a sea of students.

Then the line carries him forward to the first of several registration stations along the cafeteria's wall. Brian

Doran, Sam's friend from Gregory Heights, spots him in line, hurries over and hands him a green piece of paper with a locker number and combination on it. Brian, who arrived earlier, has already claimed the locker and requested Sam as a partner.

Sam feels someone touch his shoulder and turns to face Molly Paterno, an old friend from his neighborhood.

"I was thinking about you all summer, Sam," she says. "I wondered if you had the surgery."

She studies him.

"Oh, Sam," she says. "You look great."

Sam moves more easily as the line works its way from station to station. He studies his schedule.

"Sam?"

Emilie Bushlen bustles up and leans close.

"Sam, can I see your schedule?"

He hands her his slip of paper.

"Sam," she squeals. "We got word-processing together."

He blushes.

The line moves forward. The next stop is for yearbook pictures. Sam looks at the order form, trying to figure out what picture package to order. He selects Package E, the one that will give him two extra prints. One will go to Dr. John Mulliken, the lead surgeon in Boston.

The other has a place waiting for it on Dr. Jennifer Marler's wall.

He hands the form to the photographer, who tells him where to sit and how to pose. "OK, kiddo," the photographer says. "Here we go."

He lifts the camera.

Sam Lightner looks straight ahead. This is for the yearbook. This is for history.

He smiles. Broadly.

And a brilliant flash illuminates his face.

Writers' Workshop

Talking Points

1) An effective piece of writing has a single dominant message, what English professors call the theme. In his interview for this book, Tom Hallman describes the role theme plays in his writing. How does this device influence the information he chooses to use in "The Boy Behind the Mask"?

2) Hallman describes the pivotal role that his editor, Jack Hart, played in shaping this series. In one of his most important contributions, Hart acted more like a reporter than an editor. What surprised you about what Hart did? Read the passage on page 4 that resulted from their collaboration and discuss what makes it effective. How does Hart's behavior differ from stereotypes about the way an editor works?

3) For Hallman, scenes are the building blocks of narrative and a key element in engaging the reader's interest. Draw on examples from each of the series' four parts to illustrate how scenes fulfill his objective to bring readers into the heart of the story.

4) Martial arts have played an important role in the development of Hallman's approach to storytelling. Discuss how he applies the principles to his work.

5) The English novelist E.M. Forster described two sets of characters in literature: round and flat. Round characters are multidimensional, complex, and complicated, while flat characters have one side, such as a personality trait, occupation, or other role. To keep his narratives focused, Hallman limits the number of round characters. Decide whether the people appearing in "The Boy Behind the Mask" are round or flat. Discuss the possible reasons the writer made those decisions.

Assignment Desk

1) In his interview, Hallman describes his use of analogies, similes, and metaphors, such as Sam "moves like smoke," "His left ear…a purple mass the size and shape of a pound of raw ground beef," and comparing Sam's surgery to working

on plumbing with the water on. Go on a treasure hunt for other examples in the series and in your other reading. Come up with analogies and metaphors for elements in your stories that could benefit from comparing the unfamiliar with something better known or imagined.

2) "Conditions of difference," says Kenny Irby of The Poynter Institute, "are components that shape the human experience. As journalists, we must become smarter about differences and learn to understand and accept them as they are." Study Irby's webpage explaining this concept at http://www.poynter.org/dj/tips/vj/difference.htm. In that sense, Sam's facial deformity is a condition of difference. Consider other conditions associated with physical attributes such as obesity or dwarfism. Report and write a story chronicling how the condition affects a person's life.

3) Coach a fellow writer on a story by modeling your behavior on the way Jack Hart interviewed Tom Hallman to produce the passage about Sam's face. When the two of you are finished, both answer these three questions: What surprised you about the experience? What did you learn? What do you need to learn next?

4) If you're not doing it already, begin identifying the themes of your stories the way Hallman does. Use theme as a benchmark to guide your reporting, planning, drafting, and revision.

5) Using Hallman's definition of scene—"the places for the reader to watch and feel and experience the story"—draw borders around the scenes in "The Boy Behind the Mask." What are the signals that a scene is beginning or ending? Rent *Dirty Harry* and study how the filmmakers convey information about Clint Eastwood in the opening scene that Hallman describes in the following interview. Observe someone in action and write a scene using only dialogue, physical description, and action.

A conversation with
Tom Hallman Jr.

CHRISTOPHER SCANLAN: How did Sam Lightner enter your life, Tom?

TOM HALLMAN: This story was dropped into my lap. I'm sitting at my desk. I get a phone call. This man says, "I've been reading your stories for years, and I think I've got a good one for you. Friends of our family have a boy with a deformed face." I had this 3-by-5 index card sitting on my desk—I still have the card—and I wrote down "boy with deformed face, Sam."

The caller said, "This family is very private. They've never talked to anybody about it, but if they ever did, I think you'd be the kind of guy to tell their story." So I said, "Why don't you tell them that I'd like to just come over and meet with them, tell them the kind of stories I do, and see how they feel about me doing a story."

About a week later, he said they had given him permission to give me their home phone number. I called Debbie Lightner, introduced myself, and told Debbie I'd like to come over and meet her. They knew my work even though they didn't really know much about the newspaper business. So we talked for a while and I could tell she was checking me out, getting a sense of what I was all about. And then she asked, "Would you like to meet Sam?"

By this time, we were sitting at the dining room table. She called Sam, and I heard these footsteps coming down the steps and then this boy came around the corner. I was stunned. I knew Debbie was watching me to see how I reacted to Sam, and Sam was looking at me, and seeing his face—this is such a cliché—but it took my breath away. It stirred up something in me. I realized this human is different than me.

Sam sat across from me and we talked for a while and I talked about the kind of stories I do, and then—over the years I've sensed when it is time to let people alone—I knew it was time for me to leave the house, to let them talk about it. If I hung around any longer they might say,

"We really don't want to do it." I just knew it was time to go. I said I appreciated the time and I'd let them think about it and I'd wait to hear from them. A few days later, I got a call from Debbie who said, "Sam has decided to tell the story and he's decided to let you tell it."

You say you've learned when to leave, to back off, to give people some space. How do you know?

This story required me to use every skill I've learned in my 20-some years in the business. I spent 10 years at *The Oregonian* covering police; you've got to talk to people in tough situations, accident scenes or fires, people who've lost loved ones. You get a sense of when to approach them, when not to, when to back off, when to let the tears fall. It's a skill that's learned, like asking a girl out on a date. You've got to learn when to ask again or when to realize you've been rejected. These personal skills are as important as notetaking and knowing what questions to ask. I had great practice trying to get tough old robbery detectives to talk to me about their cases and let me wander in the squad room and learn the rhythms of people. You don't get that covering city hall or places where people want to talk to you all the time. You get it by being rejected on a daily basis.

What do you tell people like the Lightners that you're going to be doing?

I'm going to be asking a lot of questions. I'm going to be asking questions that don't make any sense. I'm going to be hanging around the house. I really get them to be part of the process. I sell them not only on the story but on my being there. I'd come to the house and hang out with Sam and his brother and sister after school; I'd walk to school with Sam. They were used to me being around. And so when the story started to move to its more emotional moments, I was part of the family and they were used to me being there and they talked openly.

Early on in the story, I had to build four relationships: I had to build a relationship with Sam. I had to build relationships with his mother and with his father, and with the entire family as a unit, and if any one of them wanted to quit this story, the project would have ended. And by doing it that way, I feel that I got the family to become advocates for me and for the story.

This paid off in part three. We've committed a bunch of time. I've spent hundreds of hours with the family. We go to Boston for this surgery. Sam goes to the place where you register. I'm there with him, the photographer's there with him. A receptionist says, "Who are you?" I said, "I'm here from *The Oregonian*." She picks up the phone and calls the PR department. Some vice president comes running down and says, "You can't be here for this operation. You should have called me. This is just not going to happen." She goes over to the Lightners to tell them, and they say, "No, that's Tom. He can be here." And so that relationship forged months earlier paid off right then.

Do you ever worry that you're taking advantage of people?

In the most blunt terms, I *am* taking advantage of them. I'm taking their life and writing about it and getting paid, and the paper is publishing it and getting paid for running those kinds of stories. At that level, I truly am a salesman selling myself to them. Once I get that access, that information, then I am a messenger telling their story and trying to do something with a greater purpose.

What is the greater purpose?

To remind people that we're all part of the human race, that really there's only a handful of emotions and we all feel them. These kinds of stories cross all boundaries of race and gender and income and where you live—you can live in a rural area and be moved by Sam and his family. You can live in the inner city and be moved by Sam and his family. That's not the case with stories about the environment or city hall. These types of stories touch something universal and remind us who we are. That's where the power comes from. The higher purpose for me is that they're about people, not about institutions.

How important is theme?

Theme is what drives my stories, the universal that comes from the handful of emotions that we all have: wanting to fit in, or love, or death. The choice the writer makes is figuring out what theme do I see and then reporting to see if that's right. If it is, that theme guides the reporting from that moment on. If you use that structure the way I do, it makes reporting much, much easier. If the theme is Sam wanting people to know that there's a boy behind this mask, that theme guides me when I walk to school with him or I'm with his friends or his family. Does this show my theme? Does this make it resonate more with readers?

That way you don't get caught up in writing a whole bunch of stuff about Sam the athlete or mainstreaming kids. You don't come back to your office with 300 pages of notes from one day thinking, "I've done a lot of work." But when it comes time to write, you don't have anything. You have a bunch of facts. You've got great individual scenes. You've got some wonderful quotes. But what's this story about?

How do you find out?

I think about the story. When I met Sam that first day, I drove over to a Safeway parking lot, stopped the car, got my notebook out, and just thought about this boy and his parents. I thought about my own daughter. What would it be like for me as a father, the heartache I would feel if my daughter was like that? How I'd want to protect her from the world and be mad at the world. I wrote these things down. I wanted to do a story that touches on those things. I'd discard some of them, but I was very aware of how I felt. Not, I want to do a story about a kid with a strange face. It had a deeper meaning. I walked to school with him one day. He crosses a very busy street early in the morning, and I felt embarrassed to be with him. I felt all these people looking at me, and part of me wanted to say, "Hey, I'm just a reporter. I'm not with him. I'm just doing my job." I realized that that's what this kid goes through every day. I wanted to get the feelings on the page. I really let my feelings guide me in the reporting and the questions I ask. The theme emerges out of that.

What's the theme of this story?

We all want to fit in. We all have a mask. You have a mask, I have a mask. The guy wearing a Rolex is sending out a message to the world, the guy wearing the suit, the guy wearing the Birkenstocks. But we can make our masks subtle. Sam Lightner could not. His mask was right out there. I wanted to show people the kid behind the mask, but get them to realize the strength and courage he had to have to go beyond his mask. We all have to get beyond our masks. You don't want to hit readers over the head with it. It's got to be subtle, very quiet bass notes. And then you've got the melody and all the other stuff that sticks in the reader's ear; but the real quiet, keeping-the-beat thing is we've all got these masks. That's what struck me early on.

Those bass notes seem to be in the deck heads on each day of the series.

Oh, those were great. The story was all laid out in a conference room and (executive editor) Peter Bhatia and (editor) Sandy Rowe walked around the room and looked at the stuff. We were originally just going to have "The Boy Behind the Mask," but Peter said, "You're going to have something...subheads?" Subheads! It turned out to be a brilliant decision because (managing editor) Jack Hart wrote those subheads. They became the theme for each day, especially for part four: "I am Sam; Sam I am." You get foreshadowing there and it comes back at the end of the story. That came out of an editing suggestion.

What does it mean that your editor could capture the theme in each of these stories?

Good writing requires good editing, and any writer that says he doesn't want to work with an editor is a fool. The reason Jack could write those is because he knew this story the way I did. I'd come back to his office and we'd talk about these ideas of themes and fitting in. It helps me refine what I'm thinking about, what I'm feeling. Then I go back into the field and do more reporting.

Jack knew the story. He wasn't just taking a piece of

copy and looking for typos or sentence structure. He was intimately involved with what this story was about. In the opening I was going to write about this kid's face. In the editing, Jack asked, "What is it about this kid that moves all these doctors? What is it about him?" Jack became a reporter. He got out this yellow legal pad and he said, "Tell me about Sam. Why do you think that is?" I started talking and then he swiveled around to his computer and he typed in basically what I said, that you find yourself drawn into that eye. You find yourself looking past the deformity and you see yourself in that eye. You see the child you were. Jack pulled that from me by just being a reporter. To me that is one of the most powerful paragraphs in the entire story. For a reader who gets to that point, the theme is just hammered home.

That's where great editing comes in, because Jack knew we had to do that, but I was so immersed in the story I couldn't pull that out. Then he tested it. We got a picture of Sam and went around the newsroom. We would walk up to people and say, "Look at this picture. What do you think? What do you see?" And all of them talked about that good eye. So we knew we were on the right track. That is a mark of a great editor; it has nothing to do with editing in the traditional sense. He's thinking about the story.

What is it about *The Oregonian* that makes this kind of work possible?

It starts at the top. You have to have top editors who understand the time commitment. Too many people look at narrative stories as simply the guy turning on a tape recorder, getting them to talk; it's an expanded Sunday feature. The best editors realize these require as much investigative reporting as traditional investigative stories. You're looking into people's lives and hearts and minds. That's no different than digging out some SEC document. So you get the time.

At *The Oregonian* if you look at any very good writing, you're going to find a very good editor behind the writer. They're assembling good teams. There's so much emphasis on how to help writers be better; there's very little on how do you grow a good editor. It's not just somebody from the copy desk. It's not just taking a reporter—I'd be a lousy editor. An editor requires a certain set of skills, temperament. The very best papers realize that and put those people in the right spot and then help them grow, too.

At some point do you make an outline, present a plan?

I wrote something up for Jack. I said, "Day one, I'll be with him going to this open house and to see Dr. Campbell." I told Sam's mom I needed his history and she said she thought they had these journals in the basement from when Sam was in the hospital. She went down there and dug them out for me. I knew that I wanted to incorporate those in part one. I knew part two would be going to Boston. Part three would be the surgery, and part four would be going to school. That was kind of a loose structure. My goal was to have the ending be him at the first day of high school.

But when I went with him on registration day, I realized there was no better ending than that. There were a couple of times in this story when the hair stood up on my arms. One was in that operation. Two was when Jennifer Marler walked into the room. And when I watched Sam get his picture taken. Right after he had his picture taken, I went back to the office, I wrote down my notes, and I knew that was the ending. I didn't care about the first day of school.

What role do scenes play in this story and in your approach to writing narrative?

Scenes make the story come alive and pull the reader into the heart of the story. If you read a story that's all summary narrative—here's what happened—it's like some kid banging one note on a piano. It's monotonous. Scenes allow you to manipulate the reader, in a very good way. It allows you to bring them deeply into something, feel something, watch something. The places in between the scenes are the time for readers to catch their breath, to get information. The scenes themselves are the places for the reader to watch and feel and experience the story. If you don't have the scenes, you're left with a bunch of information. Writers who don't really think scenically struggle to make people feel something. They fall into the trap of trying to find the right word. I really feel that they're manipulating me and I don't like that. I like the subtle manipulation where you use the craft to make the reader feel something.

How does one think scenically?

Being a police reporter is the best training ground for that because you become an observer. You go out with the vice squad and watch them picking up johns. There's a scene there. What does the guy's car look like? What's he like? What's he wearing? What is this telling you? And then you learn how to tell the scene. You go home and you tell your friends, "They arrested this middle-class guy from the suburbs and here's what happened." You're telling the story scenically. It's learned by practicing it. It requires a lot of reporting because nobody says, "Okay, we're starting scene one; get your notebook out." Scenes blend into one another.

That's what makes each person's writing different; it's what you see and choose to see that makes the story. You have to get in the habit. I wish I had done more of this early in my career. Nobody talked about writing or scenic stuff. It was the inverted pyramid, getting good quotes. I look back at some of the city council things I covered in this small town. There would be great scenes, but no, I'm writing about the new sewer district going in and not getting any of the flavor of the people talking, the people in the audience. It could be practiced on routine "boring" stories. And if you do it, you'll find that readers respond.

What do reporters have to get in their notepads to write a scene?

What's not being said. When the door opens and the person walks in, the way they're dressed, the way they move, the way they sit in a chair, and what does that tell you about them and what does it mean for what's going to happen. One of the great scenes is the opening of

Dirty Harry when he's sitting in the coffee shop and the bank robbers are out there and he says, "Call 911. There's a robbery going down." The scene is him walking across the street, shooting, and then the line, "Do you feel lucky?" It tells you everything about the character without somebody else telling you. Movies have to rely on real-time action. They can't take a break and say Dirty Harry was divorced and this is why he is the way he is. That's a trap we fall into sometimes in news stories. Because we can do that, we don't carry the scene to its full potential. It can't just be details. A scene has to have a beginning, a middle, and an end, and a point, and then lead to another scene. The story always has to be moving forward. If it doesn't move forward, then it becomes a pileup of details.

Analogies, metaphors, and similes seem to play a really important role. "He moves like smoke." "His left ear was even more abnormal, a purple mass the size and shape of a pound of raw ground beef." Why do you use them?

When other writers have read this story, I say, "Tell me what works for you and what doesn't, because it helps me figure out what I'm doing right and wrong." And so many of them have talked about "he moves like smoke." Jack (Hart) has always talked about finding specifics to talk about universals, so I'm aware of that. Everybody knows what a bunch of hamburger looks like, so again, that makes the reader do the work. Moving like smoke—you know what smoke moves like. I try to find things that trigger something in the reader and they do the work for me. At that point they're no longer reading the story, they're living it, and if you can get them living the story, then you're on your way.

How much ends up on the cutting room floor in these stories?

A lot. I want the readers to do the work for me. I don't want them to get distracted. If I write "chocolate chip cookies and Coke," I don't want them to suddenly start thinking about chocolate chip cookies—"I haven't had those for a while." That's why I don't like putting things in about songs. I don't want them to start hearing the song in their head. I want the details to be specific enough to conjure up a feeling, but not so detailed that it gets them off track.

What's the hardest part of a story like this one and how do you overcome it?

Beginning the story, actually having to put something down on the computer screen. I love reporting, I love thinking about it, talking about people, stopping at Jack Hart's office. But when I sit down and start to write, the story and I, we're in a struggle now. I'm in a boxing ring. I put a CD on and I listen to music and I start to write and I don't like it, and I go get a cup of coffee and I wander around. All that time is not being wasted because the story is starting to filter through me. I'm at home, I'm taking a shower, I'm on the bus, I'm walking downtown, I am thinking about this story nonstop. I come back and write a little more. An outline is forming in my mind, and then I get a sense of where I'm going and I'm off on this journey. There are going to be detours and roadblocks and all kinds of things, but I got a sense of where I'm at.

When's the best time?

I've started to take control of the story and started to use the tools to manipulate the readers. I'll get to a scene and I'll read it to myself and I'll feel tears in my eyes or I'll know the readers are going to feel this. One of the most wonderful moments is before I turn the story in. I'm the only one who knows about the story. Once I turn it in to Jack and it goes to the public, it's no longer my story. That's why I'm a very easy person to edit. I don't fight over words and my words aren't locked in stone. If you can make the story better, let's do it. But the hard part is that rough draft.

I got an e-mail today from a writer looking for advice on a story: "I feel like it's a gem and the perfect narrative opportunity, but I can see I may get quickly overwhelmed." What would you tell her?

You're going to be overwhelmed, and if you weren't, the story wouldn't be worth telling. One of my favorite lines in a movie is in *A League of Their Own*. Geena Davis wants to go home. She tells Tom Hanks it's too hard. He says the hard is what makes it great. If it was easy, everybody'd do it. It has taken me 25 years to really understand that. When I read a Rick Bragg story or a Tom French story, it looks easy. It looks like Tom just sat down and wrote it, but I know—because I've done them—that he was pulling his hair out. I'm hoping he had some doubts because he's too good to be perfect.

We are all on the same ship and some of us are farther along than others; but if you quit too early, you'll never realize what you could have done. I don't believe it comes down to talent. God isn't tapping people on the shoulder and saying, "You have the gift." It's just a lot of hard work.

For someone who wants to start out, I would say don't take some big Sam Lightner story. Take something smaller and work on parts of the craft. Once you've done a few of those and you feel like you have a handle, take one of those big stories. You will be overwhelmed, but it's kind of like being in love. You don't know where your head's at. But you sort it out, and that is as much a part of the writing process as polishing or editing or reporting.

We do not talk about the feelings we have as writers. When we talk about those feelings, we admit we're weak, have doubts, and a writer is only as good as his last story. To say you've got doubts implies you might not ever be able to do it again. I'd love nothing more than to spend the next 20 years talking about Sam Lightner, but I know in three weeks, I'll be working a Sunday shift and I'll have to write another story and I might be able to use some of the narrative techniques in a 15 to 20-inch story. Who knows? Maybe next week I'll get another phone call and that'll be my next Sam Lightner thing.

How should this writer proceed?

What's the story about? If you can't tell me what the story's about, you don't know the story and do not start writing until you can tell me what the story's about. If you do start writing, you will get caught up in what I call the tricks of nonfiction literary journalism—dialogue and scenes and all that. You'll think you're really doing something, but it's to no purpose. It's like when you go to a guitar store on a Saturday. You get all these young guys in there practicing. Doing all these licks and distortion. Hand them a guitar and say, "Play me a song." They're stumped. They know the licks, the cool stuff they see on MTV, but they don't have a sense of a song.

As a writer you have to know what your song is about, and then start to tell it. The feeling of being overwhelmed will go down dramatically if you know what the story's about. Then it's just figuring out what you've got in your notebook to help tell the story.

You won this award in 1997. What have you learned since then?

To trust my ability to see a story. That's because I'm living life more. That helps make you a richer writer. Journalists hang out with other journalists, go to lunch with other journalists, talk about who's going to be the next managing editor. We don't get out enough among regular people or just walk downtown and ponder.

Do prizes help you or hinder you?

All my awards are in a box at home. They're not hanging on the wall. I've been meaning to put them up for years. Don't get me wrong. I like getting them, the recognition. But there's always a part of me that realizes that I still don't know what I'm doing. I feel like I've come full circle. I started out as a police reporter, terrified about losing the job; now I've won all these awards, but I'm still at heart that police reporter figuring out how to tell the story. It's a lifelong journey and that's what makes it so rich. It's not like I closed the big real estate deal in town and now I get commissions off it for the rest of my life.

I think the very first one I won told me: You can do this. The Livingston Award. This is how naïve I was. I won the Livingston Award. I go to New York to the ceremony. I'm standing there in my brand new suit, and somebody comes over and says, "The managing editor from *The New York Times* wants to know what you're doing tomorrow, if you'd like to come down." I thought he wanted to take me on a tour of the place. I said, "Can my dad come?" and they said, "No, they want to talk to you about a job." Journalism is one field where you can continue to grow and get better and wiser as the years go on. The awards are milestones. They're nice, but to think that they're the be all and end all, you're only fooling yourself.

Are you still learning?

You bet I am. I could not have done this story five years ago. The way I relate to it is like for 20 years I've dabbled in the martial arts. I've taken karate, tae kwon do, aikido. In martial arts, you practice techniques over and over and over, punch and block, so when you have to use it, it's instinctive. That's what this story was. I had spent 10 years covering crime. I'd done hundreds and hundreds of stories. I was mugged by Sam Lightner. When it dropped into my lap, I had the tools in my toolbox to do the story the justice it deserved. Five years ago? Ten years ago? I might have fallen into the trap of deformed kid, it's a sob story, or maybe I'll go out and spend a day with him.

You're always continuing to learn more about the craft every day. The parts that I'm working on are boring stuff: transitions, exposition. How do you tell something that happened 10 years ago? Those are hard things to learn.

Where do you go to find out?

I read other people and think, "Oh, my God, I should just quit." All writers are insecure. We don't want to admit it, but we've got these self-doubts we're grappling with. We don't talk about the doubts and the insecurities and how we always are thinking we're frauds and we're one step away from really not being able to do it. We all think the other guy's full of confidence and I'm not.

That's the mask writers wear. Behind the mask, it's hard, it's time consuming, it tests your confidence, your heart, your soul. But if you work on the craft, then when you get the big Sam Lightner kind of story, you don't have to think so much about some of the tools. You can think about what it means. I play guitar and I've been taking lessons for five years. There are times I don't want to practice, but if I don't do the scales and the weird fingerings, when it comes time to play for people, I can't do anything. That's the same as it is with being a reporter. Every story presents you the opportunity to work on a part of the craft. You cover a city council meeting—and I covered many when I was at a small paper. You learn how to get the boring guy to stop talking to you, keep the interview on track. You cover a cop, you learn how to get him to help you out. All those things are part of the craft, and if you try to hurry the craft, it just doesn't work. I remember the first time I saw one of these *Best Newspaper Writing* books. I'd think, man, they're at *The Washington Post* and they're doing all these big things, and here I am covering city council in a little town in Washington.

I hope that whoever reads this is working on a small paper in Iowa or Tennessee. The message I'd give them is to hang in there and work on the craft. You don't have to come out of college and go to *The New York Times* or *The Washington Post*. Work at those small places, honing the craft, learning how to interview people. It ultimately pays off, because these stories are out there. You'll be ready when it happens.

Sun Journal

Michelle Kearns

Finalist, Non-Deadline Writing

Michelle Kearns has been a staff writer for the Sunday edition of the *Sun Journal* in Lewiston, Maine, since October 1999. She started her career in 1989 in the features department of the women's magazine *First*, where she was promoted from editorial assistant to assistant features editor. After a couple of years of writing and editing articles and a popular culture page, she got a job writing for *Redbook* as an associate features editor. There she became interested in newspaper journalism, which led to a job as a night desk writer for the Portland (Maine) bureau of the Associated Press.

Kearns went on to work as a reporter for *The Times Record* and *Press Herald* in Maine. She earned a bachelor's degree in English from Colorado College in 1986 and has studied Greek culture and history in Athens and French at the University of Grenoble. She lives in Freeport, Maine, with her husband, Robert F. Bukaty, an Associated Press photographer and a fellow Buffalo, N.Y., native.

In "Death of a Lineman," Kearns looks behind the tragedy of a blue-collar worker's accidental death to find the story of love, the cost of a hard-driving job, and the scarred memory of a father who thought his son deserved better.

Death of a lineman

MARCH 12, 2000

A windstorm had been ripping power lines for a day and Brent Churchill had barely slept in two nights when he passed his parents' house, toot-tooting his horn as he always did. From the window, his father saw him. His boy was on his way again to bring back electricity for someone.

"He must be pooped," Glendon Churchill said.

His wife, daughter and grandson kept putting ornaments on the Christmas tree and said nothing. Long hours were normal for Brent. They didn't see him for weeks after the ice storm two years ago, just the laundry he'd leave off in garbage bags.

Half an hour later the phone rang. Then his father was driving down the road. Past the blinking lights. Past the person who tried to hold him back.

"No, you ain't," he said. "That's my boy." He found his son hanging from the top of the pole by his straps while a minister stood nearby.

"For God sakes, get him down," Churchill said.

Maybe he was still alive. But there was just a minister and a power company meter reader and they didn't know how to climb 30 feet up a pole.

Then Churchill was on his way home to tell his family. Back in his driveway, he wept so hard he nearly fell out of the car.

Brent's mother, Donna, screamed loud enough for her 6-year-old grandson to wonder at how she could make such a sound.

She kept screaming, "I don't believe it. I can't feel it. It's not happening. It's not him."

Never would she have imagined this. Her son drove past the house on the way to his death?

He had just fallen in love, planned a June wedding. He was going to live behind her in his log cabin in the woods and have children.

Again her husband made the five-minute drive along the wooded curves of Route 43 to the pole by Clearwater Lake.

"Brent," he said, calling up, "talk to me."

His son's body was still. No answer came. A rescue worker had already checked for a pulse and there was none. The electricity was off.

"Please take him down," Churchill pleaded.

Lineman Tim Cummings had arrived and decided to get his gear and climb. But he was stopped. He heard someone say there was no rush.

The fire chief and a Central Maine Power Co. supervisor who were standing by decided it would be safest to use a ladder truck to take Churchill down. And so Glendon Churchill begged and waited, as his son hung by his straps for nearly an hour.

For some reason, Brent Churchill had grabbed a 7,200 volt line at about 12:15 that afternoon.

FINDING FAULT

Ten days later, the company's investigation faulted the nine-year veteran for not wearing rubber gloves, failing to check the line for electricity, neglecting to attach grounding wires and not looking to see if the fuse was blown—the standard procedures for the situation.

"It only adds to our sadness," the company said in a statement, "to learn that, for reasons we'll never know, he apparently overlooked some vital safety steps..."

But government findings indicate the company overlooked a few things, too. Churchill's mother would describe it more harshly. She believes the company worked her son to death.

Churchill worked for 28 hours straight, according to an investigation by the Occupational Health and Safety Administration. In his last 55 1/2 hours of work, it concluded, he had about five hours of broken sleep.

Twice he went to bed and twice the CMP communication center sent him back to his truck.

In addition, CMP received an OSHA $7,000 fine for violating federal rules by letting Churchill repair the high-voltage lines without help from another lineman that day. In teams, lineworkers can watch out for each other and keep each other safe. They prepare for rescues every year by practicing cardiopulmonary resuscitation and carrying a 225-pound dummy from a pole top.

A lineman rescued by his partner after touching an electrified line works for CMP still.

In acknowledgment of its failings, last month the company reached an agreement with the union to make safety changes that might have saved Churchill's life had they been in place sooner. The changes included: hiring 20 more linemen, appointing nine safety coordinators, employing a lineworker to supervise field work, sending linemen out in pairs to work on high-voltage lines and requiring seven-hour rests after 17 hours of work. In emergencies, the seven-hour break will come after a 24-hour shift so that workers can bring as much power on as possible.

COULDN'T AVOID LONG HOURS

Brent Churchill died on the fifth day of his seven-day stint as the Farmington Center's lineman on call. His turn to be "duty man" came up every six weeks on a Wednesday and he was in charge of responding to every assignment after day shifts ended at 3:30.

Co-worker Jerry Phillips had heard Churchill complain about this job. He felt peer pressure to keep working even if he was tired. He didn't like the idea of saying he'd had enough, because that would mean someone else who wasn't on duty would have to come in and maybe that person would be mad at him for giving in.

"You shouldn't let things like that bother you," said Phillips, who himself had refused duty work more than once because he was tired.

During those on-call weeks, Churchill's fiancée, Kathy Bohlman, would wait on the couch for him to come home late at night, and he would tell her he hated this duty man business as much as she did.

She dreaded the long hours and so did other girlfriends and wives.

Linemen and their families tell stories of how when a storm comes, work can go on for 36, 37, 40 hours in a row. That's how it was for everybody all the time. There have been men who have driven trucks so tired that they got back to the service center and couldn't remember who was at the wheel. They talked, slurring words as if drunk. Going 34 hours without sleep could make a man put his head in his hands and weep, thinking work would never end.

Churchill was known for resisting the long hours. His family said he made $20,000 in overtime last year, even though he turned down extra work, got caller I.D. to screen company calls and was the lowest overtime earner at the Farmington service center.

Two small scars by Churchill's lip and cheek were reminders of the job's hazards. He'd been hit in the face by a spray of electric fire last summer.

His glasses had been blackened and his nose and lips swelled.

The week he died, Bohlman had decided she didn't want her fear to weigh too heavily on his mind. She'd made an effort to look happier when he was on his way out and he noticed and thanked her for it.

In the afternoon on Friday, Dec. 10, Bohlman left work thinking of her 30th birthday on Monday. She had asked Churchill to take the day off. He'd still have to start going out on duty-man jobs at 3:30 p.m., but she thought that until then he could at least sleep.

She told a co-worker that turning 30 would mark the beginning of her life. Churchill had a good heart, a good mind and she was lucky.

She'd been trying to persuade him that at 30 he wasn't as old as he thought he was. It wasn't too late to go back to school and study to be a history teacher if he wanted to. They could manage on her income as an insurance specialist for Social Security.

He admitted he didn't want to be a lineman all his life. He was a big, strong man—6 foot 3, 230 pounds. Even so, climbing poles and freeing lines by chainsawing trees was hard on his body.

CHURCHILL HAD SAFETY CONCERNS

In the past year, Churchill had also been troubled by company policies that he thought were unsafe, and he complained loudly.

"If we don't change the way things are done around here, someone is going to get killed," was something, he told his fiancée, he had voiced at work.

The company was keeping track of everybody, timing how long workers spent running a line to a customer's house or planting a pole in the ground.

Churchill had told Bohlman he didn't like the new pressure that he was feeling to work fast.

While there were others who felt as he did, some were unbothered by the pressure.

The company later said its goal wasn't to make people work faster, but to manage work better and improve efficiency by 25 percent. CMP officials said they didn't want to compromise safety, but did want to control costs and keep rates down for customers.

Churchill would be the second man to die since CMP's safety department was changed five years ago following the layoff of 37 lineworkers.

After that, there were fewer people to send out to work on energized pole-top lines and there was no longer a person who went from region to region doing spot checks and explaining accidents and near misses so linemen would know what to avoid.

Without a roving safetyman, linemen met, talked about safety among themselves and looked over write-ups from company e-mail and newsletters. Employees know their jobs better than people from the central office, reasoned the company.

However, if a co-worker did something unsafe, there was no fear that the "safety police" would show up and notice. Linemen were supposed to say something to their co-workers or report it to a supervisor.

Churchill told Bohlman this made no sense to him: Linemen know their lives depend on each other, so why risk alienating someone in their own district?

"This isn't safety," he told Bohlman when he came home one night. "It's just a big joke."

But he didn't have a job to replace this one yet. Besides, it made him feel good when he could help people by turning their power back on.

The money was nice, too. He was single. He didn't need more than his regular $40,000 salary. He built a house. He bought snowmobiles for his parents and kept two of his own. He had an ATV, a new motorcycle and his red truck was new, right off the dealer's lot.

THE STORM

On the afternoon of Friday, Dec. 10, Churchill had worked his regular eight and a half hours by 3:30.

Before he could get home, he was sent out again.

At 5:25 p.m., he called Bohlman from his house in Industry to say he was about to make the 25-minute trip to her house in Jay.

At 6 he called again as she was making lasagna.

He was coming to pick her up and take her with him to a new call he'd been given in Jay.

It turned out not to be much of an emergency. Something so small that a lineman shouldn't have gone at all: Someone had called to say their electric bill was high, so the com center dispatched Churchill.

Instead of leaving when he heard the homeowners had a problem with their bill—a problem better suited for the business office—Churchill stayed.

It was raining, Bohlman waited in the car and Churchill checked their wires, their meter and went inside to talk.

By 8:30 p.m. the couple were at a restaurant eating french fries and sandwiches and talking about spending money on the wedding instead of a family-sized SUV that was going on sale that weekend.

Before bed, he held her face in his hands and told her he'd love her always. It was 10:30.

At 1:11 a.m. he woke to a com center call to go out and fix a broken pole in the windstorm that cut power to more than 11,000 CMP customers.

He was back at Bohlman's by 5 trying to sleep. The phone rang again at 7:45 a.m. and Bohlman, who'd been up, went in the bedroom and saw that he was already awake. It seemed to her he hadn't slept much and she told him she wanted to let him rest, but it was the company calling.

She saw Churchill for the last time that morning in Wilton at 11:30 when he passed her, pulled over in the company truck and got out to talk. She was on her way to go shopping with her son and she stayed in the car and told him she really wanted to see him.

Maybe, he said, his job would be quick and easy and he could swing over and see her before she left for a Santa train ride in Unity with their mothers, her son and his sister and nephew.

She said she loved him and asked him to be careful. As she turned to drive away, he blew kisses through the window.

AN UNSETTLING FEELING

Bohlman had been feeling strange all day. She told her mother after the train ride that she liked Churchill's family and she couldn't figure out why she spent the whole time wanting to get away from them.

"I can't calm down," she said.

By 6 p.m. a "bird dog" worker was assigned to Churchill.

The assistant usually installed and read electric meters, but during a storm his job was to drive ahead and find poles and wires that needed fixing.

The Farmington service center had an odd number of linemen, so they couldn't all work in pairs. This outage was major and every man was needed. The two men worked through the night.

At 5 a.m. Sunday they stopped for breakfast. They still had work to do.

By 6 they were getting updated orders at the CMP office in Farmington. At 6:30 Churchill was calling Bohlman.

He hadn't been to bed in 23 hours. The first thing he said was, "Baby, my ass is dragging."

"Please come home," she said back. He couldn't, he said. He was duty man.

He told her she'd been on his mind; she asked him to be careful.

At 7:15 lineman Steve Laney from Skowhegan, called in and offered to work. The supervisor at the other end of the line told him, no, they didn't need him.

The company had left a message at Laney's house the night before, but he'd been out for his birthday.

During storm emergencies, workers from one district are called in to help out in another, but when Laney called in, problems were winding down, the company later explained. The windstorm was over and that supervisor was thinking of only Skowhegan, which is a satellite office of Farmington.

At 10 a.m. when the line clerk radioed to ask how he was feeling, Churchill said he was OK, company investigators would later find. CMP left it up to lineworkers to decide whether they could keep working or not. Men had filed grievances with the union for being forced to go home.

Yet, Churchill thought he had to keep going. He had told his family that he heard what a supervisor said one day when another lineman announced he was done. "You can go home," the boss had said, "but when you come back, you might be looking for another job."

THE BEST THREE MOMENTS

Bohlman stopped in a shop to buy a card on her way to church at about the same time Churchill was getting the radio call. In the six months they'd been dating, they'd been exchanging romantic words instead of gifts.

He had surprised her by keeping the first card she gave him in his truck, reading it before work and then again before he went to bed. She'd written that his gentleness made her melt and that she'd never leave him.

She figured that while he slept Monday, she would write another card and give it to him when he woke up.

Church got out at 11:30 and Bohlman fought an urge to drive to Churchill's house in Industry. But she knew he would come to her house when he was done. Going to Wal-Mart to shop made more sense.

It was a minute after noon when Bohlman bought a salad at the lunch counter and began to eat alone while her mother and son looked for Christmas trees.

One or two bites and the sick heavy feeling she'd been having all weekend got worse. She pushed the salad container away.

Lasagna was waiting in the refrigerator for later. She made it the way Churchill loved, with three kinds of cheese and a sweet sauce.

He would often sit in the kitchen and watch her work. He admired her perfectionist way of spreading mayonnaise back and forth on a piece of bread so it was even, like frosting on a cake.

He would tease, "Girl, why haven't you married me yet?"

He would repeat what the three best moments of his life would be:

When they married, when she gave birth to their first child and when they were old. He said he would sit with her on a wooden swing and he would get off, kneel down, hold her hand and ask her if he'd been a good man to her.

"If you said 'yes,'" he told her, "that would be the third happiest moment in my life."

FATAL ERRORS

It was about 11 a.m., when Churchill's assistant arrived on a camp road by a smattering of houses rimming Clearwater Lake in Industry.

A line was broken by a fallen birch, the power was reported to be out at the houses, but the fuse rod was in its place at the top of a pole on Route 43. The foot-long tube pointed up from its hinge, a signal that power was probably running down the wires.

Churchill arrived at the downed line and sent his assistant to check the fuse instead of doing it himself.

Churchill put a sledgehammer in the back of his assistant's truck and, the man later told investigators, Churchill asked him to pound on the fuse pole on Route 43.

If the fuse was blown, the rod would likely fall when the pole was struck and that would mean the power was off.

Both men were tired, the assistant would later tell police, but he felt fine enough to be working. It had been 18 hours since the man started and 28 since Churchill left his fiancée.

The assistant drove away, pounded on the pole and, he would tell company investigators, returned and let Churchill know that the fuse didn't fall.

The man said he heard Churchill reply, "OK." Churchill, who was hard of hearing in one ear, then went to the downed wires and put his climbing hooks and belt on.

Sometime after noon, the meter man told investigators, he stood and watched from about six feet away from the pole as Churchill belted himself in at the top, near the electrified line, and made adjustments to set his hooks and get comfortable.

The assistant figured Churchill knew the line was live, he would later tell police, because he was experienced.

Churchill then reached toward the wire with his right hand, the assistant told company investigators. A ball of fire went at him. Churchill fell and hung limp, tied to the pole by his straps.

The meterman ran to the truck and radioed for help. It was about 12:15.

LOVED BY A TOWN

At the wake four days after his death, Churchill's sister, Terri, looked at him in the casket and thought he still seemed tired. The makeup didn't mask the black circles she could see under his eyes. Four hundred people came—one of the biggest turnouts the Adams Funeral Home in Farmington had ever had.

He had been known as a star football player in high school, getting chosen to play tackle for the state all-star team, going to the playoffs with Mt. Blue.

Her brother had a way of befriending everyone from the "high muckety-muck to the low muckety-muck." From the banker's son to the person on welfare.

Their father drove a school bus and Terri Churchill would marvel at how her brother didn't let class barriers separate him from others as she sometimes did. He was the person at parties people would gather around.

For fun, he would kiss the men he cared about right smack on the lips. The two high school classmates who were football captains with him came to the funeral home to put their old jerseys in the casket with him.

The next day police led a convoy of 70 CMP trucks past his log cabin in Industry for a memorial service the company organized.

At the Henderson Memorial Baptist Church in Farmington, people filled the pews and the Sunday-school rooms off to the side. Many in the crowd cried softly.

By the altar, leaning against easels, were giant pictures of Churchill; in one he was laughing, in the other he wore a company uniform.

Glendon Churchill was in a front pew while his wife sat on a folding chair in the back near the door, so she could leave when her sobs overtook her, as she knew they would.

Terri Churchill stayed at home because she was too angry. She was mad that her brother was dead, mad that he stayed up on the pole for almost an hour and mad that her father had to wait beneath her brother's body.

"I wish I could take that image away from my father," she said.

After the Thursday service, two linemen and three managers resumed the work they'd started on their investigation into why the accident happened.

Churchill's lack of rubber gloves and his neglect to check the fuse, test the wire and ground the line were named "root" causes.

These were the things that were clear, the managers said. How much sleep a person got and how that affected a person, those factors were harder to measure, harder to know.

Tiredness affected everything and it was clearly another reason, the two linemen argued. But they were outnumbered.

Dale Blethen and Dave Ellis put their coats on and threatened to walk out two or three times as they tried to make their perceptions prevail. They wanted the fact that Churchill was teamed with an unqualified worker listed as a root cause; they wanted work pressure considered.

"If you don't want to take this seriously then we're out of here," Ellis said he told the others before they managed to compromise. Fatigue and the unqualified assistant were eventually given the lesser rank of "major contributing factors."

Inconsistent safety enforcement and work pressure were also part of that list at the report's end; Ellis said he even had to fight to include the word "major."

The company would later signal the importance of these factors by focusing on them in its effort to ensure that such an accident never happened again.

NO CONSOLATION

The Churchills wanted to sue. The company blamed their son too much, they said. It made him sound careless.

"They still don't admit that some is their fault," said Glendon Churchill. "I just can't stomach that."

They consulted lawyers from as far away as Kansas City, but there wasn't any way around the state's workers compensation laws that protect businesses by forbidding lawsuits.

They now want the company's new linemen safety rules made into state law so that they can't be removed as contracts are renegotiated in years to come.

Their state representative, Walter Gooley, a Farmington Republican, offered to review linemen safety laws in other states and sponsor a bill in the fall.

The company has said it's sorry the accident happened and that it mourns the Churchills' loss. It also has kept President Sara Burns' promise to make safety changes to prevent another death. "I think there's responsibility on all parties' part," said company spokesman Mark Ishkanian.

But the family continues to want something else—a more personal admission that CMP policies contributed to their son's death.

Why, they had earlier asked President Burns, didn't someone relieve their son? No other workers answered company calls, they remember her saying.

And it was true, the company said, the holidays were near and people were out Christmas shopping.

And what about the government rule the company broke by sending Churchill out with a meter reader instead of a lineman? The rule is confusing, the parents say Burns told them.

If 10 people read the rule, they'd come to 10 different conclusions, they heard her say.

In fact, the company did send a letter objecting to the OSHA citation, along with a check for the $7,000 fine.

The line wouldn't have been dangerous if Churchill had followed the company's safety rules, it said.

But OSHA believed that when a lineman prepares to work on an electrified high-voltage line, he should have another lineman with him to watch out for dangerous missteps.

Even so, the OSHA penalty is not much of a punishment, Glendon Churchill said. "Seven thousand dollars don't mean anything to CMP."

A LASTING IMAGE

It nags at Glendon Churchill that the company has refused to let him talk with the man in charge who waited for a ladder truck rather than tell the lineman to take his son down from the pole.

"We'd like to know the reason why the man didn't go up," said Glendon Churchill.

It was just one more frustration when the man returned Churchill's phone calls and said that he'd been
advised not to talk. CMP has said it wants to spare the
man from any more upset.

But Churchill hasn't been satisfied by the company's
explanation for the man's actions—that he wanted to
avoid hurting anyone else because there may have been
some electricity running through the lines, from a gen-
erator perhaps.

The memory of that afternoon two months ago when
Churchill stood by the pole pleading still makes him cry.

"You don't know what it feels like," he said, as tears
ran down his nose like drops of water. "I begged."

He's all right so long as he doesn't think about it, but
it's impossible not to when he drives along Route 43.
Eight times a day he takes the road, going back and
forth to work in his car, and back and forth in the school
bus.

He can't help but look. There's nothing to block his
view. Each time he glances toward Clearwater Lake, he
sees his son hanging, bent backward from the waist.

Lessons Learned

BY MICHELLE KEARNS

This story began as an idea to write about the culture of power company lineworkers. It was several weeks after Brent Churchill had electrocuted himself after getting little sleep in two days. My editor wanted to understand why a man would agree to work so many hours. Was he trying to rack up overtime to earn extra Christmas spending money?

The family had not yet agreed to give any interviews, so instead I interviewed other lineworkers' wives and families. They told me how fearful they were that their own husbands and sons would die. Getting a call from the company to keep working after a long day, or taking orders to go out again after a short time at home was an expected part of the job.

The more I learned, the more I wanted to talk to Churchill's family. Finally, his cousin agreed to take me out to the pole where Churchill died. After we'd talked and tromped around in the snow, I asked if he'd tell the Churchills that I'd like to talk with them. He called from his car phone and they agreed to meet.

■ **The first lesson:** Don't be rigid about a story's premise. Start the research, and if you find something better than the original idea, change the plan.

At my first meeting with the family, the living room was full of people sitting around a table: Churchill's parents, sister, uncle, and girlfriend, Kathy Bohlman. They all had a lot to say about what happened and it was hard to talk with anyone in depth without making everyone else wait in silence.

I decided that I would go back to talk with them again. First I wanted to review my notes and think the story over.

■ **The second lesson:** Sometimes the best material comes on the second and third interviews, after people have had a chance to relax and get used to talking to you. And working with people in smaller groups, or one-on-one, allows for a more detailed conversation.

When I called Bohlman to arrange a follow-up interview, I wanted to talk with her at a place where she'd spent time together with Churchill. As Bohlman stood in her kitchen, she told me how Churchill would sit by the counter, watch her make a sandwich, and tease her for her perfectionism. She then looked out the window at the deck and described how they'd sit outside and Churchill would recite the three happiest elements of his life: their marriage, their first child, and growing old together. Their love story and its poignant details added a layer of complexity and depth to the story.

■ **The third lesson:** When people are talking about someone or something they care about, it is important to meet in a place that fits the story's context. That way you'll be able to observe elements with meaning to the people you're writing about.

By the time I was ready to write, I had reams of information: interviews with lots of other lineworkers and their families, the Churchill family's memories of their son, and the work rules and accident investigation's findings. The morass was daunting.

As I wrote story drafts, I structured the material around the time leading up to the accident. I was lucky enough to work with the paper's former writing coach, Willis Johnson, who has trained me for years and who reviewed draft after draft after draft, recommending cuts where the story drifted with irrelevant details or repetitive over-explanations of the facts. This brings me to...

■ **The fourth lesson:** The true writing of a story happens in the rewrite. For good stories, avoid filing your first draft. Find time to hone the story with a colleague or editor so that you can pare it down. This makes for stories with enough momentum to keep readers hooked to the last line.

Charlie LeDuff

Finalist, Non-Deadline Writing

Charlie LeDuff has been a reporter on the metro desk of *The New York Times* since 1998. He originally joined the *Times* as an intern in 1995 and became an intermediate reporter in 1996.

Previously, LeDuff had been a reporter for the *Alaska Fisherman's Journal* in 1994. Before that he was a school teacher at a middle school for "troubled children" and a gang counselor in Detroit. He was also a cannery worker, a bartender, and a baker.

In 1999, he won Columbia University's Graduate School of Journalism's Meyer Berger award for distinguished writing about New York City for his profiles of Mike Sheehan, who spent 25 years as a police officer and a detective before becoming a reporter for WNYW-TV, and 81-year-old Ruby Jean Johnson, a prominent personality during the Harlem Renaissance who was found strangled in her apartment in 1998.

LeDuff graduated with a bachelor's degree in political science from the University of Michigan and a master's degree in journalism from the University of California at Berkeley. He was born in 1966, is married, lives in New York City, and is a member of the Sault Ste. Marie Chippewa tribe in northern Michigan.

LeDuff steps deeply into the lives of those in his stories and tells the imperfect, raw, and sometimes disturbing tales at the core of everyday life. The stories have the authentic ring of a reporter who got out of the office and put his notebook aside to listen and learn.

For migrants, hard work in hostile suburbs

SEPTEMBER 24, 2000

FARMINGVILLE, N.Y.—When dusk comes, the streets empty and the *esquineros* hurry to the homes they share with 15, 20 and sometimes 30 others to drink beer and eat supper.

The *esquineros*—the men of the corner—used to walk home alone from the corners where they gather each morning to be hired out for yardwork or other day jobs. Now they walk in groups. At one house, where the Guatemalans live, the door is punctured with bullet holes; a white man recently drove by and unloaded a pistol.

The next block over, there is a white man who put his house up for sale after 20 Mexicans moved in next door. As he pulled into his driveway, he stared at his unwanted neighbors. He is a tough-looking guy, and he did not turn his eyes away. One of the Mexicans wore a second-hand shirt that read, "We don't like you either."

Up until now, the culture divide of the suburbs has been more a cold war than a hot one, an uneasy peace with periodic clashes over public issues like limits on the number of boarders allowed in a house or a proposal in Suffolk County to sue the Immigration and Naturalization Service to more stringently enforce immigration laws.

But when two Hispanic immigrants seeking work were lured to an abandoned building on Sunday and attacked by two white men wielding a knife, a crowbar and a shovel, the assault was a sobering reminder of the lives of the unwanted strangers. The divide plays out in towns like Brewster, Mount Kisco and Yonkers, N.Y., and Freehold, N.J.

But the emotions are rawest in Farmingville, where it is estimated that in the summertime, one in 15 residents is a migrant worker. When October comes, a few men stay, but most follow their money home.

The violence last Sunday shocked some whites and even prompted the formation of a community group by politicians and church leaders looking for ways to ease the tensions. But if the violence was a revelation to many whites, the hostility behind it was hardly news to the brown men in the Goodwill T-shirts and muddy jeans who come to the corner each morning.

ANGER ON BOTH SIDES

Dionicio Urbina walked quickly through the white neighborhoods. He is 20 years old and was shocked when some white teenagers just a few years younger than he hurled an ethnic slur and squealed with cracking voices, "Speak English," and "What are you doing here, Mexican?"

In the safety of his worn-down house, Mr. Urbina lay on his bedroll and listened to a light rain pelt his window—a bad omen for work in the morning.

"You don't know what it's like to be in a town where they hate you," he said in nearly perfect English. "The place is so weird to me. The suburbs. I never knew that word. In other parts of the country the Mexicans fight the Mexicans. Here, it's the white people who don't want us. It's not the country and it's not the city. It's strange, but, man, the money is here. I never dreamed about $100 a day."

There are plenty of jobs in this tree-lined hamlet in central Long Island that is home to 15,000 residents and acres of blacktop and strip malls. Mostly they are menial jobs like cleaning pools and landscaping, and like a quarter of all jobs in the United States, they pay about $8 an hour.

The Latinos have come in great numbers over the past four years to take the jobs locals are unwilling or unable to do. Most are here illegally, and it is their illegal status that most irritates local residents.

The people taunt each other. Some Americans picket the Latinos every Saturday as they stand on the corners waiting for work. The *esquineros* have become schooled in the ways of America. They picket back. And after the ambush of the two workers, more than 500 of the illegal immigrants took to the streets demanding their civil rights.

Every morning a throng of Latinos stands on a small mound denuded of grass but choked with poison ivy. It is known as the *esquina*, or corner, and it is the best, most visible corner around. Some men walk two hours to get to this spot at Horseblock Road and North Ocean Avenue to be picked up for some work. It is an hour if you run.

Farther back from the mound are some trees where men go in the sweltering mornings to relieve themselves or smoke a little marijuana. Next to it is the 7-Eleven, and even though there is a sign in front of the store that says "Welcome to Farmingville," the *esquineros* know that they are not welcome.

Here, 300 brown men on the corner are as obvious as a herd of ostriches.

Before, they accepted their lot as unwanted outsiders. But the beating of the two men has made the *esquineros* angry. "Man, they want you here in the mornings to do their animal work and then at night they want you to disappear," said Carlos Antonio, 19. "If they want war, if they want Pancho Villa, then I can be Pancho Villa."

The American dream for the *esquineros* is to find a way off this corner. They tell the legend of the two brothers from Hidalgo who found their way to Farmingville 20 years ago. The brothers worked as stone masons and returned to Mexico with a fortune. Others followed, and now the *esquineros* come from all corners of Mexico and Central America.

Lalo Cervantes, 37, comes. He is from Mexico City. He has gold in his teeth, and when he has no money in his pocket, he looks for a little work. Carlos Antonio comes too. And Gabriel Jimenez. Mr. Cervantes and Mr. Antonio speak good English. Mr. Jimenez, 23, comes from the mountains. He is a peasant and understands little English beyond push, pull, lift, over there, how much? and, do you buy lunch?

Often a carful of young white women drive by and whistle at the men. Sometimes they give the men the finger. Either way, the men shout back with dull agitation. They have grown used to it. White people have complained to the police about the men harassing American women.

"I wouldn't let my woman walk by here either," Mr. Cervantes said. "To tell you the truth, the whole scene does look bad. But it all gets mixed up in racism. It's not because we're Mexicans. It's because we're construction workers, because we are men."

The morning traffic must make a right turn out of the 7-Eleven. And when the Americans make the turn, they look left and avoid looking right at the *esquineros*.

When they do look, their cars are swarmed with workers. One American woman looked with purpose and lowered her power window. "I only need one," she said. She had some yardwork. When a man jumped in, the ribaldry began.

"Big gringa in a big car," said Armando Perez, rubbing his palms together. "Thick and soft. That's your American girls. Their husbands go to work and I think they are lonely just like us."

The *esquineros* would like a woman of any kind. There are few Mexican women out here, and the only companionship for them arrives in vans on Friday and Saturday evenings from Queens. The price is $20.

A DAY'S LABOR FOR $100

A white man pulled up in a big white truck. He was new to the corner and had never hired *esquineros* before. Messrs. Jimenez, Antonio and Cervantes piled in. The patron spoke loudly, as if the sheer volume of his voice would increase their understanding of English. "Boy, that's a zoo, huh? A free for all? You do that every day?"

He took the men to a chic neighborhood in Port Jefferson. You could smell the saltwater first, then you could see the boats. Then, over a slight hill was the patron's dream house. It had a pool, and it cost $25,000 just to clear the trees. Where the trees used to be were 24,000 square feet of bald earth where the men were to lay the sod. Lalo Cervantes, with his nice English, became the crew chief. The boss's wife was very particular about her grass. But Mr. Cervantes was assiduous. He calmed the woman.

The day was hot. The boss kept saying it wasn't too hot. Mr. Cervantes kept asking how much money he would be paid.

"I'll take care of you," the boss kept answering. The workers grew suspicious that they would not be paid.

Most workers will return with $100 in their pockets

after long, dirty hours. A few will get nothing. They will get stiffed, and when they return home, all they will carry is malice in their hearts and a vague promise to get even with that gringo boss.

This boss had nice cars and two grown sons with Adonis-like bodies. They like to go to the gym, the woman kept saying. One son drove a Mercedes, the other a Porsche, and they lifted no sod.

"It's strange," Mr. Antonio said in Spanish. "These guys don't know the value of what they've got. Big bodies and no work. This must make the old man sad."

When the work was done, the boss handed two new $50 bills to each man and said: "You boys know anything about air-conditioning? I fired my whole crew because they're lazy. You guys like to work hard. I'll give you that."

He handed out his card and dropped the workers on the corner.

"Oh man," said Mr. Antonio, tapping the card with his nails. "It's my dream to get off the corner. Here's my ticket." He never did call the man.

THIRTY MEN, ONE HOUSE

The men walked down Horseblock Road to the Brewery, a cantina with gray walls that is one of the few places the cultures overlap: the American war veterans, the Portuguese-American contractors and the *esquineros*.

A man named Alex Martinez held his head in his hands, his elbows on the bar. He stared into his plate. He had problems with his American girlfriend, he said.

"She just doesn't understand," he told any stranger willing to listen. "All the things. The car. She wants more. I tell her, 'I work for these things. Do you know the value of work?' I don't think she does. We come from different places."

There is a ranch house off Horseblock Road. In the house are 9 bicycles, 13 toothbrushes, 30 men, a big bottle of bleach, a pot of boiling chicken and five lingerie catalogs. The rain began to fall again. Some men sat around the dirty kitchen drinking beer and complaining about work.

"The boss, he tells me he's going to pay me only $50

because he says I don't work."

"Fifty dollars? The garbage. So what did you do?"

"What could I do? I took the fifty."

In the morning, more rain fell, and work was scarce. Across the street, white people picketed, as they do every Saturday, with signs that read "Go Home" and "Stop the Crime." A man drove back and forth taking photographs of the *esquineros*.

"I've got nothing against immigrants. Immigrants built this country," said the photographer, David Drew, 48. "But these aren't immigrants. They're criminals taking advantage of a good thing. It's like putting bread out for the birds and the rats eat it."

The Mexicans understood his English. "This guy, he's not stable," Cesar Perez said.

The *esquineros* have learned to stick up for themselves. Encouraged by men like Carlos Canales, an outreach worker for the Work Place Project, the *esquineros* have staged demonstrations at the County Legislature when it considered passing laws aimed at them. They hold news conferences and picket the homes of contractors who do not pay their employees.

During one of these vigils, among taunts of "You make me sick," and "My father came here legally," a group of Latino men with varying shades of skin spoke with two white women, one old, the other young.

"Listen to me, please." the older woman said. "I've got nothing against you personally. But you are here illegally. There are too many of you. We're inundated. You take the money home and make no life here. You don't learn English."

A brown man responded in clumsy English, "But Spanish is the second language of the world."

"And guess what the first is," the woman said. "It's the language we speak in this country."

PAY THE RENT OR ELSE

When the white people showed up at the corner with signs on a wet Saturday morning a few weeks before the attacks, the *esquineros* pulled out their own banners and signs. They crossed the street to confront the white people. The white people ran away to the taunts of "*fascistas!*"

By 10 a.m., the rain was still falling and the men went home. At the ranch house on Horseblock Road, the landlord arrived wearing a dime-store badge. He had a siren in the window of his car. He was fond of telling the *esquineros* that he was a federal agent. He told them that if there was any trouble, if any man moved in without paying the $250 rent, then he had the power to arrest him, even to shoot him.

This made the Mexicans laugh. "It's really unbelievable, the life here," Mr. Urbina said. "These are the things the men go home to tell their families about America."

Lessons Learned

BY CHARLIE LeDUFF

■ It's the small things, the important moments, that make a good story true. Keep a good eye but keep a distance. Sympathy gets in the way. Mucks it up. Cheapens the person.

■ Skepticism leads to good journalism. For instance, people of a particular ethnic group don't think in the same way. Cynicism is better suited for college campuses and government offices.

■ Writing in scenes with real dialogue, it seems to me, presents people and their way of life much better than the explanatory style. Don't be afraid to slash and burn stuff you've already written if it doesn't work.

■ If your editors are wrong, tell them. You were there. On the other hand, admit when you're wrong.

■ Don't be a vulture. Swooping around the edges won't draw people to you. Walk up to them, without fear, explain that you are a reporter and your reason for being there. No one likes a creep.

■ You must then be able to explain to a potential subject what's in it for him. His name in history? The promise that she will be heard, even if it is only for a day? Be honest about your intentions.

■ Don't run from a story, but when you are treated with hostility, remember that you have the right to be respected, too.

■ In today's America, it's good to know Spanish. Even poor Spanish. It shows an effort on your part.

■ "Yes, sir" and "No, ma'am" are better than "Hey, man."

■ Read books.

■ Write up your notes every day in journal form. Then you have blocked-out pieces of a story when you are done reporting instead of scads of notes.

Leonard Pitts
Commentary

Leonard Pitts knew he wanted to be a writer when he
was 5 years old. That's when he began reading and developing a love for words. That passion for words led
him on a writing path that helped him evolve into an
award-winning syndicated columnist. When he was 18,
Soul magazine became the first publication that published and paid him for his writing. He spent a decade
free-lancing for a variety of publications, including the
Musician, and for radio stations in Los Angeles, where
he grew up. He also became a writer for the "Casey's
Top 40 with Casey Kasem" radio show.

The *Miami Herald* hired him as a music critic in 1991.
Until then, Pitts primarily profiled people and reviewed
music. The *Herald* offered new writing opportunities
using music to explore other topics.

His writing style caught the attention of *Herald* editors.

He did a front-page piece about basketball superstar Magic Johnson when Johnson tested positive for HIV. He also wrote about the 1992 Los Angeles riots. Such articles set a precedent for writing about subjects outside his music beat. And his interest in pop music began to wane. "There comes a time when the hot artist of the day is not speaking to you, but to your children," Pitts said.

So he approached the features editor about writing a more personal, social issues-oriented column. Although the 43-year-old columnist now lives in Bowie, Md., just outside Washington, D.C., he find himself more interested in the talk at the checkout lines than in the talk of the political lines drawn in the nation's capital.

His engaging, passionate, and compelling columns address a wide variety of topics, especially race, family, and culture. His approach to writing displays his desire to wed the head with the heart, the intellect with the intimate. He strives to provide logical consistency within a human framework. And he does so with a unique personal voice that holds himself and his readers accountable for facing the truth—in all its complexity.

Pitts's willingness to challenge his own views becomes strikingly plain in his column about the Amadou Diallo verdict, a case in which police shot an unarmed immigrant from Guinea. Pitts's passion and historical bent play out prominently in his columns on South Carolina's flag and "Gangsta Rap's Mask a Rip-off." These and the other columns included in this book capture a conscience on public display—a voice unmasked.

—Aly Colón

Flag of lies still flies in face of truth

JANUARY 20, 2000

Masochist that I am, I think I'll talk about the Confederate battle flag again.

Last time I did so, I argued that the state of South Carolina needs to remove that dirty symbol of slavery and racism from its spot above the capitol building. Which, naturally, produced howls of outrage, loads of racial invective and not a few lamentations for my ignorance of history. As one writer put it, "If you are intelligent, and I think you probably are, then you know the Civil War wasn't about slavery."

Ahem.

If you know me, then you know I can't let that one pass unchallenged. Especially since it is repeated ad nauseum by apologists for the old Confederacy. The war wasn't about slavery, they say, because only a fraction of the Confederate soldiers owned slaves.

It's a non sequitur masquerading as logic. Put another way, I'd be willing to wager that the average American soldier had never even heard of Kuwait before George Bush ordered him or her to defend that desert kingdom. Because, you see, it's not the soldiers who determine whether or why a war is fought—it's the leaders. In the case of the Confederacy, the leaders could hardly have been more explicit.

In an early message to his Congress, Confederate President Jefferson Davis flatly cited the "labor of African slaves" as the reason for secession.

His vice president, Alexander Stephens, called slavery "the immediate cause...of the present revolution." And he added this: "Our new government is founded upon...the great truth that the Negro is not equal to the white man, that slavery, subordination to the superior race, is his natural and moral condition."

Not about slavery? Oh, please.

Yet, the attempt to separate the Civil War from its dominant cause proceeds apace, without the barest hint of shame. Defenders of the Confederacy huddle behind euphemisms—"state's rights," "economic issues"—but always, it devolves to the same thing, the bondage of African people. A century and a third later, much of the South still finds it impossible to face that truth squarely.

Instead, there's this taxing insistence that if grandfather fought bravely and truly believed in his cause, then surely this must transfigure the cause, must leave his deeds somehow...ennobled. But that's just another non sequitur, another blind alley of logic. I mean, surely there were Nazi and Japanese soldiers who, during the Second World War, fought bravely and truly believed in their cause. But who among us would call their cause anything but reprehensible? Who among us finds honor in what they did?

WHITEWASH THE PAST

Indeed, some years back, when Japan issued school books that distorted or ignored that nation's wartime aggression and atrocities, American observers promptly condemned it as an attempt to whitewash the past.

Small wonder. The Japanese can never be allowed to forget how awful that past was—else they might be tempted to relive it.

What would we say to the Germans if they chose to fly the swastika above their capitol? How would we reply if they told us they were simply honoring the heritage of forebears who fought for what they believed? Would we call it a "controversy," suggesting there were competing opinions of roughly equal validity? Would we, in the manner of certain rubber-spined presidential candidates, declare it a local issue of no concern to "outsiders"? Or would we be alarmed? Would we say that here was a people too deluded to learn the hard lessons of history?

SLAVES AS 'SETTLERS'

And if that's the case, then how can we say less about the South? How can we say less about the region where, five years ago, a governor proposed educational standards that would have required teachers to refer to slaves as "settlers"? Where in 1998, a school district rejected a black history poster because it included an image of a lynching? Where a banner symbolizing slavery and white supremacy flies above a house of the people?

Every day that sunrise finds it there, South Carolina shames itself, shames its ancestors, shames the nation, shames the very truth—and profanes the ideal of liberty and justice for all.

Yet there it hangs anyway, a cloth lie flapping in the Dixie breeze.

Look away, look away.

Why lose yourself in group's cause?

JANUARY 22, 2000

Our question for today: How much of you belongs to you?

I'm moved to ask this by one of the students in my writing class. The assignment was to compose and read aloud an essay describing themselves and their lives. The piece this student wrote was about how confusing and painful it is to have people pigeonhole you just because you're black. It's difficult, wrote this 14-year-old, to have others always expect you to operate, be confined by, or bend your behavior to, their expectations.

What was intriguing is that the people the child was complaining about were not white, but black.

It seems my student gets a lot of grief for speaking standard English, singing the songs of a white pop group, and cultivating a rainbow coalition of friends. Some black folks in the kid's immediate circle have responded with the harshest epithet they can muster. They call the child…"white."

If this were a movie, this is the spot where you'd hear scary music and a shriek of unadulterated horror.

If you're a member of a minority—racial, sexual, cultural, religious—there's a good chance you already understand what's going on here. If not, I can only refer you to that opening question: How much of you belongs to you? You may think the answer is self-evident. Truth is, it's anything but.

The life of the American minority group is governed by a deceptively simple equation—oppression from without creates cohesion from within. People who find themselves besieged because of their sexual orientation, skin color, culture or way of approaching God tend to draw together with similar others. They circle the wagons, raise the drawbridge, close the gates and make of themselves a community—a people.

It can be a soul-saving thing, belonging to a people. You love them unreservedly for providing you an emotional home, for instilling in you a sense of worth, for giving voice to your aspirations. Most of all, you love them for standing up on your behalf when the world comes calling with reproach and accusation.

A soul-saving thing, yes. But you find, not infrequently, that you are expected to pay for this wonderful gift at the cost of bits and pieces of your own individuality. When you belong to a people, when you are born into this association that exists on a basis of mutual defense, of watching the world from a bunker and waiting for the next attack, it's easy to lose your very self to them. So easy to become the group.

Small wonder. The group enforces its cohesion strictly. Its members are discouraged from doing, saying or thinking that which does not reflect the consensus of the whole. Sometimes, one is discouraged from even associating with members of the "enemy" camp. And there's a heavy penalty for transgression: One is cast out, ostracized.

As in a colleague I once had who told me his people constantly criticized his work. Their complaint? He was "not Cuban enough."

It's a charge that finds its echo across the American demographic. Not lesbian enough. Not Jewish enough. Not black enough. The unstated irony is that all these peoples who plead for tolerance of difference sometimes have so little tolerance for the differences within their own ranks.

So sometimes, yes, a person wonders: How much of you belongs to you? Where's the point beyond which fealty to the group becomes a compromise of self?

I wish I'd had an easy answer for my student but of course, I did not. I did tell the kid this: What you are should never be the sole determinant of *who* you are. You have the right to your own taste in music, your own choice of friends, your own self. These are your prerogatives, no one else's. Otherwise, what's the point?

Someday, I hope my student will learn. That you have to honor what you belong to, yes. But you must also protect the things that belong to you.

Second thoughts following New York verdict

MARCH 2, 2000

"...[A] wallet in the hand of a white man looks like a wallet, but a wallet in the hand of a black man looks like a gun." —Bill Bradley

I was ready to jump to conclusion. Then four black women got in the way.

Meaning the four who sat on the Albany, N.Y., jury that last week acquitted four white cops in the shooting death of an unarmed African immigrant.

By now, you know the story. How New York City police officers encountered Amadou Diallo standing in front of his apartment building early last year. How he went into his pocket for something. How somebody yelled, "Gun!"

How they shot him. And then shot him some more. Forty-one rounds fired over eight seconds, 19 of them finding their mark.

Then the awful discovery: the "gun" was only a wallet.

The thing seemed cut and dried to me. Which is why the jury's verdict was…impossible. Not guilty of murder, not guilty of manslaughter, not even guilty of criminal negligence? Now New York City is steaming, the kettle of racial acrimony threatening to boil. And I'd be ready to boil right along with them, except…

Except for the inconvenient fact of those four women.

I find myself caught between—not able to believe, not able to dismiss. And I'm forced to confess that they are the only reason I'm willing to cut the justice system even that sliver of slack.

It's a painful admission. It's also an unavoidable one. How many times has an encounter with a white lawman resulted in the unjustifiable injury or death of an innocent African-American woman or man? And how many times has an all-white jury justified it anyway?

So it makes a difference—it shouldn't, but it does—that four of the jurors who vouched for the legal blamelessness of these cops are black. Granted, blackness is no more a character reference than whiteness is a character defect. But you're more willing to listen—a friend says she had to think twice—because of the race of those women.

It's a sad truth that speaks volumes about the reputation cops and courts have earned in minority communities. If trust is the currency of justice, then the justice system is bankrupt in those neighborhoods.

Fact is, black folks know a different system than their white countrymen do. Think Rodney King, smashed to a pulp by Los Angeles police while the nation stood witness. An all-white jury set those officers free. And then there's O.J. Simpson, whose defense team drew laughter with the suggestion that Los Angeles cops might plant evidence or frame suspects. Over 20 L.A. cops have recently been fired or disciplined for planting evidence and framing suspects.

Understand those things and you'll understand why blacks have no trouble believing cops could willfully execute a man in the vestibule of his own building. Or why they would distrust a jury that said otherwise.

Here's the question: If Amadou Diallo was white, would he still be alive? Would some jittery cop have been so quick to see a gun where there was none? Would they have been so filled with fear that they'd fire 41 times—*41 times!*—to bring him down?

We cannot, of course, ever know for sure. And I'm not at all convinced the conclusion I was ready to jump to is not in fact the correct one. Yet at the same time, I'm troubled by the realization that we as African-American people jump by reflex now. That experience has taught us this is the wise thing to do.

I feel sorry for those women, having to bear the weight of expectation. I don't like having to trust more in the fact of blackness than in the promise of justice.

But that's where we stand. And until courts and cops begin to work equally hard at earning the trust of all citizens, it's where we're likely to stay.

Until that moment, these episodes will continue to move with sad predictability.

White cop shoots unarmed black person. Outrage burns like fire.

And we jump.

Reparations' weight burdens soul of some black folks

SEPTEMBER 21, 2000

"Don't depend on the train from Washington. It's 100 years overdue." —Gil Scott-Heron

In January of 1865, as the Civil War was grinding to a close, Union Army Gen. William Tecumseh Sherman issued Special Field Order 15, awarding captured farm-lands in South Carolina, Georgia and Florida to former slaves. Each freedman was to receive 40 acres and the loan of an Army mule. Four months later, President Andrew Johnson rescinded the order and returned the land to the former slave owners.

But "40 acres and a mule" fired the imagination of ex-slaves and their allies. Republican Congressman Thaddeus Stevens of Pennsylvania unsuccessfully pushed legislation to give freed blacks this leg up on their new life. It was as inconceivable to him as it was to them that millions of illiterate and impoverished people would be turned loose in a hostile region without food, shelter or means.

Surely, they thought, there would at least be 40 acres and a mule. Something to get a man started. So they waited, filled with expectation and hope.

All of which adds a certain poignancy to recent news stories of a reparations hoax targeting African Americans in South Florida and elsewhere in the South and upper Midwest. In one version of the scam, old people are told to supply personal data so that the government can pay them money under the fictional "Slave Reparation Act." Another centers on a supposed $40,000 reparations rebate on 1999 taxes open to African Americans who file an amended return with the IRS. The con artists offer to do the necessary paperwork for a fee of up to $150. Dozens have fallen for it.

ARDUOUS WAIT

Small wonder. After all, these cons play on a point of emotional vulnerability. Meaning that, where compensation for the long night of our American odyssey is concerned, many black folks are still doing as our forebears did: waiting for compensation. Waiting for reparations.

It's not that I disagree with folks who argue that cause. From where I sit, their reasoning is unassailable. If it's an accepted practice that governments pay restitution to citizens they have materially damaged, if it's proper for Germany and Austria to compensate Holocaust victims and the United States to recompense Americans of Japanese heritage interned during World War II, then what argument can be made against reparations for blacks, who suffered 246 years of slavery and an additional century of Jim Crow privation?

IMPRACTICAL

But for all that, reparations is not an issue that resonates with me. It strikes me as a righteous but impractical crusade, a tilting at windmills that diverts time, attention and political capital from more pressing matters.

Where reparations for African Americans are concerned, I consider two things unarguable. The first is that they can't print enough money to compensate the crime. The second is that, even if they could, reparations would still not happen because the mood of the country would not allow it. Inevitably, it would be seen as giving some unearned thing to black people. Never mind that we've never been "given" a damned thing; that's still how it would play.

We could argue the point, I suppose. Win the debate on its merits and still never see a dime.

Or we could invest that time and energy to improve the education of our children, reconnect our men with their communities, dismantle discrimination in housing and labor, fight police profiling, rescue our boys from the maw of the criminal injustice system. Take our destiny in our own hands for a change.

I guess I've just grown tired of black people asking white people to "do" things. Tired of black folks' contentment always being held hostage to white folks' will.

Forgive me if I seem to paint with too broad a brush. I know white America is not some wicked monolith, any more than black America is. I believe in human fraternity.

But the belief does nothing to still that fatigue—marrow-deep and newly exacerbated by the thought of scam artists preying upon this emotionally vulnerable spot.

We've been looking for those acres and that mule for 135 years. I guess I'm just tired of waiting.

Gangsta rap's mask a rip-off

OCTOBER 26, 2000

"We wear the mask that grins and lies."
—Paul Laurence Dunbar

The great black vaudevillian Bert Williams is supposed to have been a very funny guy. "The funniest man I ever saw," W.C. Fields once said.

Offstage, Williams was reputed to be exceedingly intelligent and reserved to the point of snobbishness. He was a great reader, too, favoring the likes of Twain, Goethe, Kant and Voltaire.

Onstage was another matter. Every night before he went on, Williams put on his mask. That is, he applied to his face gleaming black cork and whitewall tire lips. Then he shuffled out there, a shiftless ne'er-do-well, slow of foot, slower of mouth and slowest of mind. He and his partner, George Walker, billed themselves as "Two Real Coons" by way of assuring white audiences that they were getting something they were not: authentic black comedy.

This was obligatory behavior for black performers a century ago.

I was reminded of Bert Williams' life as I watched Spike Lee's movie. *Bamboozled* is easily the most controversial release of the season, a satire about the rise and fall of *The New Millennium Minstrel Show*, a TV variety show built on the coarsest racial stereotypes you can imagine. Two shiftless clowns, grinning from blackface and red lips, perform in a watermelon patch. Featured players include Aunt Jemima, Sambo and assorted pickaninnies. It's all the brainchild of a disgruntled black television executive who only wants to get fired. Instead, he gets acclaimed. The show becomes a sensation.

It's not a great movie—the final act is a mess, and the characters are sometimes unrecognizable as human beings. And yet *Bamboozled* is, at times, strangely compelling.

One scene in particular. You watch the characters played by Tommy Davidson and Savion Glover burn the cork black, mix it with water, then apply that paste to their faces. Watch them draw lips with lipstick the color of firetrucks. Watch them disappear behind the mask. Then they take the stage for the first time, these human caricatures straight out of a segregationist's fever dream. There's a moment of stunned, airless silence. White members of the studio audience turn hesitantly to black ones, looking for a cue, wordlessly asking if they should find this funny.

And, softly at first, the black people laugh. That laugh stays with me. There's something in it both troubling and true.

Because the better part of a century later, the "coon" act has changed and yet remains disturbingly the same. Consider that some of us now sell a crude, violent, values-free music that's supposed to be as definitively black as Bert Williams' shuffling jive.

Consider, too, that we still wear masks: A few years ago, there was a church-going ballet student who, seeking success as a rapper, remade herself as a foul-mouthed, malt liquor-swilling homegirl called Boss. Then there's the guy who began his career wearing lipstick and eye shadow until that went out of fashion and he transformed himself into a crude street punk called Dr. Dre.

Some of us still wear the mask that grins and lies. Only now they do it not because they have to, but because that's where the money is. Because black kids—white ones, too—will pay good money for fake lessons in authentic blackness.

"Keepin' it real," they say. And it's hard not to hear a ghostly echo of Williams and Walker: "Two real coons."

I'm not mad at Bert Williams. Not mad at Mantan Moreland, Butterfly McQueen, Nick Stewart, Stepin Fetchit or any other black performer who had to shuffle his feet, bug his eyes, slur his words or wear blackface because the white men who did the hiring would not accept them otherwise.

But I am mad at gangsta rap. And at those of us who passively accept the insult. Have we, African Ameri-

cans, become so numb, dumb, despairing or disconnected that we've forgotten who we are? Forgotten how to
give a damn?

Or have we just worn the mask so long we've forgotten the face that lies beneath? Forgotten everything except the rictus grin of the clown. And betrayed ancestors'
sacrifice in the process.

Because there's only one difference between Bert
Williams and Dr. Dre.

Bert Williams had no choice.

Writers' Workshop

Talking Points

1) Pitts says he is addressing two audiences when he writes about race. After reading his columns, can you identify the audiences? How does he approach them differently?

2) Pitts writes alternately as someone absolutely sure of what he thinks, as in the "Flag of Lies" column, and as someone still struggling with an idea, as in the "Second Thoughts Following New York Verdict" column. How does this alternating style affect his effectiveness? Is he more or less credible because of it?

3) Columnists can play many roles. They can preach, teach, guide, cajole, lambast, nudge, convene. What role does Pitts play in each column? What role would you envision playing if you were to write a column?

4) Pitts believes he has to put a human face on the issues about which he writes. How has he done that in the columns included in this book?

5) Pitts says he pays a personal price when he writes about race relations. What does a columnist risk in writing about this subject? What would it cost you?

Assignment Desk

1) Pitts scours the Internet to find news stories about people in such cities as Biloxi and Detroit. Surf the 'Net. Find stories that are interesting to you. Write a column based on one of those stories.

2) Voice plays an important role in defining a columnist. How would you characterize the voice Pitts uses in these columns? Think about a topic that's important to you. Take five minutes to write down your thoughts. What does your voice sound like?

3) Read the "Why Lose Yourself in Group's Cause?" column. Think of a group to which you belong. Write down how you are different from, and the same as, the group.

4) A good columnist, Pitts says, has "to give up something" in writing, surrendering a part of himself. Think about something that's had a personal impact on you. Explore that event deeply. Write a commentary that forces you to give up something.

A conversation with
Leonard Pitts

ALY COLÓN: In each of the columns published in this book, you focus on race. What prompts you to focus on race issues in your columns?

LEONARD PITTS: Well, the first thing I should tell you is that the majority of my columns are *not* about race. But it's probably the strongest, or one of the strongest subjects that I write about. In terms of what prompts me to focus on race, there are two things. One is the fact that I have a personal stake in the issue, given that I'm African American and I'm raising kids who are also African American. So there's a personal interest in the issue and how it affects my life and their lives. Then there's also the intellectual. It's just such a fascinating intellectual puzzle to me. The contortions that people take in terms of logic, and in terms of emotion, in dealing with this issue are just endlessly fascinating to me.

Do you have a sense of how often you do write about race?

Often when I write race columns, there's a certain type of white reader who is irked by those and I always am confronted with "you write about race all the time." So I've taken accounting just so I can know at any given time how obsessed I'm being. If I write 100 columns a year, 20 to 25 will be about race, maybe a few more.

What do you want your readers to understand about race as a result of reading your column?

I guess there are probably two major points. I want my white readers to quit wishing this under a rug. Quit saying it's all over now. And quit assuming that we have come further along the path toward enlightenment and the Promised Land than we actually have. I mean the statistics that I often cite to disprove this point are not anything that came from me. They didn't come from the

NAACP. They didn't come from the Nation of Islam or any other group with an ax to grind. They came from the federal government. So it's the federal government telling me that housing discrimination exists. That there are sentencing disparities in the justice system. That job discrimination, loan discrimination, and all these things are realities. Don't get mad at me for writing about them.

More to the point, don't try to tell me that it's my imagination. I think for a lot of white readers it is very difficult to read about race without feeling personally indicted. It's been the unmistakable subtext in a lot of the responses that I get. I got an e-mail from a gentleman the other day. He wanted to thank me for something that I'd written on men, on fatherhood. But he also wanted to chastise me for a column on race: "Why are you always harping on race?" I wrote him back that it's interesting that when I've written about a subject that touches him personally, it's rah-rah. When I write about an issue of race, it's something that he can't deal with and he's antagonistic toward it. It touches a place emotionally, intellectually that he would rather not be touched. I hear all the time that I write too much about race. This is from white readers.

I write almost as much about family issues. In all these years of doing this, I have not once been told I write too much about family. Given that I write about the two subjects with almost the same frequency, I can only conclude that race touches these people in a way that they prefer not to be touched. That's what I'm dealing with with my white readers. With my black readers I'm trying to inspire them, trying to inspire us to look past the paranoia, the knee-jerk responses we sometimes get trapped into. That's a different kind of frustration. I wrote once years ago about a black kid one of my sons went to school with. The kid told my son, "I can't get ahead because the white man is keeping me down." This kid's 14 years old. My column was basically that the white man doesn't know you're alive, Junior. Any white man interested in keeping you down, you've just done the job for him. You're sitting on the bench. You've taken yourself out of the game. And you're refusing to even get into the game because of some expectation that you're going to fail. I think this is a clear and present danger for African-American people, the tendency to look to the forces outside us that are already against us to the exclusion of dealing with the internal stuff that we have to deal with. I mean a lot of people place it as an either-or dichotomy. Either the problem is racism from outside, or the problem is that black people have not done what they should be doing from the inside. I consider that a false dichotomy. I think both are the problem. I think that African-American people need to be more proactive in dealing with things that concern us. We've been terribly reactive.

So do you see your column speaking to both audiences, showing each the other side to this issue?

Yes. I see myself sort of speaking to both sides. If there is a theme to my columns on race, an overarching theme, that's probably it. That there is room for improvement in both communities and it's a difficult sell sometimes.

Let's talk about how you go about determining the kinds of columns that you write. Where do you get your ideas?

You look everywhere in terms of trying to find things. I surf the 'Net. The 'Net is a godsend in that I'm not limited to the paper that arrives on my driveway in the morning. I have access to virtually every newspaper in the world. I look for small stories only familiar to people in Biloxi or Detroit or wherever. There's also life itself. There's interacting with my kids and with the people I see on the street. As a columnist you're in the moment, but you're also observing the moment, wondering, "Can I get a column out of this?" It's kind of a weird duality, but at some point you get used to it. You're living life but you're also observing yourself living life so that if a column happens to come your way, you can grab it. The thing I'm looking for is something that doesn't bore, something that is of interest to me, and something to which I feel like I can bring a perspective that's not the same as other folks.

Are there particular issues that do resonate with you?

Race and family. Then just issues of inequities beyond race. I write about sexual orientation issues several times a year, gender-bias issues several times a year also. Then there's just a potpourri of other stuff, oddities that go with the human experience. I wrote two columns on what I call "idiot warnings," warnings that appear on packages that no one who's thinking should ever really need. I do those types of things occasionally.

What columns stand out in your mind as examples of things you've felt compelled to write about?

I ended up somehow writing three or four columns on black people and Republicans and why there was such a lingering anger over the election. The last one of those was one that just demanded to be written. I tried to avoid writing that column because it was the fourth in what had turned out to be a series. It was never meant to be a series, but I kept getting responses from readers. And often a response from a reader will key another column. By the end of the third column, the responses I was getting from readers had just angered me so. There were so many that, even though I tried to avoid going back to the well one more time, I couldn't do anything else until I got this off my chest.

Those are sometimes actually the easiest columns to write, the ones that are just burning inside you and that are coming from a place of anger. There was another one that I wrote, coincidentally also about race. This also came from a reader response. The original column was on historical movies and why some people say that they find it hard to look at a *Schindler's List*, or a *Saving Private Ryan*, or an *Amistad* because it's so painful. The original column said that our forebears had to live this, so it seems that the least we can do is go and get some Hollywood understanding of what it was that they had to go through. In the context of that, I mentioned that there were three movies on black history that had not done well—*Amistad*, *Rosewood*, and Oprah Winfrey's *Beloved*. I said there are any number of reasons for this. One may be that they were flawed movies. Two, the African-American experience is so painful that sometimes it's a hard sell.

I get this letter from this guy saying the reason that those movies don't do well is that they deal solely with the black experience as opposed to the other movies that I had named, which deal with the American experience. And the two movies that he named as dealing with the American experience were *Schindler's List* and *Saving Private Ryan*, neither of which took place in America and the first of which had really no American characters in it and I don't think even American actors.

It just outraged me that he's going to point to *Schindler's List* as more "American" than a black movie that takes place in Kentucky, or Ohio, or Florida, or whatever, and that column just jumped out of me. I think the lead was: "I will try my best not to scream just at the logic of it." When readers do stuff like that, it drives me crazy. And that's the kind of stuff that makes the columns just sort of explode out of me.

It sounds like you think it's important to respond to readers and to address them. What kind of role is it that you see yourself having and what is it that you want to accomplish?

In terms of a role, I'm just a guy spewing in the newspaper, is the way I see it. I've been called a voice for black America, or a leader for black America. I don't accept either of those. I mean it's nice and it's complimentary in its way, but I am just a guy writing a newspaper column, trying to figure out what to say twice a week, and trying to make sure that he doesn't bore himself in the process. To the degree that there's any role, especially as far as the race issue goes, I think I often find myself explaining white to black and black to white because I'm on the borderline of that relationship. There's a lot of acrimony that I don't think would necessarily be there if people would simply stop and have a correct interpretation of what it is that is being said to them. So a lot of times I find myself translating those two communities to one another. But other than that, I really don't think in terms of having a role per se.

Columnists have a variety of approaches. I hear in yours a very personal, conversational tone.

That's a kind of writing I've always liked in columnists I guess, so that's the kind of writing I wanted to more or less emulate. There's a guy, who I believe still writes for the *Los Angeles Times*; his name is Al Martinez and I used to like his column, going back many years to when I lived in L.A., for the fact that there was some humanity there. I recall the first column that ever made me sit up and take notice, from an emotional point of view, of the subject of AIDS back in the 1980s. I was intellectually aware that there was this thing out there called AIDS and it's really terrible, but it's sort of like the rain forests. You have an intellectual knowledge but there's not an emotional connection. He wrote this column about a girl who was dying of AIDS. He put a face on it, and he put a body on what for me was this abstraction. It was just a very human approach and it hit me emotionally.

That was one of the things that really awakened me to what a columnist can do. You can make logical arguments, and I certainly try to make sure that my arguments are logical. But if you're making logical arguments in a vacuum, or logical arguments in the abstract, then you're not going to get people. You're going to get people in the head, but you're not going to get them in the heart. And you need to get them in both places, I think, if you're really going to move them at the most profound level.

What do you see yourself doing to help make that happen? How do you find the way to put a face on these issues?

I make sure the face is already there. I get calls from people, from publicists and from just regular people, asking me to write about this issue or that issue. I seldom do it unless I can find something human that's already there. If there's something human there, or if something in me as a human being resonates with it, then I'm more likely to write it. But I tend not to write stuff that is solely about an abstract thing because there's not a lot that I can do with it. If I have an emotional or human connection to it, or I know of somebody or there's somebody in the news or whatever who has an emotional or human connection to it, then it's more compelling for me as a reader and more compelling for me as a writer.

Do you do reporting for your columns and do you talk to people to bring out that story?

I don't do a lot of reporting. There have been occasions when I felt like I needed to call somebody to bring something in, either another voice or a fact. I think it's almost more interesting to imagine what someone feels than to actually hear the quote. I think it would have been more profound to try to get people to imagine how that feels. I think that would have been the visceral punch in the gut to really sort of open people's eyes to what that experience was like.

Do you see yourself as a proxy for the individuals who are experiencing the inequities or the challenges that are taking place? Do you work it out in a way that allows you to convey both the idea and the way you feel about it at the same time?

I suppose you could say that. There have probably been a number of occasions when I was that. But I think every columnist, or at least every good columnist, is at some level a proxy for "every man, every person," however you want to put it. One of the compliments that I get occasionally when people like a column is that they say, "How did you get inside my head? This is exactly what I've been thinking." That's pretty cool.

What enables you to get inside their heads?

I have never consciously tried to get inside anybody's head. It is a matter of learning to trust within your own head and your own heart. A lot of the columns I've gotten that compliment on have been ones in which I've said, "This is weird, this is my madness and no one else is ever going to follow this, and I'm about to get crucified here." And then you get these calls and these e-mails and you discover that, if you're crazy, you've got a lot of company. I think that a lot of times we as human beings and we as writers specifically tend to think that whatever it is that's going on in our heads is somehow unique. If there's anything that writing the column has taught me, it's that the opposite is true. A lot of fears, frustrations, doubts—whatever I grapple with in daily life—are things other people are dealing with, too. I think a lot of times columnists tend to pull away from that and deal with issues only in the abstract and in the theoretical. But when you deal with matters more closely, I think you find all of these human connections that are really just wonderful.

What does it take to write what will resonate with readers?

Well, I think the best writing always costs you something emotionally, requires you to give up something. The more you are willing to give up, the greater the rewards. I've written stuff that was quite painful. Before this column, when I was writing my music column, I wrote this piece on my mother's death. It was very painful to write because it took me back to her death, which as you can imagine is not a pleasant memory. But the thing that happened was that I got all these letters from people, very gratifying and very intimate letters.

What I hear you saying is that to be compelling and touch people, you first have to be touched.

Yeah, I think there's something inherently selfish in the act of writing a column. I can honestly say I've never written a column with the expectation of touching somebody. When I write the columns that seem to touch people the most, I've usually been trying to deal with something that was in me. So you've got to learn to trust that thing in yourself, that personal madness that all of us deal with.

Who are your favorite columnists? You mentioned Al Martinez earlier.

Erma Bombeck. I read Erma when I was 11, 12 years old. And it's funny because I went to a symposium in her hometown of Dayton about a year or two ago. A lot of people were surprised that this middle-aged, white housewife had something to say that was of interest to an 11-, 12-year-old black kid. But there was a humanity to her writing. She was writing about her experience. It wasn't my experience. But she was writing about her experience with honesty, with hope, and with humor. That transcended all of the differences to me. It's just the humanity of her stuff. Also Dave Barry, I guess. I always mention Dave. He's one of my current favorite columnists.

And his appeal to you is?

Juvenile humor. My highbrow answer is that I read Dave for the craftsmanship and to sharpen my own humor writing. I think that one of the things that you have to do is to read other writers to learn, to make yourself better. But my lowbrow answer is that I enjoy his stories of exploding cows and plumbing mishaps and whatever.

I notice you include history in your columns. What do you hope that kind of historical data does for the reader?

America is not a nation with a deep sense of history. A lot of us are very ahistorical. I love history in the sense of the stories that are told. We didn't just spring here. I think you can't have a true understanding of what is going on around you unless you have some historical perspective. Unless you have some sort of long view, you are really only half-educated on any given issue. For instance, people talk about black paranoia toward government or distrust of government medical news, medical experiments. Well, that sounds perhaps illogical until you consider it in the context of the Tuskegee experiment where these guys were basically allowed to die of syphilis by the United States government. When you have that context, things begin to change. You begin to get a little bit of an understanding, and that's the thing that I'm always fighting to bring to people in those columns.

In some of your columns, you expose readers to the twists and turns the subject can take when you examine it carefully. Is this reflective of your own thinking process?

When you see that, that's probably me trying to wrestle with two sides of an issue and trying to figure something out. One of the things I don't like about column writing in general, or columnists in general, is that if you know where he or she is on the political spectrum, you could pretty much guess what he or she is going to say on a given issue. I find it a lot more challenging to think through each given issue as if it is fresh. Sometimes I've been surprised where logic took me. Sometimes I've wound up thinking the opposite of what I had thought before.

I hear you saying you have to have a sense of integrity about yourself and about what you write.

Well, what's the point otherwise? This is why I bristle when people say you're a voice for this or you're a voice for that. I don't see myself as a voice for any given cause. I see myself as just a guy trying to make the intellectual and the logical ducks line up in a row, and sometimes they don't want to. That's a tricky thing. I see myself as somebody who's trying to achieve some sort of moral and logical consistency in the stuff that he does, and that requires a vigilance over your own thoughts. That requires a willingness to hold yourself to the same standard that you're out there holding everyone else to.

Tell me when you know that a column works for you.

I read a column over and over again, making changes and polishing it each time. When I've read it a few times, and I haven't made any change, and it's actually starting to bore me, that usually means it's time to press the send button.

How much revision do you do?

It's not uncommon for me to read a column 20 times before I send it to the editor. And then read it a few times after she's had a look at it just to make sure that everything is right and everything's the way it's supposed to be. I'm sort of an obsessive polisher, I guess.

How helpful is the editor? How do you see the editor's role for a columnist?

There was a younger writer I was talking with once, and he said that his aim was to send a column to his editor and have it published in the paper as is. The editor wouldn't have to touch a thing. I told him this has happened to me on occasions, rare occasions. But I told him that when that happens, it scares the hell out of me because I'm not that good. It tells me the editor must have missed something. My feeling is that once it's in the paper, it's in concrete. You can't change it. So while you have this opportunity to make it perfect, then you have an obligation to yourself and to your readers to do so.

I see the editor as a cooler head looking at my words. The thing about editing your own stuff is that if you have some time to get distance on it, for me at least, I think I'm as good an editor as anybody on my own stuff. I can be as merciless and as exacting on my own stuff as anybody. But the thing about newspaper writing specifically is that you don't have that time. When you've just written it, you're in love. If you've written something that you like, you're just enjoying your own wit and your own brilliance, your own turns of phrase or whatever. An editor is somebody who can say, "Well, maybe you're in love with this, but it doesn't work." Or an editor is somebody who says, "I think I understand what you're saying here but I'm not sure," which is the kiss of death for me. If nothing else, you've got to be clear.

A lot of people see it as an adversarial relationship. I don't. I see it as two people united in the same purpose, which is to make the copy better. We don't necessarily have to be friends, but as long as we are both on the same wavelength as far as the copy, then everything else is cool, everything else is fine. If you're here to help me make my copy better, then we're buddies, we're fine.

Tell me something about the language you use in writing and what kind of language you think is important.

I love the language and I guess my writing is probably a mix of the highbrow and the lowbrow in that regard. I love colloquial stuff, stuff that is written as people talk, and then I love using stuff that you will never find in everyday language. That's because I like the sound of the words. I guess I tend to mix it up. I like to think of myself as having several different voices. And you choose the one that you're going to use depending upon the subject matter and how you've chosen to approach it.

How do you change that voice? How do you capture it so you feel that it's authentic?

It depends on the subject matter. There's a column I just wrote on adolescent daughters with crushes on the cute guy in the boy band. I guess you could have written that as sort of an abstract thing. But to me, the only way to approach that was through my daughter, who has a crush on Justin Timberlake of 'NSync, and let me talk about how that feels. So it's sort of a very homey column with kind of a sweet tone to it. It wouldn't have been right to approach that in perhaps the same way that I did the column on the South Carolina flag, which was angry, or some of the other columns, which lean more toward hard logic. This was an emotional pitch with light humor in it, which is what you'd want for something like that. I like to vary the pitches only because that's a way of keeping me interested and it's a way of keeping the readers just a little off balance. I like them not to know what to expect when they open up my column.

You want them to be surprised in some way at what they'll be finding out.

Right, exactly. I don't want it always to sound the same way. If you gather any three or four or five of my columns, the one thing I am proud to say is that they won't all sound the same. There was a column I wrote not too long ago that had a spiritual or quasi-religious theme to it, not something you read on the op-ed pages a lot. That pleased me about it. And there's sort of a whimsy to that column that you would not find in a lot of the other stuff I've written. I like doing that. It sort of keeps the palette fresh. If all I was doing were columns that employed sarcasm or gimmick, columns like the

Elmer Fudd column I wrote not too long ago, I would get tired of myself before anybody else got tired of me. So I like to do a bunch of different things.

I'm struck by the fact that you want to be different in your approach and yet you also want the readers to know that it's you. How do you accomplish that?

We tend to think of a person as one thing. I think that all of us are many different things. What you're getting when you get the angry column is a facet. The whimsical column is a facet. The sarcastic column is a facet. I think that's probably the best way to think about it. I'm not whimsical all the time, any more than I'm angry all the time. Whatever the column is, it tends to be coming out of whatever the emotional state is at a given time.

Do you think that columnists need to recognize that they are part of a group—a racial group, for example—that affects them and the way they write?

Oh, yeah. As an African American—forget as a columnist—as a black man. I was a black man for 30-some-odd years before I was a black columnist. This is something you have to deal with, you have to grapple with, and come to terms with. The thing as a columnist is that you know now you are a black man in a much more high profile position. So the question is how are you going to balance the group with your own personal, individual beliefs in this public forum?

There's a belief in black America that we do not criticize our own where white people can see. We don't air our dirty laundry in public. I don't buy it. I refuse. That's caused difficulty sometimes. I used to get these calls from these guys in the Nation of Islam accusing me whenever I'd write negatively about Louis Farrakhan that I was "kowtowing to my Jewish masters." Most black people would recognize that as foolishness, but most black people would not say it publicly. I wrote a column basically mocking these guys. I laughed at them, and I got a call from a lady who said, "Well, you know, you were right. I don't disagree with what you said. But why'd you have to say it in public?"

And so that's where the group thing comes in. But at the same time, I have to tell you I wrote a column—and I take responsibility for the tone of it—that was actually fairly obnoxious. Although I didn't realize it at the time, it annoyed a lot of white readers. There was a big furor in Miami over this column, and somehow there was a rumor that I was going to lose my job over this. To that point, I had never known what kind of black readership I had. One day I get a call from this lady who said she represented such and such black group and they had heard I was going to lose my job over this column and they were ready to march in front of the building for me. Just tell them when. This is out of the clear blue from people I've never met, known, didn't even know they existed.

It's such a great thing to know that they always have your back, that they support you. See, that's the other side of the group. I don't want it to sound as if it's just a negative thing. I know that if something happens, that I'm being treated unfairly and it's racial in terms, or if it just looks racial, there are going to be people who are going to give me support. There's going to be white people there as well. But there are going to be black people who are there very specifically as members of the group to support me. That's a good thing to know. That's a good thing to feel. That puts some wind in your sail. So it's like the group is a blessing and a burden at the same time. It's a difficult thing. It's a very subjective thing.

If someone is interested in writing commentary or being a columnist, what do you think is important for them to recognize?

I don't know that we haven't brought it up, but I don't think it can be said enough: To thine own self be true. Be whoever it is, whatever it is that you are. I mean I never calculated what would work to what effect in writing the column, or even in writing the music column that came before it. I just figured I would write stuff that I would like to read. That was the whole thing. That was what I said when I first sat down in front of the computer. What can I write that I would like to be sitting down reading two days from now? That's still what I do. I tend to believe that's how the good columnist approaches it.

Colbert I. King

Finalist, Commentary

Colbert I. King is an editorial writer for *The Washington Post* where he writes commentary on national, local, and international topics and a weekly column. Before joining the *Post* in 1990, King was a banking executive, U.S. representative to the World Bank and a deputy assistant secretary of the treasury in the Carter administration, and a U.S. Senate staff member. He has a bachelor's degree from Howard University, where he did graduate studies in public administration.

King brings fearless honesty to a wide range of subjects, from racism and crime, to government and human relationships. In "Who Remembers Ray Davis?" King followed up the letter from a distressed reader alerting him to the death of a young activist. As part of his ongoing effort to keep Washington, D.C.'s, murder victims on the city's radar screen, King calls people to account: city leaders, ordinary citizens, even his own newspaper.

Who remembers Ray Davis?

FEBRUARY 12, 2000

Anthony Cooper made it 15. Andre Wallace and Natasha Marsh, the two Wilson High seniors slain this week, were the 13th and 14th. But when 16-year-old Cooper took a bullet on Valley Avenue SE around 11 o'clock Thursday night, he became the 15th D.C. public school student murdered since classes started in September.

Now I ask you, in all the histrionics and acting out across this city over just about every issue under the sun, in all those sermons and speeches that you've heard in the past six weeks by D.C. preachers and politicians, how many of them have devoted even two seconds to the number of murders of public school students?

In my column on New Year's Day, I wrote, "Celebrate? Maybe I'll rejoice if this city gets through this first month of the new millennium without setting another record for homicides." We didn't make it. Twenty-five people were murdered in January 1999. By the end of last month, 26 victims of D.C. violence had given up the ghost.

Now, dear reader, while those bodies were falling, what, pray tell, has been the major preoccupation of those highly paid, puffed-up peacocks strutting about in One Judiciary Square—our town's city hall?

What is it that seems to have gotten our city council and mayor so worked up and full of anger? Could it be the "senseless" killings and spiraling murder rate?

Naw. Since January our leaders have been growling and spitting over whether or not the Rev. Willie Wilson should be given a seat on the board of the University of the District of Columbia. Their backs were up over the mayor's preferred method of funding pay raises for unionized city workers. And now they're in high dudgeon, nursing revenge, convinced they have accounts to settle with each other, because the mayor doesn't like the council's simple-minded plan for changing the way the school board is selected.

You'd think they would be concerned about the criminality claiming young lives in our city. But this is a political leadership consumed with self-image and the picayune. The only issue of consequence, the only cause that takes on life-and-death importance with them, is their survival at the polls. Teenage slaughter is nothing to think twice about, as far as D.C. officialdom is concerned. That is, unless there is a high-profile slaying and word gets around One Judiciary Square that there will be loads of TV cameras, reporters and a big crowd at the funeral, and then, dear reader, open the door and clear the way—the next sound you hear will be the thundering footsteps of D.C. politicians as they herd toward the front of the church so they can sit in the best seats with, of course, appropriately long and drawn faces.

But it's not just the politicians who have been giving short shrift to the slaughter on our streets. A recent letter from Zahara (Joan) Heckscher hit me right between the eyes.

"The *Post* has not mentioned one word about Ray's death—or his life."

Heckscher had written to me about Raynard Davis, a D.C. native and 1985 Oberlin College graduate whom she met in 1987 when they were working with the D.C. Student Coalition Against Apartheid and Racism. Along with other community activists, Heckscher and Davis protested together, got arrested together and took their lumps together in their struggle against racism.

Following the release of Nelson Mandela and the demise of South Africa's last white government, Ray continued his activities with antiracism programs and multi-racial causes, co-founding the D.C. Student Coalition Against Racism. According to Heckscher, he earned a name for himself building bridges among the region's diverse ethnic groups—blacks, Latinos, Asian Americans and Native Americans, as well as white people.

Davis worked particularly hard to build collaboration and goodwill between African Americans and Jews, she said. He dedicated much of his life to working with high school youth, involving young people in the anti-apartheid movement and supporting initiatives to promote racial healing and justice in our own community.

"Raynard Davis," she wrote, "a graduate student at Howard University, was murdered last April 7 by an unknown assailant."

Heckscher expressed sympathy for the friends and family of murder victims Michele Dorr and Donna Dustin (6-year-old Dorr disappeared nearly 14 years ago; her remains were found last month. Dustin was slain 26 years ago; her murder is still unsolved). "I am distressed, however, by the contrast between how the murders of young white girls are treated by the *Post* and the way the *Post* treats the murders of young black men.

"As a white woman, I do not object to your reporters covering stories of murders of white girls. But the *Post* should be ashamed that the deaths of young black men are relegated to a paragraph in the Metro section—or are not even deemed worthy of coverage at all."

The force of her questions backed me up: "Where was the front-page story about the tragic loss to our city when Ray was murdered? Where was the Style appreciation of Ray's short but passionate life? Where was the follow-up story about how Ray's parents are dealing with the loss of their only child, and how the young people of this city are continuing the work he started?"

"The Post has not mentioned one word about Ray's death—or his life."

Can that be? Surely she's wrong, I thought. Let's knock the mayor and the D.C. Council for their inattention. Let's zing the clergy for their escapist retreat from real life. But the *Post*? There must be at least a brief reference to him somewhere in the paper. I went to the archives, and got a hit on "Raynard Davis." Aha!

But it was a 1986 story about the Vanderbilt-Alabama basketball game in which Jamie Dixon made an off-balance 39-footer at the buzzer with Raynard Davis hanging onto him.

It wasn't Heckscher's Ray.

She was right. The Raynard Davis who had given so much of his life to the kind of racial progress this city sorely needs had passed our way, and out of our world—"lying on the sidewalk suffering from multiple stab wounds," in the words of the D.C. police press release—without even an incidental mention in *The Washington Post*.

His parents, Hayward and Jean Davis, are determined not to let his life end like that. His father said in an interview this week that they are trying to keep his memory alive through a living legacy named the Raynard T. Davis Memorial Fund to assist a minority student in anthropology at Oberlin and the Youth Leadership Support Network, a D.C.-based advocacy group.

Jean Davis, struggling with tears as she spoke about her son this week, recalled what he was like growing up. "He was my buddy, my traveling companion, he was quite a kid." The crowd that packed Howard University's Andrew Rankin Chapel for his memorial service last July 31 thought so too. Former South African political prisoner Dennis Brutus was there. So was Ray's Oberlin classmate and mezzo-soprano Denyce Graves, who sang three songs.

But he didn't make our radar screen.

And so with this column, Ray Davis joins the long list of D.C. residents whose murders have appeared in this space. His case also carries the same police department notice: "No motive or suspects have been determined at this time, and the case is currently under investigation by detectives of the Department's Homicide Division."

Would that those unfortunate D.C. murder victims were still with us. Would that we could have made this a safer city for them. But at least they got their names in the paper. Ray didn't. And for that, I say to Ray's parents, Jean and Hayward Davis, his family, friends and especially Zahara Heckscher—I'm so sorry.

Newsday

Paul Vitello

Finalist, Commentary

Paul Vitello joined *Newsday* in 1981 as a beat reporter covering the Babylon area. In 1982, he became a general assignment reporter and has been a columnist since 1986. Vitello was born in Chicago in 1950 but grew up on Manhattan's lower East Side. He graduated from Trinity College in Hartford, Conn., and has worked at the Chicago City News Bureau, the *Knickerbocker News* in Albany, N.Y., and the *Kansas City Times,* and was a free-lance writer in Rome, Italy.

Vitello earned the 1977 New York State Associated Press Award for spot news and the 1982 *Newsday* Publisher's Award for non-deadline writing. In 1984, Vitello won the feature writing award from the Society of the Silurians, and in 1988, 1989, and 1990 he won *Newsday*'s Publisher's Award for commentary. In 1992 and 1993, he won the first-place Associated Press Award for commentary. Vitello lives in Baldwin, N.Y., with his wife, Carol Polsky, a *Newsday* reporter, and their children Sam and Anna.

As he follows fallen politician John Powell on his way to incarceration, Vitello shows the power of understated irony. His commentary is driven by a simple notion of what's right as he critiques the Italian-American stereotypes found in *The Sopranos*.

Sopranos not in my range

Out of respect for other people's feelings, and to be honest, a deep-seated fear of sounding ungrateful to Hollywood for keeping people of my particular ethnic background in acting jobs where they get to emote profanely, I would like to mind my own business about the HBO series called *The Sopranos*.

Everyone loves *The Sopranos*. *The Sopranos* is a show with nuance and great writing. Average people, mobsters, repeat violent felons, upper middle-class achievers, even some of my best friends, are addicted to it.

So I should swallow my disquiet about what makes this show so popular. Change the channel. Read Dante if I'm such a stickler about Italian culture, right?

Of course I should.

We only got the cable box a couple of months ago. We got it for the basketball games, to be honest. We didn't get it to watch *The Sopranos*.

But I watched the show a few times. I heard it was good. I watched it three and a half times, to be exact. I didn't make it through the fourth.

I think I got up to the part—maybe you remember this—where one guy in a black T-shirt is standing with his face in the face of another guy in a brown cashmere jacket with a black T-shirt underneath it. And the first guy is saying, "____ you!"

Then, I believe, the other guy says "____ you!"

It was very good writing (author! author!) but it didn't feel like an original dramatic experience to me. I had a strange sense of déja vu.

Then it came to me in a flash: Joe Pesci. Al Pacino. Martin Scorcese. Robert DeNiro. They have been doing this schtick for 30 years, haven't they?

On the other hand, I am not a knave or a fool or a Minnesotan. I acknowledge that Italian-Americans sometimes must interrupt their trips, taking their daughters to visit the colleges they may wish to attend, in order to murder some bum who is talking to the ___ feds. This was the story line of one episode.

I have seen this happen many times. Once, my Uncle Booboo, rest in peace, tore a guy's head off with a lightning slash of his sharpened right pinky nail when the bum just looked like he was thinking about talking to the feds.

And I know that as a group, we Italian-Americans have more animal magnetism, more talent for homicide, more zest for sex and bucks, and all that, than the average citizen.

But on the other hand, haven't we had enough of this movie already?

The mob, from what I have seen of it in real life, is filled with very unkind and ugly people, none of whom are remotely like this bearishly lovable killer, Tony Soprano. Some of these people may see themselves the way the producers of *The Sopranos* see them—as killers who love their children and their mothers. Or who, at least, have all the same ambivalent feelings about their loved ones as the rest of us do.

But, in fact, as they should know, mobsters destroy their children. Look at all the children of mobsters in the news: This one is going to jail. That one is losing her house. A whole nuclear family worth of mobsters is going down with that guy Gravano. They are not getting into Brown University and Sarah Lawrence College.

Tony Soprano's line seems to be about high-stakes card games, killing off stool pigeons, collecting debts from reprobates, and generally enforcing a certain moral order in the underworld. How about an episode where Tony Soprano organizes a drug ring selling Ecstacy to children? Or an arson ring whose dirty work causes the slow and painful death of innocent people?

But I am being too literal, I know. This is art, after all.

The fact that *The Sopranos* goes over the same dramatic territory that Francis Ford Coppola did better, and Scorcese did darker, is fine with me. Television is a wasteland where something that just imitates originality is a welcome breath of air. Take it. Give it an Emmy.

But as an Italian-American who has no mobsters in his family, and who doesn't know anyone who is a mobster, it makes me uncomfortable to realize that the only

portrayal of Italian-Americans in the Hollywood reper-
toire comes off this same old template.

African-Americans have the same complaint, and
justly so; but Italian-Americans haven't even had a Cos-
by show, to prove the rule by its exception.

I never used to watch sports. But I have found that I
like it more and more. You never know what will happen
in a game. It's real drama. There are no award-winning
scriptwriters in sports.

I should just watch sports. How about those Knicks?
I should just hold my tongue about *The Sopranos*.

The last gasp of a kingmaker

APRIL 16, 2000

John Powell, the former Suffolk Republican leader, strode with confidence up to the federal courthouse, an expensive lawyer at each of his well-tailored shoulders. He looked buffed and polished in his suit, white shirt and tie, wearing that commanding look he wears, even in jeans and running shoes. It is the look he will take with him into the yard at Allenwood federal penitentiary.

"Got a haircut this morning," he said, stopping to chat with reporters outside the courthouse in Uniondale just before his sentencing Friday for extortion and racketeering and the bamboozling of many thousands of people who trusted him. All the reporters snapped a clean page into place. But he didn't say anything more.

He smoked a cigarette like tough boys do in high school, pincering the filter and covering the rest with the closed hand. His mother was there. His wife, his brother. All the men smoked that tough-guy way.

At the metal detector inside, he plunged his hands into his pockets like Charlie Chaplin and came up with his Marlboros. He placed them on the conveyor belt.

Powell is the kind of person who, when he puts his cigarettes on a conveyor belt, you watch to see what comes out the other side. Will it be cigarettes, or a top hat filled with silver dollars?

On his best days, Powell pulled off stunts as good as that. On Friday, just cigarettes came out the other side.

"Do you have anything to say before this court passes sentence?" asked the judge a few minutes later.

"No, your honor," Powell said, disappointing anyone who had nursed a hope that he would explain.

Some people may wonder why I was taking cash in envelopes when, as undisputed political boss of an undisputed Republican kingdom, I could have made money in sleazy yet legal ways pioneered by so many of my predecessors. Well, here's why…

That's what I had hoped for. Instead, he let one of his

lawyers say a few words. The lawyer, Benjamin Brafman, said Powell was "a fundamentally good person who committed a bad act."

It is probably a true enough statement, which you could also apply to eight-tenths of all convicts—bank robbers and drug sellers included—though few of them will get the white-glove treatment Powell received on Friday: There were no marshals, no handcuffs, no escorts into custody. There was no custody, in fact. He went home after the sentencing. He is scheduled to surrender to begin serving his time on June 5.

Perhaps that was why there was no evident emotion in the courtroom as Powell stood silently and received a 27-month prison sentence from U.S. District Court Judge Jacob Mishler, one of the sharpest, if oldest, judges on the federal bench; a man whose successor Powell might have hand-picked, had things been different. And praise be, they weren't different.

Powell is, or was, that most dangerous of political creatures: a charismatic crook. The foot soldiers of his party organization—highway workers, secretaries, truck drivers, laborers for the Town of Brookhaven— loved him for his commanding presence, for his understanding of the working life, which he earned as a truck driver and heavy equipment operator, for his Tammany Hall style of patronage-dispensing, for his intelligence.

He was the real thing, in many ways. He liked nothing better than to get on a snowplow in a snowstorm and clear snow. To boot, he knew how to spin that into the gold of the loyalty of others. At his urging, they would pull out the vote on election night better than any organization in the state.

His charisma worked like a stain-remover on his life. When questions were raised about the lavish house built for him by a contractor who did work for the Town of Brookhaven, they didn't hurt him. When questions were raised about the public jobs he doled out to his family and friends, nothing happened.

Nothing might ever have happened if his voice had not popped up—commandingly, profanely and completely unexpectedly, say investigators—on some FBI tapes. The FBI was secretly recording people they suspected were operating a stolen-truck ring based in

Brookhaven. Powell, it turned out, was in the ring.

That was the end for a kingmaker in the making, a boss who to that point was the political muscle behind a county executive, a district attorney, a half-dozen county judges, a dozen town officials and, some say, even the election of the governor.

People said he could have made president someday, with all that talent and magic in him. He might have put the cigarettes into one end of the conveyor belt, so to speak, and gotten gold from the other.

Lucky for us, only cigarettes came out; and the man will smoke them in prison.

Lessons Learned

BY PAUL VITELLO

The pieces reprinted here are examples of two different kinds of news column—one based on a news event, one based on the unwavering confidence of the column writer in his or her right to complain about stuff. Whether by coincidence or because these are the kinds of columns that tend to capture readers' imaginations, both pieces are about myths.

The column on the sentencing of John Powell is about the myth at the center of a local political organization. In describing the way Powell held a cigarette, the rabbit-in-the-hat way he dug into his pockets, I was trying to capture the power of illusion that was part of his boss personna. He was a guy who spun modest material—a background as a payload operator—into formidable accomplishments in politics. Then, presto, it seemed, there he was, spinning his gold back into the dross of a 27-month prison term.

The Sopranos column is about the myth of Italian-American life that is at the center of one TV show and one-too-many movies. It is a different kind of column—less reportorial and detailed, more like a monologue delivered to a roomful of friends, presuming one had so many friends after writing a newspaper column for 15 years, as I have.

The column talks directly to the reader. I employed the tongue-in-cheek tone partly because that's how I think and partly because it puts a little comic space between my strong feelings and the reader's ear. I don't want to yell at people who happen to like *The Sopranos*. I just want to show them *how much I really, really hate this tired old stereotype of Italian Americans* while, if possible, making people laugh.

The myths around us—identifying them, poking them, occasionally debunking them—probably make for a good beat for any columnist. It's a staple of all departments in the newspaper, though columnists are especially well-equipped for it because myths are almost always in the subtext of stories, hardly ever in the lead.

On most days, I gather information for a story just as I would as a reporter; but when I write the column, it's the subtext that I'm trying to get right, not the text (though you want to get that right, too, please). Subtext is, according to my definition, the part of the story that none of the players ever mentions. It's the election politics in the prosecution of a murder case. It's the way angry people on different sides of a controversy, standing to face the flag before a hearing, emphasize different phrases in their reciting of the Pledge of Allegiance. It can be in the way two people look at each other across a courtroom before one testifies against the other.

For me, subtext is where the action is in any story. It's hard to say where the action should be for anyone else. I have written a news column for a long time, and I have to admit that I often have no idea where the action is in a story until I start writing it. There is an element of channeling here, as the New Agers say.

For instance, I'm not sure I knew what I would do with John Powell's cigarettes, which I made notes about on the day of his sentencing. I made a note about that; but also about the way his mother and wife stood together, but not with him; about his brother; about the many party workers who showed up in support. I made notes on the judge, who is a rich character in his own right. Any one of those ideas might have carried the column in a different direction. The cigarettes, though, suggested the barrenness ahead for John Powell. It suggested the solitude and the prison yard. I'm not sure I thought of it in those terms until it was on the screen (or page, as we used to say). At that point, it seemed like the right detail. So I proceeded to the next paragraph.

The same was true in *The Sopranos* column. I knew I didn't like the show, and I knew why. But until I started to address an audience—one I imagined to be in love with Tony Soprano and his family—I had no idea that I would assume the posture of the reluctant intruder. In retrospect it made a certain sense. It's a device every reporter has used. I have used it in getting interviews with all kinds of people, including, on more than one occasion, the family of a killer. How fitting to employ the old foot-in-the-door on the fans of Tony Soprano.

Let's be honest. It's an odd craft. You write for people you never see, about things they may or may not care about. You become a vacuum cleaner of buried stories, stray facts, court dates, book reviews, local political lore, details about little-known lives, tenuous threads of connection between your circulation area and natural catastrophes in the farthest reaches of the world. You burn bridges, make and lose irate readers, expose yourself ruthlessly for the sake of a single funny story in the Tuesday paper. Then there's just two more columns to go for the week, one with a little extra oomph for Sunday.

It's not a particularly natural state of being. During vacations of more than a week, I swear I wake up sometimes in a strange room and realize that I have forgotten, completely, how to write a newspaper column. I might as well be the proverbial monkey at the typewriter. Luckily, it comes back under the pressure of the deadline.

Did we talk about the deadline yet, and its role in the making of a column? We may be running out of time. Suffice it to say, its role is large. Nothing commands the channeling powers, referred to above; nothing is more essential to the organization of the vacuumed-up detritus in the brain, referred to above; nothing makes things make sense more effectively than a deadline. Hurray for it. There are big myths and little myths, good columns and bad; but the deadline is the truth as we know it at this time, amen.

If not for the deadline, in fact, neither of the pieces reprinted here would ever have...

Top photo: (front row) Angela Stewart, Kate Coscarelli, Ted Sherman, and Carol Ann Campell. (back row) Russell Ben-Ali, Matt Reilly, Bob Braun, Sue Epstein, and Rudy Larini. Photo by Robert Sciarrino.
Bottom photo: (left to right) Kelly Heyboer, Guy Sterling, Rebecca Goldsmith, John Mooney, Mary Jo Patterson, Steve Chambers, David Gibson, and Robin Gaby Fisher. Photo by Noah K. Murray.
Not pictured: Mark Mueller, Bill Gannon, Sue Livio, and David Cho.

The Star-Ledger
Team Deadline News Reporting

As the tragedy of fire and death at Seton Hall University unfolded in the early morning hours of January 19, 2000, reporters and editors began what seemed an unremarkable day. A reporter hit the treadmill. Another listened to the car radio. An editor slept. Within minutes of hearing the news, though, *The Star-Ledger* staff had mobilized editors, reporters, photojournalists, and graphic artists to capture the drama, heartbreak, and intrigue of a small but deadly fire.

The coverage package opened with the rewrite work of senior reporter Mary Jo Patterson, whose hands-on style of managing information helped broaden and deepen the reporting of her colleagues in the field. Thanks to that collaboration, her story had the urgency of a hard-news daily buttressed by the powerful quotes, tight transitions, and fine details characteristic of a Sunday feature. Patterson, a native of Buffalo, N.Y., is a 24-year *Star-Ledger* veteran who holds undergraduate and advanced degrees from Ohio Wesleyan University and Columbia University.

Robin Gaby Fisher's story about the three students who died in the fire was another example of what happens when unselfish team reporting is filtered through the deft touch of a talented writer. Fisher, a journalist for 16 years, went on to write "After the Fire," a gripping narrative account of what happened to two of the young men badly burned in the Seton Hall dormitory. The package earned photojournalist Matt Rainey a Pulitzer Prize and Fisher the distinction of a Pulitzer finalist.

The Star-Ledger's deadline coverage also included dogged reporting by Guy Sterling and Bill Gannon on the police and fire investigation, a deadline column by Bob Braun, and a range of stories covering everything from injured students to the safety of other school buildings in the area. With more than 35 journalists working on the next morning's paper, credit for the excellence achieved was spread far and wide. Among those singled out for praise by editors and reporters were Kate Coscarelli and Kelly Heyboer, two of the first reporters to arrive on the Seton Hall campus. Their contributions added drama and heart to several stories. Graphic artist Frank Cecala reported from the scene and combined with Andrew Phillips to offer readers a strong visual story not easily told with pictures.

The Star-Ledger team also included Russell Ben-Ali, Carol Ann Campbell, Steve Chambers, David Cho, Sue Epstein, David Gibson, Rebecca Goldsmith, Rudy Larini, John Mooney, Mark Mueller, Matt Reilly, Ted Sherman, Angela Stewart, and Sue Livio.

—Keith Woods

Fire kills 3 in Seton Hall dorm prone to false alarms

JANUARY 20, 2000

By Mary Jo Patterson

A small but intense fire sent acrid black smoke through a freshman dormitory at Seton Hall University in South Orange before dawn yesterday, killing three students and sending hundreds of others on a flight for their lives.

Fifty-eight students were injured, four critically, by the flames and thick smoke that billowed from a third-floor lounge. The smoke blinded and choked 18- and 19-year-olds as they felt their way, or crawled, to stairwells. Others, terrorized, remained in their rooms, crying and begging for help. At least one jumped from his window before firefighters could extend rescue ladders.

Nearly a score of false alarms in recent weeks had caused many students to disregard the fire alarm at first. Then, as the smoke filled the building, they realized this was no prank. "I heard people screaming... 'This one's for real! This one's for real!'" said Jason Esposito, a resident of the dormitory, Boland Hall.

Alison Liptak was one of those who discounted the alert. "I just thought it was another false alarm. I just laid there, kind of ignoring it, until I heard someone running down the hall," said Liptak, 18, of Clifton. The pajamas-clad freshman escaped from her fourth-floor room to find another horror scene outside. She looked up to see students leaning out windows, pleading for help.

As of early this morning, investigators had not pinpointed the cause of the fire, but they had ruled out careless smoking and faulty electrical wiring.

Authorities identified the three dead students as John Giunta of Vineland, Aaron Karol of Green Brook, and Frank Caltabilota of West Long Branch. Two of the three were found in the lounge, burned beyond recognition, according to sources at the scene. The third, whom fellow students tried to revive, was found in a bedroom nearby.

The most seriously injured were three of 12 victims admitted to the burn unit of Saint Barnabas Medical Center in Livingston, and one victim at University Hospital in Newark.

By day's end, 45 students had been treated and released from seven area hospitals, most suffering from smoke inhalation.

The six-story Boland Hall—built in 1952 as the university's first dormitory—is home to 600 Seton Hall freshmen.

University officials said that 18 false alarms had been registered at the 350-room structure since Sept. 1, fewer than in previous years. Still, a number of students buried their heads in their pillows at the sound of the alarm. "I didn't think anything of it. We've had fire alarms going off all the time during finals week, and I figured, 'More of the same,'" said Tom Semko of Howell.

Hellish sights and sounds confronted fleeing students.

Anthony Neis, an 18-year-old from Staten Island, passed a young man who was clad only in shorts, covered with burns, and moaning. "He must have been in such pain," said Neis, who escaped unharmed.

Carrie Fleisher, a freshman from Hillsborough, saw a teen-ager on fire. "He was totally blackened. Some kids were hitting him with a jacket. He was conscious and hitting himself, too," she said. Jumping from the ledge outside, one teen-ager hung by his hands from a window sill. Another, Nicholas Donato, a 6-foot-1 freshman, walked to his window ledge and jumped, breaking an ankle and wrist.

Yatin Patel, 19, of Jersey City, trapped in his room, heaved mattresses out his window, with his roommate's help. Paralyzed with fear, he was standing at the window, contemplating jumping, when a firefighter burst into the room. Patel wet a sock, put it over his mouth and nose and—grabbing the kneeling fireman's left leg—began to crawl out into the corridor. His roommate held Patel's leg in turn and crawled behind them. The trio moved slowly through the darkness, under flames licking from ceiling tiles, to a stairwell.

Down the hall, Virginia Wannamaker dialed 911 on her cell phone as she waited in fear with her roommate.

The 18-year-old from Irvington heeded the advice of the fire dispatcher, stuffing a comforter under the door and sealing it tight with packing tape. They opened windows and turned on a fan.

South Orange fire sources said they were alerted to the fire at 4:28 a.m. by the college's public safety department and had the fire under control by approximately 4:45 a.m. Officials on the scene could not pinpoint exactly when the blaze started, however. Seven other municipalities also responded to the general alarm fire.

University officials said the building's occupants included 18 paid resident assistants, one priest and four professional staffers. In the event of a fire, resident assistants are to knock on every door, said Lisa Grider, a spokeswoman for Seton Hall. South Orange firefighters conducted an extensive primary search of the dorm, followed by two more, she added.

Still, two freshmen slept through the entire ordeal undetected and emerged unscathed hours later, at 2 p.m.

The blaze was confined to a lounge area off the elevators, open on two sides to student rooms. Students use the area—furnished with three plush velour sofas, a rug, a cork bulletin board and pay phones—to socialize and study. Sometimes they nap there, too.

University officials said smoking is allowed in dorm rooms but prohibited in the lounge. In the fire, the sofas were completely burned; the ceiling, cinder-block walls, and low-pile rug were singed. Fire officials speculated that the two dead students found in the lounge had left their rooms and became disoriented.

Boland Hall is one of six dormitories on campus and one of two without sprinklers. It is equipped with smoke detectors and 55 fire extinguishers, one of which was found, used, near the fire, university officials said.

"This is a heartbreaking tragedy for Seton Hall University, for our families, for all the Seton Hall family, and for the larger family of the state," said Msgr. Robert Sheeran, president of Seton Hall, a Catholic university founded in 1856. Some 2,200 of its 10,000 students live on campus.

Sheeran suspended all classes, activities, and events through Sunday pending further notice.

Gov. Christie Whitman, who visited the scene, called

the fire a "huge tragedy."

By all accounts, the hours immediately before the fire passed like most nights at Boland Hall—except for the lingering air of jubilation caused by Seton Hall's unexpected win, 78-70, over basketball archrival St. John's. The new semester, which began last Thursday, was fresh and new. Students were up late, as usual. There were parties here and there.

For example, Tiffany Hill, an 18-year-old from Maryland, had spent the night alternately studying her economics textbook and bouncing between friends across the hall and in the lounge. Around 3 a.m. she finally called it quits and retired to her room. She dozed for about an hour, when her roommate woke her, saying she needed to talk. Exhausted, Hill put her off and fell back asleep, but woke not many minutes later.

This time her friend was in her face. "Tiff, get up, get up," she yelled. "It's real." Hill had not heard the alarms, but she smelled smoke as soon as she shook herself awake. Someone banged at the door.

"We put on our stuff and ran," Hill said, interviewed hours later as she walked across campus, carrying the teddy bear slippers she had put on to escape the fire.

Michael McCaffrey, a roommate of victim Aaron Karol, was still awake when the alarms sounded. He was not in his third-floor room but on the floor above, watching movies with friends.

"My bed is on the other side of the lounge wall," McCaffrey said. "If I was there, I probably wouldn't be here right now. And when I heard the fire alarm, at first I didn't react much. I was very nonchalant. There's a fire alarm almost every night sometimes, it seems. It's those idiot frat pledges who are constantly pulling the alarms."

Rob Cardiello, who lived two doors from the lounge, was one of the few students to report actually seeing fire. He hadn't heard the smoke alarms, having put on earplugs before going to sleep. Suddenly he awoke, wet and sweaty.

"I looked to the right, to the lounge, and saw (orange) flames," he said. As he exited the building in the opposite direction, the sharp black smoke penetrated his lungs like acid. "I could feel the whole way down the hallway: Your lungs are burning," Cardiello said. The 18-year-old freshman from Clark was treated at Mountainside Hospital in Montclair for smoke inhalation.

As Cardiello ran toward safety, he smacked into two students who were running and screaming. He pushed one toward the right direction, grabbed the other, and charged down the hallway. The smoke was so thick, he said, that they ran past the exit, into a wall.

Once outside, Cardiello ran around campus, looking for a missing friend. "I didn't really realize how I was feeling until I stopped," he said hours later.

All four of the students listed as "very critical" were on respirators last night. The three at Saint Barnabas, all males, had second-degree burns covering from 15 to 56 percent of their bodies. Only one, Alvaro Ilanos, was identified.

At University Hospital, the patient was Dana Christmas, a resident adviser who suffered severe burns and respiratory distress. Christmas, 21, of Paterson was unconscious and attached to a ventilator to ease pressure on her smoke-damaged lungs. Doctors said she had burns over 60 percent of her body, including her face, back and extremities.

"She has fairly extensive injuries. Her condition is being monitored on a minute-to-minute basis," said Sanjeev Kaul, the trauma physician attending to her.

News of the fire hit the airwaves early, frightening parents.

In Teaneck, Roderico Sumilang and his wife, whose alarm radio had been set to an all-news station, heard about the fire the second they woke up. Sumilang turned on the TV. He dialed the number of the cell phone he had just given his son, Romil. The son's roommate answered.

"He said, 'I can't talk, the firemen are trying to get us out,'" the father recalled. "I said, 'Where's my son?' He said, 'He might have gotten out the back.'"

Sumilang called the college but got a recording. Again, he dialed his son's cell phone. This time, a different voice delivered the news: Romil had been taken away in an ambulance.

The couple learned that some students had been taken to Saint Barnabas, and they left for the hospital.

They found their son in the intensive care unit. "I'm okay," Romil told them, then asked about his friends.

Many parents endured hours of agonizing uncertainty.

Others counted their blessings to find children alive. So did their kids.

"I think God had his arms around me this morning," said Nicole McFarlane, 19, a freshman from Summit who lived on Boland Hall's fifth floor. "That's why I got out. I had God's arms around me."

Mourning the loss
of 3 perpetual smiles

JANUARY 20, 2000

By Robin G. Fisher, John Mooney, and David Gibson

John Giunta was where he liked to be best last Sunday—sitting at a dinner table with his big Italian family.

There didn't need to be an occasion for the Giunta clan to gather, but this time there was: the golden wedding anniversary of John's grandparents.

As always, the boy they all called "Johnny" was the life of the party that afternoon at a Chinese restaurant near the Giunta family compound in Vineland. He told hilarious stories about his college escapades, made fun of his relatives who ate sushi, and teased his 14-year-old cousin, Lou, about girls.

Yesterday, the Giuntas came together again. But this time it was to mourn. Johnny, the tall, sandy-haired freshman with the perpetual grin—the second eldest of five children—was one of the three young men who died in the Seton Hall dormitory fire on Wednesday morning. The other students, also freshmen, were Frank Caltabilota of West Long Branch and Aaron Karol of Green Brook. Their bodies were discovered in the third-floor student lounge where the fire started.

Giunta was trapped in his dorm room and died from smoke inhalation, according to his aunt, Crisilda Giunta Rucci. She said his brother, Peter, a junior at Seton Hall, was frantic to find him, but couldn't in all the commotion.

"Petey and Johnny were inseparable," she said. "They weren't just brothers, they were soulmates. You couldn't get any closer—they just loved each other so much."

Yesterday, Caltabilota's high school football coach could only think of his former player's broad smile—and about how the former wide receiver would always rib him in the hallway. "He would always be laughing at me. He was just a great kid," said Mark Costantino, the eight-year head coach of the Shore Regional High

School's Blue Devils in West Long Branch.

"He had a great sense of humor, a happy-go-lucky kind of guy," said his coach. "I don't know anybody who didn't like him."

Caltabilota, the second oldest of four children to parents Joanne and Frank, had been an altar boy at St. Jerome's Roman Catholic Church. He also had a pierced ear, like a lot of teens, and something even more distinctive: a tattoo of the Chinese symbol of ascension on his left shoulder.

The family is active in the community, and Caltabilota's father had always been a fixture at his son's high school football games at Shore Regional High School—oftentimes working the game clock.

The team won the state championships two years ago, and the division championship last year—Caltabilota's senior year.

But while he was a fine athlete, Caltabilota was just as revered among friends for supporting his teammates.

One of his good friends was Peter Vincelli, a halfback and fellow defensive back at Shore Regional who now attends Gettysburg College in Pennsylvania.

"I have so many films of them playing together, slapping each other congratulations," said Louis Vincelli, Peter's father and a family friend. "He was just a real unselfish player, that's for sure."

The news about the fire started as rumors in the small Monmouth County community where Caltabilota grew up. First, the word was that the boy was just missing. By afternoon, though, Vincelli and others realized that the kid they knew as "Frankie" was gone.

Even his parents had to wait. They were told at noon that their son had been in the area of the fire, but were not officially notified of his death until 5 p.m. when he was identified through his dental records.

"He was just a terrific kid. I can't believe it, I can't believe it," said Theresa Everhardt, a second cousin who spoke outside the family's one-level ranch house.

The Caltabilota family home sits on a quiet dead-end street. Last night the street was lined with the cars of visiting friends and relatives.

Dorothy Cross, who lived a couple of doors down, said she thought the worst when she heard Caltabilota hadn't called in the morning when the news of the fire was on every television channel.

"He wasn't the type of the kid who would not call," said Cross. "He wouldn't let his parents worry."

Caltabilota's mother came outside but would not speak to a reporter. She wore a pin reading "Mom."

In Somerset County last night, family members and friends of Aaron Karol tried to take solace in their memories of him.

"Everyone loved him—he was a good son," said Candy Karol, sitting with her husband, Joe, in their Green Brook home.

Candy Karol said that when the telephone didn't ring early yesterday, she knew her son was dead. He would never have let his family endure a day of excruciating uncertainty by not calling to say he was safe.

"As the day wore on, I knew he was one of the fatalities," she said. "He would have called."

Karol's girlfriend of a year, Aliza Olive, a student at Watchung Hills Regional High School, rested her head on Candy Karol's shoulder and cried.

"I think they would have gotten married," the mother said. "I feel so bad for her. I had him for 18 years—she only had him for one."

Dan Root was Karol's soccer coach for his last two years at Watchung Hills.

"As a junior he was a quiet, shy kind of kid," Root said. "You could see he wasn't very sure of himself. But as a senior he came in with a confidence he didn't have before—not only athletically, but socially.

The coach said Karol blossomed into a strong defender and was an integral part of a team that came within a hair's breadth of winning a state championship.

While Karol could have pursued soccer at the college level, Root said the fast-maturing young man decided that academics trumped athletics. "He just decided that soccer wasn't his top priority."

Going to college was important—Karol was a psychology major whose dream was to become an FBI profiler—but so was remaining close enough to home to stay in touch with his parents and older sister.

"Seton Hall was the perfect place for him to be," said a distraught Joe Coletti, a Watchung Hills senior and teammate who was Karol's friend throughout high school. "He was one in a million. It's like losing a brother."

Coletti had seen his friend just a couple of weeks ago. He recalled how they used to listen to Aaron's CD collection of R&B and jazz—John Coltrane was a favorite.

At college his tastes grew even more expansive. "He had very eclectic musical tastes. He liked techno. He listened to a lot of rock. He was a great dancer and loved going to raves," said Karol's college roommate, Michael McCaffrey of Bergenfield. "He also wrote great poetry. His stuff was really amazing. The poems he wrote were very moving."

McCaffrey had known Karol only since September, but at 18 that's a long time.

"He was a very cool roommate to have," McCaffrey said Wednesday night. "He was such a nice person. He was a good friend, and a much better student than I was. He was always helping me with my studies, and because I'm kind of lazy he was always getting me going and motivating me."

McCaffrey was on the fourth floor of the dorm watching movies and "hanging out" with friends when the fire broke out. He had last seen Karol about 8 p.m. Tuesday night as he was heading out to a party at Montclair State University. McCaffrey also saw Frank Caltabilota about that time. Caltabilota was leaving Boland Hall with his father. Eight hours later he would be dead.

As McCaffrey spoke, a friend came up and hugged him. McCaffrey broke down in tears.

"All this, it just hasn't sunk in at all," he said. "I feel like I'm stuck in some sort of sick dream."

Mystery of blaze includes 3 visitors

JANUARY 20, 2000

By Bill Gannon and Guy Sterling

Careless smoking and faulty electrical wiring have been ruled out as likely causes of the fatal fire at Seton Hall University, investigators said.

While authorities said publicly there was no indication that the blaze that killed three students yesterday morning was suspicious, law enforcement officials disclosed they were looking for three people who had been asked to leave the dorm about 45 minutes before the fire was discovered.

Essex County Prosecutor Donald Campolo, who is heading the investigation, said statements were being taken from anyone who might have witnessed the fire or events leading up to it.

Among the other agencies investigating were the State Police, the federal Bureau of Alcohol, Tobacco and Firearms, and local police and fire departments, Campolo said. "We're looking into every possible aspect and every possible cause of this fire," he said at a news conference, adding, "I have no information to determine this is suspicious."

Other law enforcement officials, however, reported that a resident adviser at Boland Hall had asked three young men she did not recognize to leave the dorm less than an hour before the fire broke out. They did leave. Police said they were trying to identify the visitors so they could question them.

Fans of Seton Hall basketball had swarmed over the campus after its upset victory over St. John's at the Meadowlands Tuesday night. Spontaneous celebrations broke out throughout the dorms, keeping students up well past midnight.

The fire began just before 4:30 a.m. in the windowless, third-floor common area of the co-ed dorm, one of the largest buildings on the South Orange campus in Essex County. The room is a white cinderblock area with two pay telephones and a cork bulletin board on two walls.

The area, which is open to the elevators, was sparsely furnished with cheap, wood-framed, foam couches upholstered in green plush fabric.

Arson investigators said they have ruled out smoking as a probable factor because there was no apparent sign of smoldering—telltale evidence of a cigarette—on any of the couches in the lounge. There had been speculation that a student fell asleep on a couch with a lit cigarette, but investigators noted that the two victims found in the lounge were discovered not on a couch, but on the floor. Officials believe both had left their rooms and became disoriented and trapped in the dense smoke.

Tests to determine whether the blaze began with an open flame or smoldering materials were expected to be completed today.

There were no indications of an electrical short-circuit, and dogs trained to sniff for flammable substances could detect no indications of an accelerant like gasoline, those close to the investigation said.

One of the building's 55 fire extinguishers had been used to try to put out the fire, to no effect.

Campolo said, "It's difficult to say how useful that fire extinguisher would have been, because this was a pretty fast-moving and intense fire."

Whatever the cause, Boland Hall seems to have been well-known to the South Orange Fire Department.

In just the past four months, the village had responded to at least 18 false alarms at the dorm. The building's antiquated fire hoses were so old, they were being hauled out of the residence hall last week. The old, brick structure, meanwhile, had a history of small blazes that had forced the evacuation of students.

In 1996, someone set fire to a couch on the fourth floor of the building, causing serious damage. At least 11 students suffered smoke inhalation.

And in 1995, a television set in an unoccupied dormitory room caught fire, causing five people to suffer smoke inhalation and the student residence hall to be evacuated.

The dorm was not equipped with fire sprinklers, but because of its age—nearly 50 years old—it did not have to be, under the state uniform construction code.

State officials said the only fire code requirements at Boland Hall were lighted emergency exit signs, fire extinguishers, and smoke and fire alarms, which were all in place. School officials said the fire alarm system was not linked directly to the village of South Orange, but to campus security officials, who then call for emergency aid.

Officials said that the university is required to undergo a fire inspection once a year. South Orange fire officials would not say when the last inspection of Boland Hall had been conducted, or how the building had fared.

According to university officials, the building's smoke alarms and pull stations were last tested Tuesday by an external inspection company as part of a routine inspection performed every other month.

The building's alarm system was also in working order and is electronically checked every day, the university said. The fire extinguishers in Boland were checked semimonthly, with the last inspection in late November.

Investigators confirmed that hoses to the building's fire protection standpipe system had been disconnected and removed last week. The fire hoses are designed for firefighters' use inside the building, but had been disconnected because the equipment was no longer of use, said Seton Hall spokeswoman Lisa Grider.

Staff writers Ted Sherman and Peggy McGlone contributed to this report.

On the other end of phones, tears, terror, understatement

JANUARY 20, 2000

By Bob Braun

The phone rang, and she screamed.

Daisy Llanos screamed and the sound sliced through the silent, predawn darkness in a way that could have meant only one thing: Something horrible had happened to Alvaro.

"Alvaro! Alvaro!" The woman's two other children, Shirley, 25, and Shany, 16, awakened instantly and rushed from their beds in the small Paterson apartment on East 18th Street and tried to find out what happened.

Their mother could barely speak, says Shirley. It must have been something she heard on the telephone. Shirley thought she heard it ring but paid no attention. "She finally cried out Alvaro was in the hospital. He had been burned. We had to go immediately."

Hours later, Daisy, her face streaked with tears, still shook her head in disbelief. "How could this be?" she recalls asking the anonymous voice on the telephone, a voice that said something about Saint Barnabas Medical Center. "Alvaro cannot be in the hospital. He is safe in school. I just saw him two days ago."

The calls were not all as bad as the one Daisy Llanos received, but phones rang unexpectedly in hundreds of homes throughout the Northeast before dawn yesterday. Calls like the one received by Joyce Smith of Linden:

"Mom, Mom, listen don't be frightened, but I'm calling you from an ambulance. Everything's okay. I'm all right."

That's how she learned her son, Gabriel, was one of 54 injured in yesterday's fatal fire at Seton Hall University's freshman dorm, Boland Hall.

"Ambulance? What're you talking about?"

"Can't talk now. Going to Orange Medical Center."

Joyce found her son later at the hospital, covered in soot. She didn't recognize him, wouldn't answer the boy in the emergency room who kept calling her,

"Mom!" Finally, he yelled, "Hey, Joyce Smith. It's me. Your son."

It happened that way, again and again. The phone rang when it shouldn't, the worst sound for a parent whose kids are away. It reminded them that bad things happen.

Mostly, the kids themselves called. They knew their parents would wake to the news of the fire and the deaths. They knew it and they wanted their parents not to worry.

"She said something like 'there was a little problem in my dorm,' " says Joe Liptak from Clifton about the call from Allison, his daughter, his only child. "She said not to worry. Everything would be all right."

So Joe and Angela, his wife, snapped on the television, only to see images of a burning dorm with a grave voice-over saying three students had been killed and many more injured.

"Little problem?" Joe said aloud.

Sometimes, the calls were so strange.

"Mom, I love you." Linda Melanaphy knew the voice, but it was oddly small and tight. A frightened little boy's voice. Her son Brian's voice. He just didn't call in the middle of the night to say he loved his mother.

"Brian, what's wrong? What happened?" What a mother would say without thinking when a telephone rings when it's morning and still dark.

The voice of her 18-year-old son, a big kid, a self-assured kid, cracked into tears and he began to cry. "There's been a fire. Kids are dead. Mom, please come get me."

So Linda and her husband, Dave, raced out into the cold of the Rhode Island morning, Dave's foot so heavy on the pedal Linda swears they hit 100 miles per hour.

"We made it in three hours. We didn't think of speed limits."

Often, it was a neighbor or a friend who called, unaware they brought frightening news.

" 'Is Andy okay?' What do you mean, 'Is Andy okay?' Why shouldn't he be?" This is what Tom Landers asked a friend who called. His wife, Laurie, woke up beside him, and she also wanted to know—demanded to know—why someone was calling about Andy at this time of day.

The friend heard it on the radio and called the Morristown family. Tom and Laurie started making calls. The school. The fire department. Anybody who could tell them. Nothing. No news. As if the telephone refused to work the other way, to bring good news, calming news.

So Tom called his office, said he would be late, maybe not in at all.

That's when he heard Andy really was okay.

"Hey, I heard your kid on the radio," a co-worker told Tom. "Sounded great." Andy Landers, aspiring journalist, went to the offices of WSOU, the campus radio station, to cover the story. He answered calls from other stations. His voice was heard throughout the area.

Parents got the calls, and they came. With warm clothes because they saw television pictures of students in their pajamas, shivering against the cold and the shock. Although most knew their kids were all right, some couldn't stop shaking, thinking of what might have happened. Thinking of the telephone.

"I knew she was all right. She told me 100 times. But I had to see her. I wasn't going to believe it otherwise."

Parents came to the Dougherty Student Center to learn more, to find their kids. Faculty and staff tried to be kind, comforting. It didn't always work.

"Where's Shantay?" Doris Wyches, 72, of Hackensack asked every face she saw. She stopped students. Priests. Cops. Asking for her granddaughter. "Where's Shantay Callis?"

"She's in the hospital," answered Dinean Robinson of Vineland, a young woman dressed in a nightgown, a blanket draped over her shoulders. The tears burst from the older woman's eyes. "No, no," Dinean added quickly. "She's fine. She went there to see a friend."

Doris Wyches let the tears come anyway.

Daisy Llanos went to the student center, too, although she knew Alvaro would not be there. She and her husband and daughters had stayed hours at Saint Barnabas and the doctors said they should go and come back later. They promised to do what they could for Alvaro.

"I wanted to know what happened. I wanted to know why I thought my son was asleep in his dormitory.

Safe. Why someone wakes me up to tell me he is in the hospital."

She was not satisfied. She did not know how to explain it all to her husband, also Alvaro, walking heavily on a cane because of a recent stroke, a man who does not understand English as well as she.

Daisy and her daughters talk of Alvaro. The big guy of the family. The baseball player. The basketball player. Tall, good-looking, a kid so much in love with another Seton Hall student, so happy with his new life as a freshman, living on campus.

"Alvaro was so proud to be here," says Daisy, who, like her husband, was born in Colombia. "He got a scholarship," she says. "So smart. And a certificate from where he works."

Then they went home, because they didn't know what else to do. Daisy wandered the small apartment collecting photos of her son. Stopping now and then to look up at the many pictures of Jesus on the wall. Wordlessly asking Him to save Alvaro. "I am praying," she says.

Back at the hospital, she and her husband try to talk to Alvaro. He doesn't answer. He is hooked to machines, a tube running from the corner of his mouth, his head swathed in bandages, the skin around his eyes blackened by fire.

"I cannot believe I picked up the phone and this happened," says Daisy Llanos.

Students, ignoring peril, turn saviors to keep peers alive

JANUARY 20, 2000

By Russell Ben-Ali and John Mooney

Dozens of Seton Hall students made sacrifices large and small to protect their classmates yesterday when all hell broke loose in Boland Hall.

Some—like Justin Fox, an 18-year-old criminal justice major; Dana Christmas, a 21-year-old resident assistant; and Daniel Nugent, another resident assistant—put their own lives on the line on behalf of classmates who were in harm's way.

Others—like Celeste Banks—simply took time to lend a hand when they could have been tending to their own comfort.

Fox, a freshman from Paramus, found another student in a heap on the hallway floor, gasping for air in the thick black smoke. The student's face was burned. His hair was singed. His breathing was shallow and his pulse was faint, according to Virginia Wannamaker, 18, a freshman from Irvington who lived in the dorm. Rather than leaving the dorm, Fox pulled the unidentified male student into his own room and wrapped him in a sweatshirt, several of his friends and dormmates said. "Justin has it in his heart to do something like that," said Kerry McNeill, 18, Fox's girlfriend of the last two years. "He doesn't always show it, but deep down inside, he would definitely do something like that."

He and other students then escaped down a ladder placed against a window by a resident assistant, Dan Nuygen, who climbed up to stay with the injured student until rescuers arrived, Wannamaker said. Fox, who plans to work one day as a police officer, suffered injuries from smoke inhalation, as well as a burn on his hand, and he was hospitalized in stable condition in Saint Barnabas Medical Center. The status of the other student was unclear.

"He's definitely a good guy," said Kristie Ewall, a friend and classmate of Fox. "He knows when he's needed."

Christmas was critically injured when she inhaled smoke while pounding on doors and screaming for other students to leave the dorm, said Dr. Sanjeev Kaul, who treated her at University Hospital in Newark.

Banks, 18, of Jersey City, found a classmate gasping for air at the foot of a staircase as she was fleeing from her first-story room. The shirtless young man was covered with soot and ash from the waist up.

Banks, a distance runner on the Seton Hall track team, picked up the student and carried him outside to a group of his friends. "I just picture myself in that place," Banks said. "I wouldn't want somebody to leave me there if I was hurt."

Tears welled in her eyes as university spokeswoman Lisa Grider recounted tales of heroism on campus. She drew special attention to Daniel Nugent, a sophomore resident assistant who was in charge of third floor Boland North. Nugent, she said, began awakening his residents as the alarm sounded and led them downstairs. Then he returned to bring down more. A resident on Ward Place, near the campus, arrived with an aluminum ladder to help with the rescue, she said. Nugent and the resident used it to help evacuate students trapped on the third floor.

At one point, Grider said, Nugent, a trained EMT, administered CPR to a student until paramedics could arrive. He stayed on the floor afterwards, directing firefighters to specific rooms where students were trapped. "He went upstairs four different times," she said. "These are the kind of young people who attend this university."

Tom Feeney, Bill Gannon, Angela Stewart, and Steve Chambers contributed to this report.

For many students, fire was first brush with tragedy

JANUARY 20, 2000

By Rebecca Goldsmith

Dazed and numb, they spoke to one another through tears, searching for solace in the embraces of parents and friends.

Behind yellow police tape, their dormitory, Boland Hall, sat empty but for investigators seeking the cause of the blaze that killed three students and injured dozens more.

Death had come to Seton Hall University, and for many of the young adults who escaped and watched the quick, intense inferno, it was their first brush with tragedy, an unbidden descent into terror and grief in the darkest hours of a brutally cold night.

Throughout the day, they watched as their South Orange campus was transformed into something they usually saw only on television. The circle of grass at the center of campus, normally off-limits to cars, became a parking lot for emergency vehicles. Dozens of news trucks lined other campus drives. "You hear these things happen in old downtown buildings, but on a college campus, you would think they're safe," said Evangeline Williams, a sophomore from Delaware. Williams said she always felt her school was immune from such destruction.

The student center's auditorium, home to perfunctory activities such as registration, drew hundreds of students and parents every few hours for official responses to their questions: Who died? Who was injured? How seriously? Where were they taken? Where is my kid?

Don Ballard was among them. After hearing about the fire on the morning news, he raced to Seton Hall from his central New Jersey home, panic creeping up his back as he worried about his daughter, whom he was unable to reach on the phone.

Ballard was one of the lucky ones. He found his daughter safe. But he watched as one man struggled for control while he waited for word of his son.

"No one knew where his son was," Ballard said. "He was beside himself. He was broken up."

With the university closed for the day and classes called off until Monday, students had little else to do than gather with friends in clusters, sharing grief and information.

"Everyone's kind of shocked. It's just too close to home," said Shawn Utsey, a psychology professor from South Orange who came to the campus offering his counseling services.

The student center became a reunion place for people such as freshman Theresa Wilk and her mother, Frances, of Neshanic, who arrived to bring her daughter home for a few days. By early afternoon, Theresa still clutched the white teddy bear she had held to her mouth as she crawled from her dorm room through smoky hallways to safety.

Elsewhere on campus, students simply milled about, unsure of where to go and what to do.

Mental health professionals tried to help those hardest hit.

One of the counselors approached a group of students watching an early afternoon news report.

"By nature you're doing what you need to do, which is to talk to each other. One of the most important things you can do right now is just to talk to each other," she said.

Theresa Berkey and Megan Koenig, freshmen from Chicago, said they appreciated the advice but had had enough talking by late afternoon. They were still lounging in the clothes they were wearing at 4:30 a.m. while waiting to find out when they could return to their dorm rooms.

Despite the official updates, many students did not know the fate of their friends for much of the day.

"You just ask around," said Lovereen Lehga, a freshman from Plainsboro. "You get little bits of information."

Deborah Gilwood, a music professor, walked around the student center with a list of names of students in her program. She had confirmed the location of all but one by early afternoon.

"It's a supportive atmosphere. Everyone's talking to one another. We're all very distressed," she said.

The fast-food court, usually a lively gathering place with blaring TVs, was somber and quiet, with groups of students mingling with parents, faculty and clergy.

The housing office took up the job of finding beds for displaced students last night, fielding offers from community members to put up students in their homes in South Orange, Maplewood and Millburn.

President's Hall, where administrators work, became the command center for information to be released to the public.

Throughout the day, members of the campus community turned to God for reassurance.

A circle of worshippers in the student center gradually swelled as the day wore on, with more and more people pausing to offer prayers.

"We're just hoping that God will heal the bodies of people that are injured," said April Richardson of Newark, a student who thanked God for sparing her younger brother, a Boland Hall resident.

Later, more than 200 people crowded into Immaculate Conception Chapel, praying for those injured and killed. About 150 others waited outside in the cold, saying the Rosary.

Newark Archbishop Theodore McCarrick offered a benediction and words of support over the faint chopping of a news helicopter overhead.

"We're all trying to be here for each other," said Amy Reina of Matawan, a student member of the Alpha Phi Omega service fraternity, which was passing out towels, toothpaste, soap and other goods to students in need. "It's just good to see that the community came together."

Scary formula: Old buildings, timeworn prank

JANUARY 20, 2000

By Matthew Reilly

Hoping to avoid the nightmarish loss of students to fire, college administrators across New Jersey say they have taken pains to ensure fire safety on their campuses, from retrofitting older buildings with modern equipment to harshly penalizing the students who pull false alarms.

Even so, many of the state's older dormitories, like the Seton Hall University building where three students died in a smoky blaze yesterday, are not equipped with sprinkler systems. Nor are they required to be. Because fire codes have evolved over time, older buildings must add sprinklers only when they undergo large-scale renovations.

Adding to the danger is a common difficulty on college campuses: Because there are so many false alarms, some students ignore the warnings, riding them out in their rooms. At Rowan University in Glassboro, George Brelsford, assistant vice president for residential life and student services, said six of the school's 11 residence buildings have sprinkler systems, including a pair of buildings more than 70 years old.

"Whenever there's a renovation, the building has to be brought up to the most recent issue of the code," Brelsford said. "I have two buildings, from 1927 and 1929, and we did a re-work of them two years ago and sprinklers were added."

The last dorm fire on the Rowan campus, where about 2,400 of the school's 10,000 students live, was six or seven years ago, he said, and was confined to one room by the sprinkler system that extinguished the flames.

Some older buildings, dating from the 1950s, do not have sprinklers, Brelsford said, because they have not been renovated and are still under the fire code in effect at the time of their construction. However, the university has gone beyond those earlier code requirements to upgrade fire safety systems in those buildings, he said.

"What we have done is hard-wire all rooms with smoke detectors and put heat and smoke detectors in hallways and common areas," he said. "These buildings are above and beyond what the original code was."

He said flame-retardant materials are used whenever possible.

The school runs formal fire drills at least twice a year but also treats any alarm, from a malicious false alarm to a simple smoke condition, seriously. Students who ignore fire alarms are subject to punishment.

The College of New Jersey in Mercer County has added sprinkler systems to all but two of its 14 residence buildings. Three dormitories built in 1931 were retrofitted for sprinklers when they were renovated in 1992, spokeswoman Sue Murphy said.

Chief Joseph Zuccarello of the Rutgers University Fire Department said his firefighters chased down 107 malicious false alarms last year.

"Every college and university has a hassle with false alarms," Zuccarello said. "It's amazing. The students go away for winter break and we don't have any false alarms, and the minute they come back in the dorm, the alarms start transmitting for one reason or another."

At least once a year, the chief said, university officials inspect every dorm room for items such as candles, halogen lamps, cooking appliances, extension cords longer than 6 feet, overloaded outlets, and posters fixed to the ceiling. All of those items are prohibited in residence halls.

All dorm furniture, from mattresses to desks, is fire-retardant, Zuccarello said.

Michael Massaro, a 19-year-old sophomore at Rutgers, said he inadvertently has tested the university's fire safety measures on occasion. In October, a smoke alarm alerted him to the melting, smoking remote control he had left on a lamp in his room.

Last year at Tinsley Hall, where he lived, the residents were fined a total of $2,000 to cover the installation of new fire alarms after some 15 false alarms there, he said.

Jamaal Lowery and Jed Herb say it can get awfully cold in their dorm room at Kean University in Union

Township, and they had resorted to using an open oven to keep their suite toasty.

But since a fire erupted in their 28-year-old dorm Monday night, they have made sure the oven stays shut.

Lowery was getting ready for bed at 12:30 a.m. Monday in his room at Sozio Hall when the fire alarm went off. He looked out into the hall and saw smoke pouring out of the trash chute. Lowery ran outside, but noticed that some of his fellow students did not follow.

"They hear the alarm all the time and just figured it wasn't a real fire," said Lowery, 21, a sophomore from Pleasantville.

Kean officials believe someone threw a cigarette down the trash chute. The blaze caused minimal damage, said Robert Cole, a university spokesman.

Herb, 19, a sophomore from Lacey Township, said he had been across the quad, at Rogers dorm, when he saw fire trucks roll in.

"I thought it was a false alarm, but no one picked up when I called our room," he said. "People don't pay attention to that kind of stuff."

The roommates estimated 10 fire alarms have been pulled at Sozio Hall since the beginning of the school year.

At Ramapo College in Mahwah, many students said it's not uncommon for residents to stay inside during alarms.

Tiffany Patterson, a 21-year-old senior who now lives in campus apartments, said she got tired of fire alarms going off twice a week when she lived in their dorms. Rather than trudge outside, she hid in the shower.

"I usually stayed in my room most of the time because I assumed they were false," she said. "Nobody wants to go outside at 3 or 4 in the morning."

Jonathan Jaffe, Greg Saitz, Alexander Lane, Jeffery C. Mays, and Mark Mueller contributed to this report.

Writers' Workshop

Talking Points

1) When Seton Hall officials began clamping down on access to the campus, *The Star-Ledger* had to find creative ways of getting to witnesses and describing the fire scene. What methods might you have used to get information under these difficult conditions?

2) In the early hours of their reporting, *The Star-Ledger* team had to get information on students without knowing for sure if the students survived or died in the fire. Reporter Kate Coscarelli said she was careful not to "freak out anybody's roommate or friend." Talk about ways you might approach getting the information without hurting people.

3) Columnist Bob Braun recreates a gripping scene in the first two paragraphs of his column, writing as though he witnessed it. Then he switches perspective and tells the story using other sources. What do you think of this technique? Talk about the pros and cons of recreating scenes and writing them as though you witnessed them.

4) With less than a day to report, *The Star-Ledger* team needed to pull in facts from a number of sources. Read Mary Jo Patterson's lead story. See if you can identify the many different sources from which the information came. Check your ideas against the interviews that follow.

5) Police would not say officially that they suspected arson in the fire. Still, it was clear to the reporters that arson was a strong possibility. Talk about how Bill Gannon and Guy Sterling handled that question in their story and how it was handled in the lead story by Patterson. Did the reporters do a fair and complete job of conveying what they knew?

Assignment Desk

1) Reporters and editors at *The Star-Ledger* said the stories were richer because rewrite reporters were able to interview reporters in the field. Working with a fellow student who will do rewrite, go out and report on a deadline story. Later, let the

other reporter interview you about the information you've gathered. What facts and details were you able to provide? What did you miss?

2) Reporters made use of official and secondary sources in tracking down the names, hometowns, friends, and backgrounds of the students who died, as well as those who were injured. Identify the official sources of such information at your school. Investigate the other places you might find information about fellow students on deadline.

3) Interview someone about a traumatic event such as a fire. Write a series of scenes, some recreated and written as though you were there, others written from the perspective of the source.

4) Investigate the fire-alarm history of a dormitory. Guided by what you learn from *The Star-Ledger*'s stories and interviews, write about attitudes and procedures at your school.

Recalling deadline with
The Star-Ledger

KEITH WOODS: Tell me how you first got word about the fire.

MARY JO PATTERSON: It was one of those mornings when I didn't listen to the news, and by the time I came in around 9:30, a good three and a half hours later, I still didn't know.

The first I knew that there had been this awful event was when an editor, David Tucker, said—I remember exactly what he said—"You're going to do the main story. You do the poetry." And I said, "What the heck are you talking about? Poetry?" And then he said, "There's been a fire." It's just one of those mornings when you walk through a fog into something happening, and at that point, people were already well on the scene.

What is it that positioned you to be the person who would write the main bar?

Frequently I'll be asked to do that, although I don't do *just* that. I try to constantly talk to people on the scene, make sure they get numbers for me to do call backs to fill in the details because they don't know, and I don't know, what are going to emerge as the best interviews five hours later.

So that becomes important for you—that when you're in touch with these reporters who are out in the field, that they provide you with not only the information that they've found, but also contact information?

Yeah. Otherwise when it comes down to the writing later, I won't have what I need. Because when you have as many people as we had deployed on the scene, they're not getting parallel information. So I always try to have the desk remember that I want to talk to whoever's on the scene. Don't get me in trouble here, but editors have a tendency to want to manage their folks on the scene, and they like the reporters to report to them. But quite frankly, although they obviously need to tell (reporters) where to go, I want them to talk to me, too. So I always say, "After you're finished, please send them over here."

Did it work out for you that way?

It must have, because upon re-reading it's clear to me that I had access to at least one and probably two of the reporters who were talking to the students, which is where the good details came from. It certainly didn't come from officials, either municipal or the university.

Now you come in and this train is way down the track by the time you walk in. What happens next?

Well, if there's anything on the wire, I read that. Quite frequently, I just start calling people myself. I'll work the phones, because you don't want to let any of that time go at all. I'll call people I know who might be familiar with, in this case, the dormitory. I called a friend whose son had spent a summer at a basketball camp there, and I asked her, "Have you been in that building? Tell me what that building looks like." So I fill in and I also write from the bottom immediately.

What do you mean by that?

I will learn things about the structure or the building, and start writing the bottom of the story very early in the game, as soon as I can. That's a big help at crunch time.

How do you manage that much information, especially when you're doing it on deadline?

Well, I guess that's one of my strengths. I am very detail-oriented and I'm very, very fast at reading and putting stuff together.

In your story, you have levels of detail that essentially disguised the fact that you weren't there.

That's why I go back so many times. Reporters who

work with me get sick of me. I try to get them while they're still around the person. I will say, "Go back and find that person," or "Tell me where I can find that person."

What was the most interesting fact you heard as you were putting this together?

I really wondered about the safety issues immediately, and I felt these children were so vulnerable because of all the elements we talked about. The fact that these alarms came so often. The fact that it came at the worst possible time of night. Kids are up late and some kids get up early, but who the heck is up at 4:30? They're young. The fact that they hadn't been at school that long. The fact that they were going to be so traumatized. The idea that they were running around and they saw kids who were literally burning up. I think that was all very sobering. And I remember asking someone to describe the kids hours later. They were kind of shell-shocked. I remember I said (to a reporter), "What did this kid have on?" and she said something like "big fuzzy slippers." I said, "What kind?" She said they had teddy bears on them.

Right. That's Tiffany Hill. Now that fact comes not because the reporter offered it up originally, but because you, in the course of a conversation with the reporter, got it out of her.

Right, right. You know sometimes the best thing to do is just interview a reporter. You know, it's not so easy to be on the scene. You don't really know what the writer wants. So if you can interview the person at the scene while they still have access to folks, you can really reconstruct something that puts the reader there.

And the interviewing, I assume, also jogs things from the reporter's memory that might not have wound up in that reporter's story.

Yeah, which is why I like to talk to them constantly.

Do you have one or two pieces of advice for some-

body who would be sitting in the same seat as you on such a big story in their community?

Coordinate things with supervising editors so that you're not sitting there twiddling your thumbs. Use every minute you can to find out what you can on your own while you're waiting to hear from people in the field. Remind people on the scene to ask interviewees, "Where can we find you if we need to?" That can be hard to remember when everything's so chaotic. Because then, when you're building the story and you want that little detail, well here's the number, call her up.

Rick Everett, managing editor/news

I found out about the fire because my wife woke me up and told me. She was getting my kid ready for the school bus; I guess it was 6:15, 6:30. So I called photo first, which is what I normally do on breaking news because you always want to get the photographer there first. And then I called the reporter who covers higher ed for us, Kelly Heyboer, and told her to make a call and then get over there. And then not long after that, Suzanne Pavkovic called me and she was also hearing it and getting people out there. I would say the first hour of mobilizing people I did from home. By 9 o'clock, I would guess we had 30 people working the story, including photographers, graphic artists, and reporters. I think we ended up with 35 different people working on it.

I just got us rolling and then turned it over to Suzanne and (education editor) Joanne Sills as far as divvying up who was doing what. Then my role through the rest of the day was making sure we had all the bases covered, deciding what was going to go outside, making sure the stories didn't overlap, and that the graphics matched up with the stories. There was enormous frustration in not being more able to learn the identities of the victims. Hours after the fire, Seton Hall wasn't identifying them. They finally did put the names out, which was 8:30 p.m. or so—45 minutes before our deadline—but they didn't put out the hometowns. And the other difficulty was our access on campus. They turned the student union into a media center and shunted all media to this place and kept them away from students. They were trying to strictly limit access, and I can't say we followed all of their ground rules. Access on campus, the inability to get interior photos, and the lack of IDs, those were probably the toughest problems to surmount in the coverage.

Deadline Tip:

Don't wait to get a lot of people to the scene. The reason I think we did a good job on this story was the level of detail we managed to come up with by getting a lot of people to the scene early. Also dividing the tasks and having clear assignments: divvying up where we wanted to go, having people do the scene in color, people do the investigation, people do the victims, I think, helped.

Suzanne Pavkovic, metro editor

We have a motto here at the *Ledger*: Hit it hard, hit it fast. Within the first half-hour and first hour, run quickly, send everyone out that you can, because you can always pull back if you don't have to be there.

One of the first things I did when I got into the newsroom was to create a budget or a digest, a list of stories, who's writing the stories, and to pair the people in the field with people in the newsroom so that we can start taking information throughout the day, as opposed to waiting until the evening. It then becomes sort of our bible in that it's a guideline for where reporters should be and where they should go. And if you look in our paper on that day, you'll see we have labels—the heroes, the victims—and a lot of those were the original slugs we had determined that morning before we went into our early news meeting.

I think that everyone worked together as a team. There was a tremendous sense of camaraderie. Essentially everyone was involved and it was one story. People who were here were willing to take dictation from the field, were willing to run down tips, were constantly running library searches to get information on people. I think that sense of teamwork and the back and forth between the people in the field and the people here is what made it work. I think also because the editors worked together as a team, everyone pulled together. I don't recall us having any disagreements or fights that day, and I guess the written budget helped a lot because everyone gets an early take: This is what we're doing. Then people can comment, "I think we need to add this," or "I think this works better as a separate story." So everyone's involved in the process because everyone can see what's going on.

Deadline Tip:

If you get a sense that there could be a big story, fan out, run quickly, send out a lot of people. What we try to do is cover every angle so that the next day people are following *us*. And let your reporters go. I mean, you can tell them where to go, you can tell them where to be, you can give them a sense of what they are expected to write. But essentially, then you have to let them run.

Robin Fisher, reporter

I remember driving in to work and I had the New York radio stations on and they said that there was a fire at Seton Hall. I remember thinking it would be one of those stories that was going to fizzle like so many stories do by the time you get to work.

Once I got here, they had more information. They knew that there were fatalities and they knew that it was a serious fire. As I recall, they immediately had Mary Jo Patterson doing the main bar and me doing the sidebar. I always get the touchy-feely people stuff. They wanted as much as we could get on the three boys who died. It was very late in the day that we got their names, so the whole day was just trying to find out names and trying to find relatives and things like that. Deadline had to be 9 o'clock, I would think. John Mooney and David Gibson, who sit around me, each had a boy. I had written from the bottom up with everything that they were giving me. In the meantime, I started making calls on John Giunta, and I was lucky enough to get an aunt who was willing to talk to us.

I told the aunt that we were writing about the Seton Hall tragedy and were trying to find out whatever we could about John so that readers would know about this boy who died in the fire. And she said she would be willing to talk about him. And I just asked away. "When was the last time you saw him? What was your last memory of him?" And then she brought up this dinner. She also put her young son on because Giunta used to tease the little boy all the time. He got on hesitantly, but also wanted to talk, and they painted a really nice picture of this boy and how he was fun and funny and entertaining his whole family just the weekend before.

At the end of the night there was a great feeling of accomplishment that it was as complete a story as it could possibly be and that we were able to tell our readers about each one of these boys. Because they were young boys and they died and they deserved at least that.

I remember editors standing over my shoulder and people throwing e-mails on my desk…it was a pressure-cooker. I'm tied to the desk, I'm tied to the phone. I have my computer screen active and e-mail popping up constantly—new message, new message, new message—and I finally said, "No, give me hard copy and put it in these two piles," and that's how it worked. That's what helped. It was having this organization. I've done that on other breaking stories, too. You take subjects or people and put all the information pertinent to that in these piles. Or you copy it from the e-mails and throw it into files with people's names on the top. The worst thing you can do is push everything into one file. I like to have the hard copy to read, and then I highlight it, the things that I know I want to use from it, and I can refer to it quickly.

I was getting calls from (reporter) Kate Coscarelli out at Seton Hall. She's out there and she's getting all this great stuff. She would keep calling, calling, calling, calling. Sometimes they'd send her to Mary Jo, sometimes they'd send her to me. The phone was ringing constantly between Mary Jo's desk and mine. Guy Sterling was constantly feeding me little tidbits of things he was getting. And you know what? I remember thinking, "I wish I could write this well when I take my time."

Deadline Tip:

Don't stop to think. Just write it. Don't labor over every word. Just write it. And in reporting, people who are experiencing tragedy want to talk. I know that sounds odd, but it always amazes me. It's gut-wrenching calling and you're thinking, "I hate doing this," and you're under pressure anyway, but they want to talk. So let them talk. Call them. Let them talk. Don't be afraid.

David Gibson, religion writer

Because it was an early morning fire, when we came into the newsroom or were called in we all knew what the story was, and it was a question of divvying up the responsibilities and the duties. I was one of those who was in the newsroom trying to help with and coordinate some of the coverage of the victims.

It was very difficult to find out the identities or to confirm the identities, which is such a delicate thing. That confirmation didn't come through until late in the afternoon. And so the bulk of this work, certainly 90 percent of our work, was done in a couple of hours. This was almost like a wire service kind of a thing. We were writing versions of stories and composing stuff, a lot of which ended up on the cutting-room floor just because the story was developing so quickly.

We spent most of the day trying to hash things out and trying to get the facts straight. And as we got some names, some rumors, or reports from kids about the names of the victims, we were able to do some preliminary research, expecting that these would be some of the names, looking in yearbooks, looking back in our own data—for example, seeing what they had done in high school athletics. It was, as is often the case here, a lot of hurry up and wait.

Any time you call a victim's family or friends, it's a difficult thing to do. Obviously for them it's the most difficult, and I'm always amazed at how open and how eager and willing to talk are the families. The families were really wonderful, the friends were really wonderful, and in a short period of time, it was one of those things where they said, "Oh, you should call this person who went to school with him at Watchung Hills Regional, or you should call his coach," and they'd give me numbers. So for me, I think I certainly had the easiest time of it with the victims because a couple of calls and everything kind of unraveled. It was just really a question of time getting to all these people.

Deadline Tip:

I think when you're dealing with spot news, when you're dealing with tragedy, being sensitive to the families and the victims is so important. I've always found that you can get more information if a family does not want to talk to you and you just tell them that you understand. Just tell them that you want to present a story of their relative, and ask if there's someone else that you can talk to.

John Mooney, state education writer

I was vaguely aware there had been a fire but it was overnight, so I hadn't been called to cover it, and I think I heard something on the radio in the morning, but I came in and, clearly, it was all-hands-on-deck right away. I did not go to the fire; it was all out of the newsroom.

We were calling anybody we knew who knew anybody who knew anybody. I mean you're just chasing these little strings you have. We had first names and things of that sort. We were each given a name and they said, "Find out everything you can in the next three hours." My kid was from West Long Branch—Frank Caltabilota. So we did a scan, found he had played football. We found the football coach and I called him and got a fair amount out of him. I found one of his best friends. I got his father. He talked about it. And then I think we got word of a girlfriend, but she wouldn't talk. There was a lot of stuff that doesn't show up.

You just tread lightly as best you can. I remember somebody telling us not to say, "I heard a rumor that he may have been killed" or something like that. You don't do that. And I've covered enough tragedies that I know the right things to say. And if they don't want to talk, they don't talk. You try to prod them in certain ways. I probably got four or five people who knew him, but it was two hours to deadline, and then you race to put together 10, 15 paragraphs. Then Robin Gaby Fisher did most of the rewrite on it, but we didn't have much time to rewrite. She said "Give me 10 paragraphs and I'll plug them in," and she made them shine.

Deadline Tip:

Details, details, details. In a case like this where you're trying to recreate a boy's life in 10 paragraphs, just try to find the details. When you're rushing, you sometimes lose sight of them because you want to get in this broad fact or that broad fact. But readers remember the details. You're talking to somebody in a tragic situation and they're saying, "He was a neat kid." They're going to give you a nice heartfelt quote and then you've got to ask the next question: "Give me an example of something he did." I remember that I had a quote from a coach that Frank was a happy-go-lucky guy, which is a nice quote, and I remember saying, "Well, give me an example," and he said something about how he used to razz him in the hallway. It wasn't a great detail, but it takes it a step further.

Kate Coscarelli, legal affairs reporter

I was one of the very first people called for a couple of reasons, one of which is I covered South Orange, the city that Seton Hall is in, when I was a municipal reporter. In addition, I have a sort of young-looking face and it means that I get called on pretty much whenever tragedies happen to young people.

I'm sure that I was probably sleeping, and one of our managing editors, Rick Everett, called me and said, "There's been a fire at Seton Hall. You need to get there." I think I might have brushed my teeth and I grabbed a banana for the ride. It was a horrible day. It was snowing and nasty. It was very cold. So I drove to Seton Hall. Needless to say, cops were already positioned there not letting people on campus. So I walked around to the front entrance of the university and just walked on campus. I purposely dressed down. I think I had on hiking boots and jeans and a skiing jacket or something.

I remember hearing what the editors' dream was: that we could have a firsthand account of what it was like inside the third floor north. I remember finding a kid, Rob Cardiello, who had seen it. I remember interviewing him in this small room that I think housed part of the university's museum collection and getting him to go through it. I was smart enough to get his phone number so that we could bother him at many other points throughout the reporting process, which isn't something I was smart enough to do on every interview. We had the firsthand account by 10 a.m., so we spent the rest of the day going out periodically and just collecting as much information and detail as we could.

I remember stopping people along walkways and trying to get more details. There was a point at which we had gotten some of the names who we thought might have been the kids who died, and we had to ask other students if they knew anything about them without saying that they were the kids who died, because we didn't know for sure.

It actually turned out that one of the initial names was wrong. But nobody ever said, "Hey, this is the kid that died," so we never had to freak out anybody's roommate or friend or parent or anything to that effect. People were very conscious of that because everybody was so freaked out. And the kids were so young. They were all really, really shaken up. I remember when they announced the names. It was in the student center of the university and the press wasn't supposed to be allowed, but my editors asked me to try to sneak in, and if anybody asked me, of course, I'd tell them who I was and what I was doing there. But if nobody asked me, then I just sort of stood in the back of the room, which I did. I think the Dean of Freshman Students made the announcement to this auditorium full of kids. And the grief was audible.

Deadline Tip:

It never hurts to go back and say, "I don't understand what you meant when you said this." You had to go back to students and ask, "Were you standing across the room or were you standing next to that person or what exactly made you afraid when you heard the alarms go off." I didn't do it all the time, but when you did it, it was important and it almost always got you a better answer. I talked to notebooks full of people and it didn't matter that they had all been through the same thing. It's easy to go through something and say, "Yeah. I got my two anecdotes, I'm done." Every time we asked a question, the story got more complex.

Kelly Heyboer, higher education reporter

By the time I drove on campus, I knew it was going to be something bigger than just a small fire. I could see parents running around already trying to find their kids. I walked up to the library where they were going to have the news conference and there was a student in her pajamas and her slippers just standing in front of the building sort of looking around in a daze like, "What am I supposed to do now?"

It was only a small pack of journalists at that point. I don't know how many other newspaper reporters were there, but it was mostly the early morning radio and TV folks. And gradually the other folks I knew from other papers started to come in, and over the course of the day, you could feel it getting bigger and bigger. All of a sudden *The New York Times* was there and then *The Philadelphia Inquirer* and then all of the New York stations were there, and I got really nervous when the network news crews started to show up.

In between the news conferences, Kate Coscarelli and I were both running out and trying to talk to students. It was already very hostile when we got there. This is a private university and they were dealing with all of these reporters, so they sort of penned up the students in the student center and were trying to keep some sort of control. Kate is very young; she looks about 14 years old, and she was able to sneak in and out of the building and talk to students. She was very successful at it, and I was partially successful at it. At the time I was 27, so I didn't look that old, and I was able to sneak in a little bit and talk to some students. But it was so hard.

We were calling in to the city desk every couple of hours and our editors were saying, "You have to find someone who saw the fire. You have to find someone who saw the flames," like it was going to be somehow simple. But there were 600 kids who lived in that building, and only a handful of them lived on the floor where the fire was. But Kate did manage to track one down and that was our biggest success of the morning.

With all the media on campus, a lot of the students were already anti-media within a few hours of the fire. The ones who were available had been prodded so often that they just didn't want to talk any more. I found most of the students, though, to be surprisingly open. I think a lot of them were still in shock and wanted someone to talk to. With hundreds of students waiting to see counselors, a lot of them hadn't had a chance to say anything yet and really opened up when we started to talk to them.

I was most worried that other reporters were going to scoop me. Once Kate and I did finally talk to the first student we found who had actually witnessed the flames and had to crawl out of the building, our main concern was getting him away from the other reporters. We schemed our way into an office in the library and interviewed him there with his parents, away from other reporters, and then physically walked him off campus to his car to make sure nobody else talked to him. That's how intense the competition was getting throughout the day.

Deadline Tip:

Bring a pencil, that's for sure. I missed so many good quotes because I couldn't get my damn pen to unfreeze. Other than that, I'd say go in expecting it to be worse than you think it could be. I've got to say I could have gotten there faster if I'd known it was going to be this big. I just didn't go in expecting it to be as bad as it was going to be, and that might have helped my reporting more if I was thinking bigger when I went over.

Guy Sterling, criminal justice and law reporter

I turned on the radio that morning and heard that there had been a fire in a dormitory and dozens of students were evacuated—smoky fire, third floor, all that stuff. About 10 minutes later they said that there had been three casualties and, at that point, I knew that my day, if not my career, was going to change drastically.

I had a number of law enforcement people I knew who were at the scene. Initially they said, "Well, let's just stay on hold. Let's see what's going to come back from the scene." And pretty early on, the paper realized that not much in terms of the cause of the fire, the identities of the victims, the identities of the kids who'd been taken to the hospital was coming back. So that was my assignment for the day and through the night, really. I had to get inside the investigation, both in terms of the origin of the fire and the identities of the people who had been killed and the identities of those who were most severely burned and had been admitted to the hospital. That's what I spent most of my day doing—contacting people I knew.

Before the afternoon was out, I was able to get that information. It turned out that Seton Hall eventually made the announcement about the identities of the students. I was able to get that information about four hours before they released it, with the hometowns of the victims. These are people I know and work with and they said, "You want the names of the dead? Here they are, and here are the hometowns."

When I knew I was going to get the identities, I started working on the cause of the fire and I started calling everybody I knew. Based upon that information, we were able to get reporters on the phone and to the homes of the victims before anyone else.

Then the other part of it was getting the names of the most severely burned kids who'd been admitted to the two hospitals. I had a source inside the hospital who provided me the names and hometowns of those kids. And the other woman who was admitted to University Hospital in Newark, I got her name and hometown from a local politician who's close to Seton Hall.

And then I pretty much went back to my own story,

which was about the cause of the fire. I worked on that story with Bill Gannon and Ted Sherman.

Deadline Tip:

Well, there's no doubt that I would not have gotten this without well-placed sources inside the investigation, and these are people I know and have developed as sources over the course of 21 years at *The Star-Ledger*. It may seem like it comes easy, but it's really the result of developing sources, of working with people, of being able to get people on the phone when you need them, and getting inside the investigation because people know and trust you. That's what it was.

Bob Braun, columnist

I was the education writer for the paper for 27 years and also have two degrees from Seton Hall—a graduate degree and a law degree—so I know the campus very well. I know the personalities fairly well, and (managing editor) Rick Everett thought it'd be a good idea, and I did too, to get over there. I got there around 8:30, 9 o'clock, and there was immediately no real sense of what I would do.

I'm a news columnist. I do off-the-news kinds of stuff. And I just wanted to try to figure out what it was that I was going to do. My kids are both grown—they're both college graduates—and both went away to school. I lived in dread of hearing calls in the middle of the night and that sort of thing. So I got a sense that I wanted to do something about the parents and I started talking to parents as soon as I got there. I noticed this couple who looked actually a little bit older than typical college parents, looking very lost and wandering around, and I stopped to talk to them.

The man had a cane; he looked not well. They were Alvaro's parents. Their English wasn't all that good and I don't speak Spanish. But we were able to communicate and we talked. There was an innocence about them that I think was part of the product of just being so stunned.

It appeared that they didn't know what was going on. There were interviews going on all over the place—you know what a media frenzy's like—and nobody was paying attention to them. It was just something about how he looked so beaten and so sad and so upset that I said, "Excuse me, were you able to find your child?" Or something like that. Of course, Alvaro was one of the most severely injured of the kids. And they told me that he was at Saint Barnabas Medical Center and I talked to them for a long time. We went to the Janos's apartment and I talked to the mother and the sisters and got some feel for where the youngster had come from and what he looked like, who he was and how the house was decorated. I try, although I'm not always successful, to select detail that is reflective of the kind of life folks who live there lead. They were very kind. I mean considering what was going on in their lives at that particular moment, they were very kind and very open and just beautiful people. They talked about how the telephone rang in the middle of the night and how Daisy, I guess it was, had screamed, and how the girls came running in and asked what's the matter. So I used that as the basic framework for the column.

Deadline Tip:

You've really got to let the story tell itself. There's a tendency to overwrite, to overthink, to overdramatize, and what I try to do is use detail, an anecdote, to tell the story without making the statement. Obviously, this is a horrible, horrible thing and obviously one of the worst things that can ever happen to a parent who sends his kid away to college is to get that call in the middle of the night saying, "You'd better get down here, something terrible has happened." So how do you say that? I mean you say it by saying, "one of the worst things," but that's kind of boring. Or you can say it by telling a life story, which is what I did.

Tyler Bridges   Sandra Marquez Garcia   Curtis Morgan

The Miami Herald

Finalist, Team Deadline News Reporting

The story of Elián González was always about much more than the tragedy of a Cuban child alone and adrift at sea after his mother and others had drowned. When U.S. Customs agents raided the home of Elián's uncle to reclaim the boy for his father, *The Miami Herald*, well-prepared for that moment, began a daylong reporting job that captured the smallest details and put them in a global context. That effort earned the newspaper a Pulitzer Prize. In their piece of the multifaceted coverage, reporters Tyler Bridges, Sandra Marquez Garcia, and Curtis Morgan covered the streets of Miami, following the fires, protests, and a trail of tear gas to give readers a vivid sense of the depth of emotions exploding in Little Havana.

Tense scenes played out
on Miami streets

APRIL 23, 2000

Five months of pent-up passion spilled over Saturday into a bitter daylong series of seesaw clashes in the streets of Little Havana between hundreds of protesters and nearly as many police in full riot gear.

Demonstrators, outraged at the seizure of Elián González by a gun-toting federal SWAT team, shouted, wept, waived flags and signs and—in isolated angrier outbreaks—blocked traffic, threw rocks, overturned bus benches and torched tires and trash bins. Police met them fast and forcefully—some say too forcefully—pumping tear gas canisters into crowds and hauling off dozens in handcuffs.

At least 268 people, including a man charged with attempted murder for attacking three officers with a baseball bat, had been arrested by 10 p.m. Scattered skirmishes were still breaking out into the night but authorities hoped the worst had passed.

"Clinton, Miami is burning!" protesters chanted around a bonfire built of old tires, a trash bin load of cardboard boxes and a shredded Florida lottery billboard at Flagler Street and Northwest 27th Avenue, an intersection blocks from the home where Elián was snatched before dawn.

But Miami, despite super-heated emotions in the streets, was not on fire.

That street blaze and at least 128 others were doused by firefighters. The shifting protests were confined to a dozen or so blocks in Little Havana. There were no reports of serious damage and a few miles to the east, the Miami Heat won an undisturbed playoff opener at American Airlines Arena. Reported injuries, topping 50, were mostly cuts and bruises.

"These are sporadic acts, isolated events, but they are ugly pictures to see," said Miami City Manager Donald Warshaw. "This is not a riot."

PRAYER VIGIL

Political and community leaders—Miami-Dade Mayor Alex Penelas, U.S. Rep. Lincoln Diaz-Balart, Spanish-language radio hosts and others—took to the airwaves appealing for calm. Penelas said he planned to organize a large-scale ceremony, possibly a prayer vigil.

"I've asked people to refrain from this kind of behavior," he said. "There is a right way to protest and a wrong way."

"Right now," Diaz-Balart said, "the worst thing we can do is give our enemies the gasoline to set us on fire."

At nightfall, tempers seemed to have cooled but the streets remained tense enough that police warned journalists that they were at risk outside the González home, prompted by a throng that knocked down the CNN tent. Exile organizers and CNN staffers calmed the crowd and a platoon of police, thumping their batons against their plastic shields, marched in. Within an hour, the strange village of satellite trucks dubbed Camp Elián had folded.

For the most part, the community paid heed but at Ground Zero—Flagler Street stretching several dozen blocks through a working-class stronghold of Elián supporters—the scene was chaotic. For much of the day, the air smelled of a stinging mix of tear gas and trash bin fire smoke. At noon, the peak of problems, protests popped up as fast as police broke them up.

CUFFED PROTESTERS

Sweeping the streets in ranks sometimes 10 across, police gruffly cuffed protesters. Dozens of other protesters and bystanders stumbled about, eyes red and burning. After one of the numerous gassings, a crowd fled to a Walgreens drug store, tearing water, soda, anything from the shelves for relief.

"The first time I got gassed I almost got hit by a car," said Carmen Cantu. "It's scary. I'm only 12. They arrested a little girl right before my eyes."

Officers also were roughed up in at least two clashes and one cruiser's window was smashed. In the most violent confrontation reported, a man was arrested on charges that included attempted murder after he allegedly attacked three officers with a metal baseball bat.

Daniel Perez, 29, of 10730 SW 28th St., drove his light blue Toyota through a police barricade at Flagler and West 35th Avenue, nearly running over two officers, according to a police report.

Perez stopped the car, grabbed a bat and started hitting officers, the report said. Three officers were injured, two with back pain and another with a shoulder injury, said Miami Police Lt. William Schwartz. The officers were taken to Jackson Memorial Hospital, where they were in stable condition, Schwartz said.

PUSHED TOO FAR

One woman said police pushed a tense crowd too far.

"They were provoking us," said Marta Suarez of Miami. "Because people are on the sidewalk chanting *libertad* there is no reason to arrest them. If the police keep acting like this it will get worse. People don't want violence but police are getting violent."

Schwartz, doing an interview outside the González home, also was pushed, pummeled and spit on by protesters before officers and others in the crowd came to his aid.

"I was surprised and angry, and ultimately gratified that people were trying to help me," Schwartz said.

The first protests began within an hour of Elián's removal. The crowd around the relatives' home, less than 50 when the lightning raid took place, swelled to hundreds. Others poured into nearby streets.

Isis Cardoso rushed from her Miami Beach home to Flagler and 27th Avenue, also known as Unity Boulevard, after her son called her at 5:30 a.m. She thought it was time to send a message.

"As long as we can't fight in our own homeland, all we can do is fight on the streets of Miami," said Cardoso, wearing a black band around her arm. She listened to *La Poderosa* radio station, but ignored the urges to stay home.

"I had it on this morning but I finally turned it off because they were calling on people for *calma, calma* (calm), but today is not a day for calm. Today is a day for action."

By 10 a.m., protesters were swarming Little Havana. Most people simply stood on sidewalks, waving flags or signs. Crowds, arms linked, spilled onto the Dolphin Expressway, temporarily blocking traffic before Florida Highway Patrol troopers arrived.

The mood among protesters was defiant—toward police but more toward the U.S. government that they felt had betrayed them again.

Juan Contijoch, holding his 2-year-old daughter Yara and waving an American flag smeared with a black paint swastika, stood in the smoke of a Flagler Street trash bin fire and expressed what seemed the prevailing view:

"This is the beginning of the end of this free society. Little by little, they are taking away our rights. Now is the time for us to take the streets."

"We are going to paralyze Miami," vowed Irma Garcia.

About 11:20 a.m., with bonfires burning on a half-dozen street corners and problems spreading, police regrouped. Patrols withdrew and returned in increased force and riot gear—batons, plastic shields, gas masks.

The city of Miami had about 700 of its 1,127 officers on the street. Miami's officers were reinforced by the Miami-Dade Police Department with 650 county officers in field units and a SWAT team from the Florida Department of Law Enforcement. FHP troopers patrolled the perimeter and Miami Beach officers assisted by providing security at the Heat game.

MANY CHARGED

About noon, officers, marching in near-military formation, started sweeping west to reclaim Flagler, arresting protesters and others on charges that included disorderly conduct and inciting a riot. At least five journalists were also arrested.

Many protesters complained that the police used excessive force. Erika Huerta said a tear gas canister fell at her feet, even though she was peacefully protesting.

"There has been rock-throwing," she said, "but at that moment, we were just walking and saying, 'Justice for Elián.'"

An old man was handcuffed and dragged on his knees. Officers knocked down and handcuffed a teenage girl. Others saw officers kicking and punching protesters.

By afternoon, with the police force swelling, tempers seemed cooler. Armando Perez helped officers remove a concrete bus bench from the street as city maintenance crews began clearing debris.

"We don't have anything against the police," he said. "If they would take off their helmets and put away their batons we would feel better about them."

About 8 p.m., nearly 300 people gathered at Southwest 17th Avenue and First Street and burned dozens of tires. Police broke it up in 30 minutes.

"This is crazy. The police are crazy. They're kicking people and hurting people," said Yvette Gomez, 30.

Police defended the tactics, saying the swift arrests and strong force snuffed potential problems.

"I think they've done an excellent job in very trying conditions," said Miami Police Chief William O'Brien. "They've arrested a whole group of troublemakers and there is no significant property damage."

Herald staff writers Charles Rabin, Ana Acle, Eunice Ponce, Charles Savage, Mireidy Fernandez, and Marika Lynch contributed to this report.

Lessons Learned

BY CURTIS MORGAN

The Miami Herald unfortunately has too much experience covering street violence, but every eruption is unique. The seizure of Elián González, as reporter Sandra Marquez Garcia described it, was "bigger than Elián. It was a loud, painful wailing over the loss of a homeland."

In the end, though, the Elián affair once again underscored the basics of the business.

■ **Start early**: In the perfect news world, every major event would start before dawn as this one did. That gave us eight to 10 hours of street reporting, the equivalent of about two normal working days. Perhaps that's a lesson for routine news coverage as well. All too often, reporters don't get marching orders until after noon planning meetings, and actual news gathering is condensed into a few rushed hours.

■ **Have a plan and stick to it**: Editors divided the duties clearly and early.

■ **Stay with key sources**: Tyler Bridges had been covering Miami city government for a year, developing a good relationship with the police chief. Instead of waiting for the news conference, Tyler was at command central by 9 a.m. That gave the *Herald* some of the first hints of how the raid came down, which included the first details that Miami police had helped carry out the raid— a fact Tyler confirmed for a team assembling a separate tick-tock story on the raid.

From there, Tyler got the chief to allow him to stay throughout the day, giving us an essential pipeline to the prime-time players. When other reporters were calling in for information and injuries, they often got busy signals. Tyler got face-to-face instead.

■ **Be street smart**: As part of volunteer teams monitoring elections in Haiti, Sandra had experienced street violence firsthand. As one of the key reporters in the field, she knew the trick was to walk the edge—get into the action without getting arrested or hurt. By sticking with small groups for periods, Sandra caught vivid scenes—old folks gassed in a bus, crowds staggering into drug stores hunting for something to flush out burning eyes. She took some risks but not foolhardy ones. She got close enough to learn one lesson for the inevitable next time: Maybe newspapers ought to stock a few gas masks along with all the cell phones and beepers.

■ **Details, details**: Editor Gene Miller, the *Herald*'s legendary two-time Pulitzer winner, doesn't want to know what a murder victim was wearing. He wants to know what was in the victim's pockets. The same rules apply in the big breaking stories. We didn't get just the official count of street fires, we knew what the fuel was for one—cardboard boxes and a shredded Florida lottery sign. Police didn't just march in, they thumped their batons on their plastic shields. One center of discontent was 27th Avenue, also known as Unity Boulevard.

Such small stuff, sprinkled among colorful quotes and dry facts, gave the story authority and enlivened the retelling with a sense of reality.

■ **Use TV but don't be TV**: The raid and uprising were covered by countless crews and broadcast live nationally. In the newsroom, the tube proved invaluable, helping us dispatch street reporters to hot spots and capturing the run-and-gun nature of the conflicts between protesters and police. But the cameras, in tight focus, portrayed a city in turmoil. The breathless reporting did the same, even at the network level.

We zoomed out. The *Herald* didn't soft sell the protest. In fact, from day one we were the only media to identify the questionable police tactics that would in weeks ahead lead to upheaval in city hall, starting with the resignation of the police chief.

But we didn't bend to the temptation of blowing it out of proportion either. We put boundaries on the protest, literally (a dozen blocks in Little Havana) and figuratively (noting the Miami Heat playoff, not more than a few miles away, went off without a hitch).

Miami had seen real riots, with blocks of buildings burning, bloodied heads, and bodies in the street. That wasn't even close to what was happening here.

■ **The final lesson**: Report with accuracy and perspective.

St.Petersburg Times

Sue Carlton

Tom French

Anne Hull

St. Petersburg Times

Finalist, Team Deadline News Reporting

It was an unusual murder case and it called for unusual reporting. So the *St. Petersburg Times* brought the strength of narrative writing to the challenge of telling the daily story of Valessa Robinson's murder trial. Accused of taking part in the stabbing death of her mother, Robinson presented the newspaper with a case about parenting, teen-agers, drugs, all bigger issues than a single criminal trial. Covered by three of the best narrative writers around—Tom French, Anne Hull, and Sue Carlton—the trial came to life as a courtroom drama brimming with three-dimensional characters and complex truths. It is informed by a wealth of background reporting woven seamlessly into each day's deadline story.

A lesser degree

APRIL 22, 2000

TAMPA—The night before the verdict, Valessa Robinson's lawyers hit Burdines.

Dee Ann Athan, Lyann Goudie and Lisa Campbell, the three assistant public defenders battling for their young client's future, swept through the second floor of the department store at WestShore Plaza around 7 Thursday.

The trio of lawyers stood out among the other shoppers. They kept huddling and whispering. They moved like women on a mission, scanning the racks.

"Oh, I think she'd like this," said one of them, holding up an outfit.

A few minutes later, they made their pick: a baby pink sweater set.

Then they hurried from the store.

* * *

The beginning of the Easter weekend had left most of the courthouse's rooms and hallways darkened Friday. But not the third floor and Circuit Judge J. Rogers Padgett's courtroom.

Vicki Robinson's mother stepped off the elevator. Donna Klug was wearing a pale suit, the last of the outfits she had packed when she and her husband had left their home in Michigan weeks ago. By now they had a stack of dirty laundry in their hotel room.

"This high," said Mrs. Klug, her hand at her waist.

Valessa's trial had lasted longer than anyone expected. Now, after two weeks, the case appeared to be teetering on the brink of a mistrial. The night before, the jurors had sent the judge a note saying they were deadlocked. The judge sent them back to their hotel to sleep on it.

A mistrial would give Valessa's lawyers a second chance with a different jury. As the three of them gathered in the courtroom Friday, they seemed re-energized.

In a matter of minutes, Padgett punctured their mood. The judge announced that he intended to revisit a question the jurors had asked two days earlier, in their first hours of deliberations. If a person is determined to be a principal in a crime, the jurors had wanted to know, is that person guilty of the crime?

The question went to the heart of the prosecution's case. If Valessa was found to be a principal in her mother's murder—that is, if she encouraged or helped the killer—the law considered her just as guilty.

On Wednesday, Padgett hadn't answered the jurors' question. Instead, he had simply repeated an instruction explaining the principal theory.

Now the judge wanted to answer their question straight out. If the jurors believed Valessa was a principal in the murder, then yes, she was guilty.

"These people are entitled to a meaningful answer," Padgett said.

Valessa's attorneys were livid. The judge was about to tell the jury something that could seal a verdict of first-degree murder and send Valessa to prison for the rest of her life.

Lead attorney Dee Ann Athan slumped into her chair. The other defense lawyers began to argue.

The judge folded his hands. He listened patiently until they were done, calmly denied the objections, then asked the bailiff to bring in the jury.

Lyann Goudie turned away from the judge.

"At this point, we should all just go home," she said.

Padgett had had enough. He stopped the bailiff from bringing in the jury, then turned to the defense attorneys.

"You know better than to say something like that with the cameras rolling," he said. "Who said it? You, Ms. Goudie?"

"Yes, I did," she said.

"Do you want me to hold you in contempt?"

"Judge," Goudie answered, "that's your prerogative."

Padgett told her that there would be a contempt hearing later.

"That's fine," Goudie said.

Finally, the jurors were brought in. The judge first gave them an instruction called the Allen Charge, encouraging them to keep trying for a verdict.

"I have only one request of you," he read. "By law, I cannot demand this of you."

Take turns, he said. Tell your fellow jurors about any weaknesses in your position. Don't interrupt until everyone has had a chance to speak. After all that, if you still cannot agree on a unanimous verdict, I will declare a mistrial.

That finished, the judge returned to the principal question. He told the jurors that he had not fully answered it for them two days before. He tried again.

"Now, if you have considered each of the instructions and if you have weighed all of the evidence in accord with those instructions, then the answer to this question is yes."

If Valessa was a principal, then she was guilty.

One of the jurors nodded slightly. The packed courtroom watched them file out.

* * *

The jury room was either hot or freezing. The jurors banged on the door for the bailiff to adjust the thermostat. They had been in the windowless room for almost three days.

Among those sitting around the table were a railroad bridge tender, a lineman, a homemaker, a salesman, a maintenance worker, a day trader. During the deliberations, the day trader had scribbled almost 50 pages of notes.

The jurors had taken several votes.

First, they had done them by secret ballot. After a while, they switched to voting by a show of hands. But they couldn't reach a unanimous decision.

There were no angry exchanges. It wasn't like the movies, the foreman would later say.

They had looked over the physical evidence, the photographs and the videos. Leaning against the wall were the shovel and pitchfork, the tools Adam Davis and Jon Whispel had used in their attempt to bury Vicki's body.

Remembering the testimony was tricky. They tried to recall precisely what each witness had said. Different memories produced different recollections.

Some jurors were troubled by the lack of physical evidence linking Valessa to the crime. They wondered about the credibility of one witness, presumably Whispel.

Miranda rights had been reviewed, and the role of LSD. They discussed culpability and premeditation.

The foreman, Gerry Siering, felt like he was putting a frustrating puzzle together. "No matter what," he'd said when they'd first gone into the jury room Wednesday, "we have to listen to what each other has to say."

They listened. But they were still stuck.

* * *

In the courtroom, the defendant was wearing the pink sweater set her attorneys had bought the night before.

For two weeks, Valessa's makeover had been the talk of the courthouse. In her old life, before her arrest, she had been the girl with blue fingernails, baggy jeans and an "A" tattooed on her right hand, professing her love for Adam Davis. She was the kid with a ferret named Slick.

For her trial, she had been remade into a young schoolgirl. At her lawyers' insistence, her long brown hair had been cut into a conservative bob. The T-shirts and jeans she once had worn were replaced with ivory sweaters, pleated skirts, tights, even a pair of Mary Janes. Whenever the jury was in the room, she kept her hands—and the "A" tattoo—clasped behind her back or folded in her lap, under the defense table.

Those who knew Valessa in her old life barely recognized her.

"She wouldn't have been caught dead wearing those kinds of clothes, any time, anywhere," said Ed Philips, one of Vicki's friends who attended the trial.

Valessa's lawyers were angered at the suggestion that their client's transformation was a ploy. Valessa, they said, was merely dressing appropriately for a courtroom. Shouldn't the attire of all their clients, they asked, show respect for the judge and jury?

"According to the media," said Lyann Goudie, "I guess we're supposed to be bringing them in naked or in jailhouse jumpers."

But Valessa's makeover went well beyond a simple gesture of respect for the courtroom. The clothes, the shoes, even the barrettes in her hair—in every detail she was being presented as a "little girl," which is how her lawyers described her to the jury.

The Mary Janes said it all. They were not the typical shoes of a 17-year-old on the verge of adulthood. They were what a 10-year-old girl would wear to church.

Day after day, Valessa's appearance and demeanor in the courtroom drove home a message of obedience, submission, innocence.

She had chosen not to take the witness stand and tell her story to the jury. Instead, she let her clothes testify for her.

* * *

An hour into their deliberations Friday, the jurors sent out a new question. Judge Padgett read aloud to the attorneys what the foreman had scrawled:

We request transcripts of any and all court records, testimony, and other usable evidence, specifically relating to whether or not Valessa held her mother down, or pinned or restrained her, in any way, during the course of the alleged murder.

Quickly, the lawyers on both sides tried to calculate what was behind the question. Padgett said there were no transcripts available, no more exhibits to review. The jury had what it needed.

He called in the jurors, told them just that and sent them out again.

An hour later, another question was handed out. It was a rhetorical puzzle.

You said "rely on your collective memory." Must we rely on our own personal individual collective memory of all the evidence OR do you mean we rely on a majority memory of the collective group as a whole? i.e. if eight members remember something one way but four remember another, are the four obligated to abide by the memory of the eight, suspending any doubts they have?

Once more Padgett summoned the jurors. His answer to their question was its own puzzle:

"You must rely on your own personal collective memory."

What was the jury stuck on? Did some jurors recall testimony or evidence differently from others? Whose memories would prevail?

* * *

They were all in limbo.

For days, those who had loved Vicki and those who still loved her daughter roamed the courthouse, wondering when the jury would end their waiting. They prayed together, snacked on blueberry muffins and Lay's potato chips, kept a close eye on the nearest TV for any news of a verdict.

Mostly, they talked. Hour after hour they talked about Vicki and Valessa, parents and children, all that lingered unspoken beneath the facts of the case now before the jury.

The question, always, was why. Why had Vicki been killed? What had gone wrong inside the Robinson home in the months and years before the murder?

Like so many people, defense attorney Lyann Goudie said she did not know.

"Nothing about it is right. It's all wrong," she said. "I think a very bad person got mixed up with this kid."

Alicia Thompson, a 16-year-old King High School student who attended the trial out of curiosity, said: "I think things escalated between Valessa and her mom. Sometimes you paint yourself into a corner. You just can't see a way out."

Chuck Robinson talked about how impressionable his daughter was. "When you start hanging around with older kids, you're gonna be in trouble. I don't care who you are. You can't be hanging around with kids four or five years older...It's enormous. It's huge."

Assistant State Attorney Shirley Williams said the answer was inside Valessa. "Vicki was trying to break her and Adam up, and she wanted her mom's money and her car and her future."

Williams also talked about teens in general. "There's this old saying: If you give them an inch they'll take a mile...The rules are different now. Parents used to be ashamed if they let their children misbehave and act up. And now they're ashamed to discipline their children."

Carlton Huff, a friend of Vicki's: "Putting those two kids together was a volatile thing. Take away one of a number of variables out of the equation, and this wouldn't have happened...Keep Chuck at home and it's not a broken-up family. Adam gets raised by his mother. Obviously, you remove Adam from the situation and maybe she's just another rebellious teenager. Take away the drugs and maybe it doesn't happen. It's a combination of factors. It's not any one thing."

Julianne Holt, Hillsborough public defender, mother

of two small children: "I think about it all the time. I just think that we as parents have to slow down our lives long enough to see and hear what our kids are doing. You have to care who their friends are. You can't say, 'There's nothing I can do.'"

Bruce Wilson, the Texas sheriff who captured Valessa and Adam and Jon, had an opinion, too.

Months ago, when he was asked about the case, Wilson talked about how much children need love, how parents need to learn to discipline and set boundaries, the difficulties of raising kids when both mothers and fathers are off at work.

As for Valessa, he said it was a simple matter of gratification.

"That's all the little girl was. She wanted what she wanted."

The sheriff paused.

"It was the boy—that's the way I got it. She wanted that boy."

* * *

In the jury room, the 12 were struggling with matching the requirements of the various degrees of murder with each juror's recollection of the evidence. The robbery charge—the one related to the use of Vicki's ATM cards, and other items taken from the Carrollwood house—was intensely debated.

In the late morning, they read the jury instructions again. More talking, more listening. Just after noon, they decided to take another vote.

The foreman looked around the room. Twelve arms were raised.

* * *

When it came, it came, and there was nothing anyone could do to change it. The 18 hours of misery—the pacing and napping in chairs and trips to the water fountain—were over.

At 12:20 p.m., the jurors told the bailiff they had a verdict. The news spread in a current through the courthouse.

Vicki Robinson's mother held a pink rose as she entered the courtroom. "This is for my Vicki," Donna Klug said. "I wanted to think of my Vicki. She loved roses."

It was the strangest mixture of dread and anticipation, walking into that room. The air was frigid, and spectators shivered against the cold and the nerves. Almost no one spoke. Stomachs fluttered.

"I think I'm gonna throw up," said a lawyer from the public defender's office.

The prosecutors sat silently at their table, watching the door the judge would walk through. They were composed, giving nothing away.

Behind the defense table, Lyann Goudie paced along the wall, arms folded, blue eyes flashing toward the door. Lisa Campbell was silently preparing a motion the defense would make before the verdict was read.

Dee Ann Athan sat close to Valessa. They were bound to each other now in ways that suggested mother and daughter.

Valessa looked peaceful. She leaned her head on Athan's shoulder. That morning, it had been Valessa who brought a Good Friday Scripture to her lawyers, reading to them about Jesus and the Resurrection.

Her face was pearly. It was a yearbook face.

The judge swept in.

Before he recalled the jury, he had something to say.

"This is the point in the trial which is seen by people as either a victory or a loss," the judge said. "And that's not the way those of us who work here look at it, but I think that's the way other people do.

"And I think it's probably fair to say that in this case it will be seen by some people as a major loss, or a major victory."

There was a beat of silence. People were trying to comprehend the meaning behind the judge's words. They were almost a warning. He then ordered all in the courtroom to refrain from any emotion or disruption.

And then everything happened in a rush.

The jury came in. The judge looked to the foreman.

"Mr. Siering, has the jury reached a verdict?"

"Yes it has, your honor."

"Hand it to the bailiff, please."

The bailiff carried the slip of paper to the clerk. Her voice was clear and strong.

"The State of Florida versus Valessa Lyn Robinson," she began.

"We the jury find as follows as to Count 1 of the indictment: The defendant is guilty of murder in the third degree.

"We the jury find as follows as to Count 2 of the indictment: The defendant is guilty of petty theft.

"We the jury find as follows as to Count 3 of the indictment: The defendant is guilty of grand theft motor vehicle as charged."

The clerk had read so evenly and so crisply that it took a few seconds to grasp her words.

Chuck Robinson stared straight ahead. He would not be walking out with his daughter. But she had avoided a first-degree murder conviction and life in prison.

There was almost no noise in the courtroom, except for the cameras whining on auto-drive. Robinson and his wife and daughter Michelle, Valessa's 19-year-old sister, stayed seated as they watched Valessa. She was handcuffed. Her expression was nearly serene.

"I love you," she said, looking hard at each family member, burning her message into them.

The judge set sentencing for May 30.

Valessa was led out.

A low moan unfurled itself from the middle of the courtroom. Vicki's friends had clustered together, arm in arm, and now one woman cried inconsolably.

Vicki's parents and brother filed silently from the courtroom. Vicki's mother was still holding the pink rose. They would soon set off on the 1,200-mile drive back to Michigan.

Before he drove off, Kirt Klug, Vicki's younger brother, said one thing.

"My sister's life was worth more than this."

In the lobby of the public defender's office, the defense attorneys were restrained.

"It's Good Friday," Lisa Campbell said evenly. "Given that the worst didn't happen, I guess you could say it's a good day for Valessa."

Dee Ann Athan was cautious, as if she had rescinded all the emotion from the courtroom battle and was now waiting for sentencing. But later, when the attorneys had gone back into their offices, through a window Athan could be seen smiling.

* * *

Valessa handed her court clothes to her lawyers and put on her orange jail uniform.

She was led down a back elevator to a carport. A jail van waited for her. So did a TV camera.

Athan walked with Valessa, still clutching the girl's hand. When Athan saw the camera, she headed for the photographer.

"No comment," she said loudly.

The photographer ignored her. "Valessa, did you get a fair trial?" he asked, his camera rolling. No comment, Athan yelled again and again. She knocked the microphone out of the way and put her hand over the camera lens.

Valessa said nothing. She was loaded into the van that would take her back to her solitary cell at the Orient Road jail.

The murder charge Valessa had been convicted of is an uncommon one. Third-degree murder, unlike first-degree, doesn't require premeditation. Nor is it a killing that the jury determines occurred during a violent felony such as rape or armed robbery.

Third-degree murder occurs when someone is killed during the commission of a lesser felony, such as aggravated battery or grand theft.

Under sentencing guidelines, Valessa faces approximately 13 to 20 years in prison. Judge Padgett has a reputation for imposing tough sentences.

A 1995 state law requires prisoners to serve 85 percent of their sentences, so Valessa could actually spend the next 11 to 17 years behind bars. She could be out before her 35th birthday.

In jail Friday afternoon, Valessa was still confused about her convictions, Dee Ann Athan said. Her lawyer tried to explain it all to her.

"She's not happy, but she's not devastated," Athan said. "She's 17 years old. She's not comprehending everything.

"She realizes it could have been a lot worse."

* * *

Tom Klug, Vicki's other brother, was already back in Michigan when the verdict came.

He thought what had happened to his niece was just.

She would be punished, but she would be able to get out of prison someday.

"I think this is what Vicki would have wanted. I think so," he said. "It's her daughter. I don't think anyone would want her child locked away forever, without a chance to redeem herself."

He hoped that one day, Valessa would sit down with her family and tell them what happened.

The truth, he said.

* * *

After Valessa was taken away and the jurors had hurried off and the lawyers had returned to the sanctuary of their offices, one thing remained unchanged.

Vicki Robinson was gone.

Twenty-two months after the murder, Vicki's loss had torn a hole through the lives of those who cared about her, those who depended on her, even those who had been convicted of killing her.

There was no sense to any of it.

If Valessa and Adam Davis were so determined to be together, why didn't they just get into the minivan and drive away? If Jon Whispel was so disturbed by the plan to kill Vicki, why did he hand over the knife?

No logic, no reason.

Whatever roles each of them played in the murder— no matter whose idea it was, who did the stabbing, who dumped the body in the woods—what did the three of them gain? A few days on the open road. Money. Drugs. Tattoos. The barest hint of freedom.

Nothing.

Nothing but waste.

* * *

In the state attorney's office, a small plastic bag sits on a shelf. Inside is the 10-carat gold ring that Adam purchased for Valessa with her dead mother's money. He bought it two days after the murder at the Wal-Mart on Dale Mabry Highway, just off the interstate. It cost $84.

According to Jon, Adam surprised her with the ring in the lobby of the store.

"What's it mean?" said Valessa.

"What do you think it means?" said Adam.

"We're married?"

"For right now."

* * *

Four days ago, Jon Whispel turned 21. He has more than two decades of his sentence left to serve. He has been working as a prep cook in the prison kitchen. He says he doesn't much like looking in the mirror.

Adam Davis, also 21, sits inside a 6-by-9-foot cell on death row at Florida State Prison. The romance between him and Valessa—the great love that Vicki Robinson paid for with her life—ended soon after the murder.

Now Adam has a new girlfriend. She lives in Starke, just a few minutes from the prison. Adam works on his appeals, reads Sidney Sheldon novels, watches the black-and-white TV in his cell, wonders when his turn with the executioner will come. Not long ago, in a letter to a friend, he wrote:

I'm probably 100 or 200 feet from the death chamber. I'm not far away.

Then there is Valessa.

In a few weeks, after the judge sentences her, she will be transported to a prison somewhere in Florida. Until then, she will remain at the county jail.

In her cell, she keeps a picture of her and her mother. It's from Christmas, not long before the murder. Vicki is smiling. Valessa is smiling.

They look happy.

Times staff writers Graham Brink and Sarah Schweitzer contributed to this report. Research by John Martin. Transcription by Michael Canning.

Lessons Learned

BY NEVILLE GREEN

■ Narrative can work surprisingly well on a breaking news story. Although it's usually thought of as an approach reserved for takeouts and special projects, it can energize and deepen a newspaper's daily coverage of an event important to its readers—particularly if that event is being covered heavily on TV and the web. Contrary to common wisdom, the sky does not fall if you don't always put the "news" at the very top. On the day of the verdict, we did not report the verdict until the 112th paragraph of the story. Only a couple of readers complained.

■ When three reporters are writing a story together, it helps to have an outline that lays out a coherent plan for how it will all come together before deadline. Tom French was our master outliner. Every day during the lunch break we began talking about our best scenes so far, and Tom would start to come up with an outline and figure out who would write what. At day's end, he updated it. Tom made simple outlines—usually one section from inside the courtroom, one section from outside, then back inside, etc.—seem varied and intricate. But they were logical and the story flowed.

■ Details are everything. When we were trying to describe the holding cell where Valessa Robinson sat for hours waiting on a verdict, we made sure we could describe that setting for our readers, down to the chill of the room's temperature, the rank smell of the toilet, the graffiti scrawled on the walls. Try to show instead of tell: the jail grub of turkey sausage and oatmeal shoved through the feed slot of Valessa's cell, the barrette in her new demure curls, the potential juror who saw all the reporters and said, "Oh, dear"—all the stuff we too often leave out of our daily stories.

■ Know when to ask questions and when to shut up. The lawyers involved in the case knew our notebooks were always open, but sometimes it was best to just sit back while a scene played out. The best example: When the jury went out, Anne Hull headed up to the state attorney's office. Vicki Robinson's parents were there, too, and then in walked Vicki's other daughter, Valessa's big sister. The grandparents had seen little of their other granddaughter since the murder of their daughter. Anne just watched and then later simply described what had happened. It was one of our best scenes.

■ Take advantage of editions to revise. We had a first-edition deadline for copy to be at the front-page desk by 9:30. Each night, we had to race to meet that deadline, but then for the next two hours we revised and polished for the midnight copy deadline of the main city edition. We made substantial changes between editions; one night we threw away the first 80 lines of the first-edition story and wrote a new top.

■ Copy editors are your saviors even more so when you are writing thousands of words on a daily deadline. We had two copy editors, Beth Navage and Ron Brackett, reading behind us every night, and they saved us time after time. Also, having the copy editors and page designers closely involved allowed us to push deadline at times. They were on board to make the story as good as possible and kept finding us an extra 10 minutes or so when we really needed it. The page designer, Amy Hollyfield, was a genius at finding solutions when stories came up short or long.

■ If you're not going to give away the news in your lead, don't give it away in the headline or front-page photo cutline either.

■ Doing a story this way takes resources beyond reporters and editors. We had two photographers, Jamie Francis and Tony Lopez, whose work instantly built the atmosphere for each day; a terrific researcher, John Martin; and an editorial assistant, Michael Canning, who taped each day's testimony and then would transcribe passages so we could check the accuracy of our notes.

■ Working 16 hours a day, dinner is not necessary. Sleep is.

Neville Green, managing editor of the Tampa edition of the St. Petersburg Times, oversaw the trial coverage.

Stephen Magagnini
Diversity Writing

Stephen Magagnini calls himself the "Rainbow Writer" of *The Sacramento Bee*, and the title would surely cover the work he does to bring the diverse world of the area's myriad ethnic groups to the *Bee*'s readers. But the title is also a metaphor for his storytelling, splashed as it is by vivid description, colorful quotes, and the subtle, complex hues of life that reside between the black and white of things.

Magagnini has been doing that kind of writing for the *Bee* since 1994, when he took over the "minority affairs" beat, a title that struck him as odd, he says, inasmuch as everybody's a minority in California. He has been writing about people whose stories needed telling all of his career. In 1978, after graduating from Hampshire College, he went to work at the *Sacramento Union*, where he teamed up with his mentor, K.W. Lee, to write the stories that helped free a Korean immigrant falsely accused of murder. He spent 5 1/2 years at the *San Francisco Chronicle* and joined the *Bee* in 1985.

Since then he has been a magazine writer, columnist, and projects reporter and has written about crime, corruption, politics, and just about every ethnic group in northern California. The consummate storyteller, Magagnini's clip file brims with tales like that of Nikolai Feitser, a successful businessman in Russia who took three English classes a day for 18 months so that he could take care of his 10 children.

Magagnini has won regional and statewide awards and has been honored twice by the Columbia School of Journalism. He was a Freedom Forum fellow in Asian studies in 1991 and was awarded a Knight Foundation fellowship at Stanford University in the spring of 2001.

Magagnini's biggest projects include "Lost Tribes," a modern history of California's Native Americans published by the *Bee* in 1997, and "Getting Along," the award-winning 1999 series about people who crossed racial barriers to become friends.

As part of his beat, Magagnini has traveled to cities and towns in South Africa, Ukraine, Belarus, Mexico, China, Vietnam, South Korea, the Philippines, Japan, Russia, Italy, and, more recently, Laos, where he reported parts of the following series, "Orphans of History."

In telling that story of a displaced people, he has pulled together more than seven years of wondering, reading, studying, visiting, schmoozing, and, in the final 18 months of the project, relentless reporting. The result is a series that at once reveals and explains the things that make the Hmong different while grounding the stories in the struggles and triumphs of our common humanity.

—Keith Woods

Family reaps bitter harvest in America

SEPTEMBER 10, 2000

At the end of Albion Way, a dead-end street in south Sacramento, Hmong children play America's game, shooting baskets on a rickety hoop.

Beyond the hoop outside her ramshackle apartment, Nou Her has transformed a field into a little slice of Laos.

On this drizzly morning, Nou Her, 56, comes alive. While a plump, wildly optimistic Hmong boy casts his fishing rod into a large rain puddle, she pulls weeds from the rows of mustard greens, onions, beans, cilantro, sugar cane and other crops she has raised since she was a child in the mountains of Laos. Her ailing husband, Yong Chue Thao, carries her hoe and helps as much as he can.

The field is their only refuge, the only place in America they truly feel Hmong.

Her and Thao, 57, have also lovingly raised 12 children, considered gifts from the heavens in Hmong culture. But it has been an uneven, sometimes disastrous harvest in America's urban jungle. Three of their sons are in prison for murder.

On Albion Way, a 5,000-year-old culture is dying.

DECADES OF TRAGEDY

In Laos, Yong Chue Thao was a captain, a war hero who saved the lives of seven American pilots shot down in the jungle.

For nearly 15 years, he and thousands of other Hmong as young as 12—vastly outnumbered and poorly equipped—battled the North Vietnamese army to a stalemate in northern Laos.

Three days after he landed in America in 1976, he went to work on an Alabama assembly line, making lawn mowers for $2.75 an hour. He processed chickens in Arkansas, stitched upholstery in Kansas and cut mushrooms in Utah.

By the time the family moved to Sacramento in 1988,

Thao didn't have much fight left.

Slowed by a stiff back and a queasy stomach, he drives his teenage children to and from school, then retreats to his apartment, watching TV shows he doesn't understand and trying to put a smile on decades of tragedy.

Like many Hmong in their 40s, 50s and 60s, Thao is a broken man, defeated first by the communists, then by brutal Thai refugee camp guards, now by the English language.

In Laos, where he fed and protected his family, his word was law. Here, he has suffered the humiliation of unskilled jobs, welfare checks addressed to his wife and total dependence on children who have never known him for the man he was in Laos.

But the worst defeat of all has been at the hands of sons Sou, Lee and Chun—each convicted of a different gang murder. Sou and Lee claim they're innocent; Chun says it was an accident.

Together, they represent thousands of Hmong American youth alienated from parents and society.

Sacramento's fastest-growing gangs are Hmong, eclipsing other Asian-American street gangs, police say. Hmong gangs have been involved in at least six shootings in the north county in the past four months. Paul Suwa, a veteran police gang detective, estimates that more than a dozen Hmong gangs with a total of at least 270 members are operating here.

Hundreds of other young Hmong are ditching school or marking time in Juvenile Hall, the California Youth Authority or state prisons.

Their older siblings remember the rice terraces carved into the mountaintops of Laos, where they grew mentally and physically tough and learned to honor their parents as part of an intricate culture built on honesty, spirit worship and clan loyalty.

But many younger brothers and sisters, raised in Thai refugee camps and America's ghettoes, know their parents only as impoverished strangers from another time and place who can't deal with landlords, doctors or school officials without their help.

Until the Thao family and thousands of other Hmong were driven from the mountains of Laos by the Vietnamese and Lao communists in 1975, they lived a tribal existence free of telephones, electricity, plumbing, banks, lawyers or schools.

Their children became adults as early as 12, expected to work, marry and raise children to help in the fields. Most never learned to read or write; they passed on their wisdom through stories, not books.

The Hmong "are unique even among refugee groups," says University of California-Berkeley professor Ron Takaki. "Their adaptation to America is filled with hazards and barriers and cultural land mines."

Unlike other refugees, few Hmong ever dreamed of coming to America. Their elders told fantastic tales of yellow-haired, long-nosed American giants who dined on plump Hmong.

But in coming to the United States, Thao never imagined his sons would turn violent here. He couldn't show them the way—he'd never even seen a pencil before he came to America—but he tried to teach them respect. On rare occasions, he struck them, as the culture prescribes. More often, he begged them to stay home. His wife, too, swallowed her pride. In a culture where love is rarely expressed, "I'd tell them I loved them as they walked out the door," says Nou Her.

Detective Suwa and his partner, Sharon McClatchy— who have known the Thao family for years—ache for them and hundreds of other hapless Hmong parents.

"If this town only knew," Suwa says. "These kids b.s. these parents so bad."

By the time Thao and his wife knew the depth of the trouble their sons were in, it was too late—the young men were on their way to prison.

THE LEFTOVER PEOPLE

Sou Thao is a thoughtful, well-groomed, quiet young man. His shoulder-length black hair flows from a receding hairline that he says dates back to the time four Vietnamese American kids jumped him in the Burbank High School library and yanked out most of his hair.

"They were in a gang; I was not," he says. And so began Sou Thao's life as "Hitman," one of the toughest, most respected Hmong gangsters in Northern California. He became an icon for Hmong youths who knew no other heroes, including his younger brothers, who followed him into the gang life.

On April 21, Sou turned 28 in California State Prison, Solano. He has just passed the six-year mark of 16 years-to-life for the murder of a Hmong youth.

Police investigating the murder found a photo of more than 40 Hmong boys and girls flashing gang signs, and a large poster titled, " 'The Leftover People'…We will never die, we just multiply."

The Leftover People. That's exactly how many Hmong, young and old, see themselves: leftovers from the CIA's secret war in Laos, a war that robbed them of their homes and their way of life. Leftovers dumped in America's worst neighborhoods, unable to read street signs, much less their kids' gang signs.

When the Thao family moved into their three-bedroom apartment at the end of Albion Way in 1988, they entered a new kind of killing field. Bursts of Uzi fire tore through the neighborhood as Crips and Bloods engaged in a bloody cycle of retaliation.

Sou and his friends, figuring they had nothing to lose, bought stolen guns and defended themselves. In America, they had no identity—they felt neither Hmong nor American—so the gangs gave them new ones: "Too Short," "Rooster," "Lonely," "New Wave." Sou became "Hitman."

Now, his identity is Inmate No. J75216. He has had no visitors since his conviction. No one has visited younger brothers Lee and Chun, either. All three say they're ashamed to let their parents see them in prison; in Hmong culture, violent criminals are disowned by their clans and families.

Sou says racism shaped his early years in America. Like many Hmong families, the Thaos moved around a lot, led by Sou's grandfather, a fertility expert who treated Hmong across the nation.

"Every time you move, you get picked on," Sou says.

When he entered Burbank High in 1988, he says, the south Sacramento school was polarized by gangs seething with racial hatred. Then, there were only a few dozen Hmong students; now there are more than 500.

After Sou was jumped at Burbank, he fled to Chico, where his older brother Bee lived, and got a job as a movie usher.

But he returned to Sacramento 18 months later to attend Fremont Continuation School. He worked as a cook at Burger King and ran with MOD (Masters of Destruction), a Hmong gang whose influence has spread from California to the Carolinas.

Sou soon became a legend in the deadly turf war between south Sacramento-based MOD and archrival AFG (Asian Family Gangsters), a Hmong gang based in North Sacramento.

In the past six years, Southeast-Asian gang-related shootings have erupted at high schools, on freeways and on streets, says probation officer Todd Winfrey. "It puts a lot of the public at risk."

Sou Thao's fury was fed by the 1993 gangland murder of his best friend, Jimmy Yang, 16.

Police say Sou became a killer on June 17, 1994, after two carloads of Asian Family Gangsters drove around Susan B. Anthony Elementary School, the heart of MOD territory, and shot at several Tiny Little Rascals, the Cub Scout version of MOD.

Later that night, Sou and other Hmong gangsters ordered some Tiny Little Rascals to get them a "G ride"—a stolen car. Then they drove to North Sacramento to exact their revenge.

Police say that at 2:18 a.m. they killed Khao Heu, a one-time Asian Family Gangster, with a shotgun blast to the head.

The key witness against Sou was his little brother Lee. Though he has made his peace with his brother's betrayal, Sou says "his story was all lies."

Sou, who finished high school in prison last year, has come to appreciate education. On the outside, he says, college never crossed his mind. No one suggested it.

Prison never crossed his mind, either. "You're so angry about everything else you don't even think about that."

"We had no mentors," he says, no one to help him feel good about being Hmong American. "A mentor that's involved in the community would help a lot, someone who pays attention to our personal problems, school problems."

His dad, like many Hmong fathers, talked to him only when he got in trouble. His mom urged him to find a wife, hoping that would get him out of the gang life, but he never had a real girlfriend.

Still, Sou—like his brothers—doesn't blame his parents for his descent into gang life. "They did their best," he says. "We didn't listen."

FLEEING THAILAND

Nou Her wears a multicolored headdress—a fusion of red, yellow, green and purple—and a face chiseled with a mother's pain. When she talks about her imprisoned sons, she cries like a wounded animal.

"The children that came from Laos seem to respect me more, while the kids that were born here seem to be out of control," she says. "They are more intelligent than I am, they know the system better than I do."

Nou Her thinks she was born in 1945, in Laos. When she was 11, her father died of a snake bite, and her mother remarried and left Nou Her on her own. At 14, she married Thao.

In the past 18 years, she has watched Thao deteriorate. A bleeding ulcer has left him able to stomach only bread and rice, and arthritis has made his body so stiff he can barely bathe himself. He watches CNN or Hmong videos on a couch under a figurine of Christ—the Thaos, like many Hmong, have become Christians, hoping to change their luck.

Thao's father was famous in Hmong circles for his ability to treat infertility by placing his hands on women's stomachs and readjusting their internal organs. In Laos, the Thaos grew sugar cane, rice, bananas and opium—it is legal there—and raised oxen, cows and sheep. "Life was good," Thao says.

But at age 16, just three days after he married Nou Her, Thao was recruited into the CIA's secret army led by the legendary Gen. Vang Pao.

Thao and his 120 men and boys battled the North Vietnamese army at the fabled Plain of Jars, giant stone pillars known as the Hmong Stonehenge. He was wounded in the hand and the head.

Sent home in 1975, he found there was nothing to return to. His family already had fled the communists, crossing the Mekong River into Thailand on bamboo rafts.

Thao found them a year later, in Ban Vinai refugee camp.

The Thaos, like the rest of the Hmong in the camps, had little choice: They could return to Laos with nothing and risk being executed by the communists, or they could take their chances in America, a place so alien it might as well have been the moon.

Most came here with no idea how to turn on a faucet, a thermostat or a stove, no notion of the joy of soaking in a hot bath. Forget about filling out a job application.

And America's institutions and agencies were totally unprepared for them, despite official efforts ranging from English classes to job training programs.

"I perceive a lack of willingness by social service providers, cops, teachers—anybody—to even try to understand these communities," says police Sgt. Fernando Enriquez, who has held gang prevention workshops for Hmong parents. "This is a cultural tragedy that we're seeing unfold. They're going to go from (being) disenfranchised to cultural extinction."

Today, most of Thao's 12 children are scattered like mustard seeds. His oldest daughter lives in Minnesota with her husband's family. Four others live in Utah, including Pai, once a star student. Now 20, she takes a few college classes, works nights sewing air bags and minds her older brother's children during the day.

Only three children are still at home, including youngest son Jer, 16, who already has had scrapes with gangs and the law.

For all his trials, Yong Chue Thao doesn't blame the U.S. government. He says the people of Laos lost the war themselves. "If I could turn back time," he says, "I would still fight." He blames his sons' troubles on the neighborhood, but doesn't quite know where else to go.

'I MISS MY FREEDOM'

Lee Thao lives a few minutes from the untamed beauty of California's rugged North Coast. But he never gets to see it. He's doing 25 years at Pelican Bay State Prison, a concrete hellhole 400 miles from Sacramento.

Lee, who stands 5-foot-3 and weighs maybe 125 pounds, is "walking the line with some of the toughest inmates in the world," says a corrections officer. In

March, 200 rioted.

Early one July morning, Lee, 22, is let out of his A Block cell to meet his first-ever visitor: a reporter.

He says his street name was "White Boy," because of his light brown hair and fair complexion. He misses his mother's plain, steamed rice and his midnight fishing trips for stripers and sturgeon, sometimes in stolen cars.

"I miss my freedom, really," he says.

Of the three Thao brothers in prison, Lee was the least violent—and the most tragic.

He was born in Selma, Ala., and grew up in Merced and Sacramento. He earned a B-plus average at Burbank High before he dropped out. "If I'd have stuck to school, I'd have been somebody."

Lee wanted to play football, but his parents didn't want him to get hurt. He says organized sports could help save younger brother Jer: "Basketball, anything where he's not out on the street like we were..." But few after-school programs actively recruit Hmong youth.

Soon after Lee moved to Sacramento, he started hanging out in Susan B. Anthony Park, where some Hmong youths administered a two-minute beating, his initiation into the Tiny Little Rascals.

Had his parents been stricter, "that would have made me worse," he says. "I had that attitude."

In 1992, he was sent to Juvenile Hall for stealing guns. "It wasn't no punishment. It was like a camp...you met all your friends."

At 15, he told Sacramento Police Detective Jeff Gardner that his brother Sou was involved in a murder. Three months later, he unwittingly implicated himself in the drive-by killing of a 15-year-old member of a rival Lao gang.

Police say Lee and his fellow gangbangers stole a van, then drove alongside the victim's car and gunned him down in front of a church on Meadowview Road.

Lee was all the cops had, at first. "I didn't know I needed a lawyer," he says. According to court records, Gardner told him, "I don't want to think that there will be any charges filed against you in this shooting."

But after Lee told police who was in the stolen van, two of the suspects he named testified against him. Lee claims that although he helped steal the vehicle, he was in Stockton the night of the shooting.

Now Lee chops vegetables in the prison mess hall for 30 cents an hour, draws pictures of knights and dragons, and counsels a Hmong gangster from Crescent City as part of Pelican Bay's "Scared Straight" program.

Prison didn't dash Lee's dreams. He never had any. "We wouldn't think past our next good time about the consequences. We really messed it up for ourselves and our family. We just lost them...We didn't see the sacrifices they made to get here."

A WARNING SHOT

Chun Thao, at 21 the youngest of three Sacramento Hmong brothers in prison for murder, represents a sliver of hope for his shattered family on Albion Way.

Unlike his brothers, who will spend the first decade of the 21st century locked up in state prison, Chun is scheduled to return home by 2002.

More boarding school than prison, the California Youth Authority's facility in Paso Robles has given Chun a real shot at redemption. He roams the well-manicured grounds with relative freedom.

It's five years since he shot and killed "Little T," a 14-year-old Lao boy whose gang crashed a south Sacramento birthday party. Chun claims he only fired a warning shot to defend the children at the party, that he didn't intend to hit anyone.

Though he says he's sorry and talks of becoming a role model for Hmong youth, prison officials wonder whether Chun has really changed. A CYA spokeswoman describes Chun's frozen demeanor at parole hearings as "flat."

By the time Chun was a sixth-grader at Susan B. Anthony, he'd joined his older brother Lee's gang, the Tiny Little Rascals. They'd skip school, steal cars, rob houses, buy guns and terrorize the neighborhood.

"The teachers would want to talk to my parents. I told them my parents didn't speak English."

He says his father and older brother Billy would whip him with a belt, then lecture him about how he could become anything if he'd finish school. But, he says, "I was a little hard ass. When they beat me, it just made me madder. I was angry at them for being right."

His parents blame the neighborhood, but Chun says he would have joined a gang no matter where he grew up. His gangster brothers tried to keep him off the streets, but they were the only ones he looked up to.

Strange as it seems, Chun says, "I'm kind of happy being locked up instead of being out there. I would have done something worse, or I would have been killed."

He calls his mom every month, and writes to his sister May. She and her husband, both ex-gangsters, now have an infant son.

Getting married is the only way your "homies" will let you leave the gang life, Chun says. When a 15-year-old friend tried to quit the gang, "they beat him up bad."

In April, Chun got his high school diploma, and plans to go to college when he gets out. He's read *How to Get a Job* and his favorite, *Chicken Soup for the Teenage Soul*.

"The message," he says, "is that everybody goes through bad times."

'WHERE'S WALDO?'

Hmong parents and their children are lost in America, even to each other. Often they literally don't speak the same language.

The Thaos' youngest son, Jer, 16, teeters on the brink of disaster. But he doesn't speak or understand Hmong well enough to share his deepest thoughts and fears with his parents.

"Where's Aunt Thao?" he asks in halting Hmong about a relative who used to live with them.

His mother responds in Hmong, which Jer can't decipher.

"My mom doesn't get what I'm saying," he says in frustration. "I can't explain…"

Mother and son, however, understand a bribe. His mom paid him $90 to cut off his Mohawk and pony tail; now he wears a flat-top fade and a new leather jacket.

On this gray weekday morning, Jer is hanging around the house in his baggy green bell bottoms, doing nothing much. He doesn't emerge from his bedroom until 11 a.m., claiming a stomachache.

Asked the last time he went to school, Jer looks at his

watch. "I forgot," he says.

Jer Thao has become the "Where's Waldo?" of the Sacramento City Unified School District. He hasn't been to school for more than a month, and nobody knows where he is.

District officials say he's at Goethe Middle School, but he hasn't been there since May 1999. Officials at Burbank High School, where he enrolled in September, say he's supposed to be at Thurgood Marshall Continuation School. But the principal there has no record of him.

"This is the biggest mystery in the world, Jer Thao," says Burbank principal Kathleen Whalen. "He was in trouble from the get-go, smoking on school grounds...Of course he's failing."

The school scheduled a behavior hearing in December, but Jer's parents didn't show up. They couldn't read the letter notifying them about the hearing. And Jer didn't tell them.

"Jer's doing everything he can for a family reunion (in prison)," says Bob Sandoval, Burbank's vice principal of discipline.

Sandoval says Burbank's 507 Hmong students include several dozen Jers, kids who drift in and out of school. In a classic Catch-22, those caught cutting class are suspended for five days.

When Jer finally shows up at Thurgood Marshall, he's bullied by several other students. "They're mad-dogging him, challenging him to fight," says Suwa, the detective. He guesses that Jer's tormentors might be retaliating because their friends were killed by his brothers.

Fighting isn't Jer's style. If he's not shooting baskets on the rusting hoop overlooking his mother's garden, you can usually find him at a friend's house, watching videos or playing video games.

"School?" he yawns. "It's not all that hard...I'm just lazy and don't do my work."

HARVEST OF HOPE

It's a sunny Saturday afternoon. Nou Her and her youngest daughters, May and Mai, are watching May's 8-month-old son, KayBe, play with a toy on the living room floor.

May, 19, has a full-time job with the U.S. Census Bureau; her husband stays home with KayBe.

Mai, 14, a quiet girl with chestnut hair, is doing well at Burbank High and has found her passion: the violin.

Nou Her wanders out to her garden to fill a few bags with mustard greens, then returns to cradle KayBe. For one afternoon, she is all hope and smiles. There will be new crops to harvest, new generations to nurture.

Activists chart path
for a new generation

SEPTEMBER 10, 2000

The six little girls giggle when Xeng Xiong writes a Hmong phrase on the blackboard, then translates it into English: "You are very beautiful."

For Xiong, 30, witnessing Hmong children say and write "You are very beautiful" (*cawhjong gaow heng*) in their native language is indeed a thing of beauty.

While the younger kids learn Hmong language, values and folk tales, Pahua Lor, a student at the University of California-Davis helps the teenagers with their homework and teaches them about affirmative action, equal rights and other American ideas.

They belong to a grass-roots program aptly named HOPES (Hmong Organization for Parents, Educators and Students). HOPES doesn't get a dime of public or foundation money—it's driven by an all-volunteer corps of community activists.

They're just part of a new wave of Hmong freedom fighters, ages 18-35, who are going to war against the demons of illiteracy, truancy, delinquency and poverty that are tearing apart Hmong society. Born in Laos but schooled in America, they are challenging police, school administrators and city officials to wake up before Hmong culture is wiped out here.

The freedom fighters are spread out around the community. Some are college students. Others are teachers. Still others are social workers.

Tsia Xiong, HOPES' founder, is among those leading the charge. Xiong, like teacher Xeng Xiong (no relation) is that rarest of birds: a 30-year-old Hmong bachelor. His life is a whirlwind of probation hearings, mentoring programs, a summer day camp, parenting workshops and visits to troubled families.

Last year, when he was given a community service award, Xiong was in no mood to celebrate.

"There's no after-school program to keep our kids in school. No Hmong teachers at Grant High (one has since been hired). Less than 10 percent of the Hmong in the Sacramento City Unified School District are reading at grade level. Our Juvenile Hall numbers keep increasing," he tells the stunned crowd. "We need to solve these problems or the Hmong community in Sacramento will cease to exist."

He's angry that city officials haven't hired a Hmong community liaison to bridge the language and culture barrier—a job he and others have been doing for free.

City officials say they can't hire a liaison for one ethnic group and not the rest. But Xiong says Slavic and Latino immigrants are much more familiar with Western law, medicine and politics than Hmong refugees, and thus adapt more easily.

Although refugee resettlement agencies have worked tirelessly to help Hmong families adjust, they've been overwhelmed by the sheer number who have come to Sacramento.

Local law enforcement officials have held community workshops for the refugees but say they have had little success recruiting Hmong officers. Schools also are struggling to understand how best to help Hmong students and their parents.

On a recent Saturday morning, Xiong helps moderate a workshop for 250 Hmong parents at Goethe Middle School. The parents complain that the district doesn't tell them their kids are in trouble, or absent, until a week after the fact.

"Each school should have a minimum of one Hmong-speaking staff member in the office," says Xiong. "I'm going to have to get on the nerves of a couple of school board members and principals." And he will.

Some problems, however, defy solutions. Over lunch, a Hmong teacher at Goethe tells Xiong of a truant seventh-grader—a good student—whose mother dragged him to school on Monday and followed him from class to class, as school officials had suggested.

By second period on Tuesday, the boy had given his mother the slip. On Wednesday, she enlisted everyone from the principal to the hall monitor to make sure he went to every class. "He was crying the whole day," the teacher says.

At fifth period Thursday, he escaped again and hasn't

been back to school since.

"The mother did her part," Xiong says, shaking his head.

Xiong and other activists know these problems first-hand. Their younger siblings and teenage children are living them.

Ka Va, another freedom fighter who made a presentation at the workshop, says his younger sister Mai was a chronic runaway who stole and wrecked all four family cars. Her behavior drove her parents to seek a divorce—from her.

Va, 33, has tried to be a good role model. He became the first Hmong teacher in the Sacramento Unified School District and the first Hmong professor at California State University-Sacramento.

But, he says, the more Mai hung around with her friends, the more stubborn she got. "She became a person that's very rude, not respectful to anybody, including me."

After Mai stole her mother's van and broke the transmission, she says her mother tied her up and called the police, who took her to Juvenile Hall.

"My parents said, 'You're dead, you're not our daughter anymore, so don't come back to this house,'" Va says.

After spending much of last year in Juvenile Hall, Mai was married in January, went back to school and got a job at Burger King. She hopes to become a lawyer, and says she's sorry for the pain she's caused her family.

What worries Tsia Xiong—who says his own teenage sister locks herself in her room rather than listen to him—is that the longer the Hmong are in America, the worse things seem to get.

At 13, Xiong was thrown into the eighth grade in Stockton with no prior education. Like other refugees, he had to work three times as hard to catch up. But his sink-or-swim experience made him stronger: He speaks English more fluently and did far better in school than most of his 10 younger siblings who grew up in America.

He got extra help because there was only a handful of Hmong students. "But now, the school system is overwhelmed by Hmong kids," he says. Few local districts have any materials in Hmong to help students maintain their cultural identity, and there is little communication between parents and school officials.

Sometimes, the most Xiong can do is offer moral support.

Early one morning, Xiong stops by the south Sacramento home of Yang Xeng Lee, whose 16-year-old son was gunned down in front of a friend's house in broad daylight a year and a half ago.

Police say Jindao Lee was a gangster; his father remembers a B-plus student who played soccer and volleyball, always came home on time and did his homework.

Jindao's father looks down at the floor, his hands clasped, his big toes interlocked. "He helped around the house, he looked after the younger kids, and he was a very good listener."

His son's death left Yang immobilized at stop signs and red lights until the incessant honking of cars behind him jolted him into consciousness.

Some Hmong parents, at their wits' end over wayward children, are turning to a centuries-old solution: early marriage.

Freedom fighter Pa Vang, a social worker, tried everything else with his eldest daughter, who was skipping out of Burbank High and hanging with gangs. "I helped her play tennis, volleyball, soccer, but that didn't solve her problem," Vang says.

Luckily, Vang says, she fell in love. When Vang asked the family court for permission to marry off his 16-year-old daughter, the court counselor gave him a withering look. "She said, 'Mr. Vang, you are a social worker. Do you think this is a good role model?' " Vang replied, "'Let me ask you, what do you want: for her to marry a good guy or stay a gangbanger?' She said, 'I guess that answers my question.' "

To solve the Hmong crisis, law enforcement, city hall, school districts and the welfare system must hire more Hmong speakers, Xiong says.

"We are crying out for their help and yet they are denying us," he says. "A lot of kids are innocent but can't afford a lawyer and end up in a plea bargain. We need to work together or we're going to lose a whole generation of Hmong kids."

The new freedom fighters aren't waiting for city and

county officials to act.

At UC-Davis, there are now 100 Hmong students who have assumed the mantle of leadership for the next generation. They include future doctors, researchers and lawyers, and they understand that education comes first: Only a handful are married, and none has children. ("I've never even had a date," confesses one 20-year-old pre-med student.)

This spring, the UC-Davis Hmong Club held a day-long conference for more than 400 Hmong high school kids from throughout northern and central California. The conference, titled "Hmong: A New Direction," sought to meld pride in Hmong culture with the new realities of life in America.

In a fiery keynote speech, Steve Ly challenged the youngsters to get their parents to fill out census forms. "It's important for local officials to see we're 25,000 strong…Each person is a dollar value, used in building new schools."

Ly, a UC-Davis graduate who works with troubled youth, paid tribute to his parents' generation: "They have witnessed death and torture in all forms." But then he chastised them for treating women like second-class citizens, and for splitting into factions that hold competing Hmong New Year celebrations.

On the mountaintops of Laos, when the Hmong had exhausted a piece of land, each village asked for volunteers to find a fresh place to farm.

Just as the fate of the village rested with these pathfinders, Ly tells the future freedom fighters, "You are the Hmong community's pathfinders. Your job is to find the path to success and show the way for your younger brothers and sisters, cousins, parents and the Hmong people."

Hmong women building bridges

SEPTEMBER 11, 2000

In the back room of a south Sacramento welfare office, a quiet revolution is under way.

A dozen Hmong women sit around a table, eating strawberries and trying to solve the mounting problems facing Hmong families in America.

Tonight, they are learning how to say "I love you" to their children. While many American parents say "I love you" as often as "Good morning," few Hmong are comfortable with the expression—as if to say it would somehow devalue it.

Slowly, the crushing burden of Hmong womanhood unfolds. Debbie is missing tonight; no longer able to cope with her 10 children or the shame of her rumored affair, she has tried to hang herself. Meanwhile, three of Nue's four teenage sons are AWOL, and after 19 years, her arranged marriage is crumbling.

Though nearly every woman in the group is in the throes of a personal crisis, an aura of strength and optimism fills the room.

That confidence is embodied in May Ying Ly, the cherub-faced founder of Hmong Women's Heritage Association, which earlier this year received a $400,000 grant from the California Endowment to help troubled families—and to help Hmong elders bridge the generation gap.

Ly's sister-in-law Nue embodies the angst of Hmong women. At 31, Nue has six teenagers (including the three who are AWOL). "She takes care of everything, the dinner, the homework, the housecleaning, the parent-teacher meetings," Ly says. "Her husband never changed a diaper."

Some Hmong men consider Ly and her confederates heretics intent on dismantling male-dominated Hmong society. But the organization is fast becoming one of the most influential Hmong groups in California.

"Some of the women say life in America is scarier than running from the war in Laos," says Ly, 32.

Many Hmong women, including several in Ly's family, "are looking at their situation and they're taking off—or trying to," she says. "They're willing to give up everything, including their kids, to do what it takes to be happy."

Hmong men won't publicly criticize the group's Hmong-style feminism, but Ly suggests they're feeling a loss of control.

"There's more rights in this country and women take advantage of it," she says. "Hmong men are actually very nervous—they blame Hmong Women (Ly's association) because there is this problem and we want some voice…We have to combine what's positive from the old culture with what's good in this country."

Ly's life is a high-wire act between old and new. Her two daughters have American names—Mercedes and Candace; she named her son, now 9, Ntuj Tshiab (pronounced *Tdoo Che*), which means "New World" in Hmong. "So he'll always remember that he has to make a difference in the world," she says.

One weekend, Ly and her children pick strawberries on her mother's farm in Merced. The next, Ly and Mercedes, 11, fly to Las Vegas for a Backstreet Boys concert. Ly has held dinners honoring Hmong clan leaders—even though they are always men—and criticized the old Hmong guard for living in the past.

She peppers her English with "yada yada yadas," yet she's fluent enough in Hmong to be author Ann Fadiman's interpreter for *The Spirit Catches You and You Fall Down*, a nonfiction book about a sick Hmong child caught between cultures.

Up at 6:30 a.m. on a typical weekday, Ly makes rice, eggs and maple sausage for her family, then changes into SuperHmong.

From 9 to noon she teaches survival skills to Hmong women who know a thing or two about the subject. One 56-year-old grandmother says proudly, "I delivered all 12 of my babies by myself and never let their heads touch the ground."

Then Ly bounces from crisis to crisis.

She rushes to UC-Davis Medical Center to visit a pregnant 15-year-old in intensive care with pneumonia and a bladder infection. "The family was really traditional. They tied strings around their wrists for good luck and called in a midwife to massage away the sickness," she says later. The hospital "gave her some antibiotics and she's doing fine."

After that, she's on the trail of her nephews, Nue's sons, only one of whom showed up at school.

Two of them, enticed by Ly's promise of "delicious, delicious food" and a $5-a-day stipend, turn up at her evening survival skills for teens class. They and eight other youths learn how to find and keep a job, set goals, solve legal problems and deal calmly with the turmoil raging in their often crowded, chaotic homes.

The most anguished part of Ly's day is yet to come. That night and the next, Ly and her husband host emergency meetings of clan leaders.

Their objective: to save her sister-in-law's marriage.

Fed up with a spouse who shoots pool five nights a week while she scrambles after her sons, Nue is nearly at the end of her rope.

"I don't know what to do," she says. The vice principal at Burbank High School told her to stick around a couple of days a week, as some other Hmong mothers do, to make sure her sons get to class. "I can't do that," says Nue, who works for a children's advocacy group. "If I don't go to my job, they don't have food on the table."

She visited a Hmong fortune teller, who tried to sell her a $400 elixir guaranteed to keep her sons out of trouble. "She said if I put it on my lips and talk to my kids, they will listen."

Instead, Nue bought a $25 bottle of "magic" water. She poured it into five cups for her sons and husband. "They said, 'What's this for?' I said, 'Just drink it.'"

The water didn't do the trick, so Nue has been salting away money from her job to start a new life.

"There's nothing good in my marriage," she says. "He doesn't talk to me, and he's not a good father to my children...If I don't get out, I'll sink and drown."

The clan leaders order her husband, Joua, to start acting like one—less pool, more parenting. He says he'll try harder. "I'm short-tempered," he admits, but says Nue's acid tongue is partly to blame. "I do 60 percent right, but that's still not good enough for her."

A WAY OUT

Like many Hmong women her age, Nue played by the rules in Laos, only to find the game of life turned upside down in America.

When she was 6, her family landed in Santa Barbara. She'll never forget the humiliation of her first day of kindergarten: She was sent home because she wasn't wearing underpants beneath her skirt. "We don't wear underwear in Laos," she says.

Then her family moved in with a stepbrother in Orem, Utah. When she was 13, one of her stepbrother's soccer buddies, Joua, paid her stepsister a $20 bribe to get Nue out of the house for what Nue thought was a baby-sitting mission.

Instead, Joua and four male members of his clan grabbed her and put her in a van. Then Joua held her hand, announced he loved her and said he was going to marry her.

Nue knew girls were kidnapped into marriage in Laos, but couldn't believe this was happening to her in Utah. He was 22; she was a sixth-grader.

She cried, screamed and begged them to let her go. But Joua's mind was made up.

Joua didn't touch her, but he spent three days in the same room with her, making sure she didn't jump out the window. According to Hmong custom, if a girl spends three days in a man's home, even if there's no physical contact, she must marry him as long as he can pay the "bride price" set by her parents.

When Joua brought Nue back home, Nue's mother wept, then told her, "Just go and learn what you have to do to be a good wife, mother and daughter-in-law."

Joua bought Nue for $1,500.

"Why do you want to sell your daughter like an animal?" Nue says. "Every time you have a fight with your husband or your in-laws…they remind you how much they paid for you."

Wifenapping is slowly fading away in America. If a Hmong girl marries before her 18th birthday these days, it's usually because she's madly in love, pregnant or desperate to get out from under her mountain of chores.

But most clans still support arranged marriages, and most husbands are still expected to pay a bride price ranging from $6,000 to upwards of $10,000. Looks are less important than a woman's clan reputation, capacity for hard work and education—though some traditionalists accuse college-educated women of using their careers as a cover for extramarital affairs.

"My uncle married a woman with a master's degree in social work; her bride price was $25,000," Ly says.

The bride price serves as an insurance policy against bad wives and husbands. If a woman dishonors her husband, some clans give him a refund. And if your clan helps you pay the bride price, you'd better not do anything to shame them or you can forget about their help in the future.

Even in California, the pressure to go through with an arranged marriage can be enormous.

Nue didn't call the cops when she was kidnapped because, tired of picking up aluminum cans for pocket change, she saw marriage as a way out of her poverty-stricken family.

It took her about a month to fall in love with her husband. "He treated me right," she says. They had six children in rapid succession.

In Laos, each child meant another pair of hands to harvest crops, feed pigs, cook and clean. There was no birth control; even in America, many Hmong know little more than what their children learn in sex education. In Sacramento, there are Hmong families with as many as 14 children.

'I LOVE YOU'

About eight months after Nue's youngest child was born, she says her husband beat her up over $20—he admits striking her but says it was over $40—that had fallen out of his pocket.

"The minute I walked in he called me a thief," Nue says. "He slapped me, then he kicked me and I fell down. The next thing I remember I was in the hospital" with a ruptured spleen.

Much of her love died that day.

Joua begged forgiveness and paid Nue's mom a $1,000 fine. A Hmong who beats his wife can be fined $5,000 by her clan, which is refundable if he treats her lovingly for three years.

Joua, 41, is not one to hide the truth. "I blacked out, maybe," he says, between games of eight ball at the Jointed Cue, a billiard parlor on Fruitridge Road that became his nighttime sanctuary starting in 1986. "I got mad, stupid, whatever."

Joua twirls on a counter stool, his trademark toothpick clenched in his left cheek. A fellow pool player addresses him as "master." Here, he is a man to be respected.

Pool hall manager Carlos Muñoz says Joua used to hang out there all the time. "They only have one car. She'd want to go and he wouldn't give her the keys."

But since the clan's intervention two weeks earlier, Joua has cut back his pool habit to Tuesday nights, and then only with the permission of "the boss," Nue snarls playfully, as she leans over the rail and blasts the eight ball at the corner pocket.

Instead, Joua takes his kids to play soccer or basketball and tries to help them with their homework. There are no more nightly shouting matches.

"I'm trying to change a lot," Joua says. "I don't want her to go; I'm really worried about it."

On Mother's Day he took Nue out on the town and bought her a $300 Hmong outfit, imported from China, at the Hmong store on Stockton Boulevard. Back home, while the family watched a video of Hmong New Year's in Sacramento, two of Nue's children brought her a teddy bear and some flowers and told her they loved her.

Then Joua told her, "I love you, too."

"I only hear that once a year," Nue says. "It's very hard for us to say that word. It made me feel special."

Joua's new role model is his brother-in-law Pheng Ly, May Ying Ly's husband, who cooks and washes dishes.

Pheng and May Ying met in Merced. She was a nerdy high school junior; he was a community college student, "this cute guy in a red shirt who had already put a diamond engagement ring on my best friend's finger."

When Pheng's engagement fell through, May Ying consoled him. They married during her sophomore year at California State University-Sacramento. She went on to become a supervisor at the county welfare office, where she saw dozens of Hmong families caught between their desire to get off welfare and their dependence on Medi-Cal health insurance.

Ly says she owes much of her success to her late father, Cha Ly Xiong, one of the first Hmong school teachers in Laos.

On April 23, 1976, he brought his family from Thailand's Ban Vinai refugee camp—where Ly remembers watching many people sicken and die—to Honolulu.

Her father, who spoke English, had no trouble finding jobs as a social worker or interpreter in Hawaii, Orange County and Merced, where he was killed in a car accident when Ly was 16.

She says the only reason she hasn't been flayed for her feminism is because her father was a war hero whose memory still commands respect from the old "generals" who were leaders in Laos.

CLOSE-KNIT CLANS

Ly has reached out to members of the old guard, offering them a place in her center where they can talk free of distractions. She has challenged many of the old ways, yet she's a firm believer in the close-knit clan structure and its moral authority. "We don't have a word for cousins—it's brother or sister," she says, and clan elders are called "uncle."

But some clan leaders still have multiple wives, which Ly says undermines sexual equality. Gen. Vang Pao, the legendary Hmong leader who led the CIA's secret war in Laos from 1960 to 1975, took eight wives from the largest of the 18 Hmong clans. (In keeping with American law, he has since divorced all but one.)

In Laos, there were reasons for polygamy: When a man was killed in the war, his brother was duty-bound to marry his widow and raise his children.

But in Sacramento and Stockton, there are still Hmong men in their 20s and 30s with two or even three wives, much to Ly's chagrin. Some Hmong husbands threaten to get a second wife, and a few have actually recruited second wives in Laos.

Although early teen marriages and multiple wives aren't legal here, some Hmong couples avoid scrutiny by not registering with the courts.

Marriage remains the most sacred event in a Hmong's life. In Laos, divorce was rare. So was theft or spousal abuse because anyone who reflected badly on the clan quickly became an outcast.

But what worked for generations in Laos often breaks down in America. "This country is so big, people can hide their mistakes," Nue says. "There isn't that group pressure."

Many older Hmong think the "Land of the Free" is too free. They complain they can't force their children to go to school, or do their homework, or even come home at night. And many Hmong men feel that women, too, are abusing their freedom of choice.

Here, women realize they are free to sleep with and marry whom they choose. They are free to pursue jobs or an education. They are free to demand equal rights and to get out of a bad or loveless marriage.

The balance of power has shifted dramatically as young Hmong women do better in school—partly because their parents are stricter with them—and often are more likely to get and hold a job than their male counterparts.

"The women are very quick—they've learned a lot about this country," Ly says. "They take their kids to Cub Scouts, learn cooking, go to church. The Hmong men are the slowest to change and they're the ones who distrust the system the most."

Power struggles between Hmong men and women sometimes turn fatal. One of Ly's shell-shocked clients is Mai Thao, who was widowed in November when, after years of frustration and financial problems in America, her husband killed their five youngest children, then himself.

Ly has heard that some men blame the association for fomenting marital strife. But she and her members say the best way to save Hmong marriages is to break with the destructive patterns of the past.

For instance, association president Sia Thao makes her son and two daughters split the chores: "Nobody is going to be anybody's maid for life."

She says Hmong mothers are the glue that holds families together. But when it comes to raising children in America, she admits she doesn't know where to start, except to say, "I love you."

Because Hmong parents rarely show their love, many Hmong children feel unloved and unwanted,

Thao says. "Tell them every morning that you love them," Thao advises the women around the table. "It really works."

A HMONG MAVERICK

One recent Friday night, Ly and her husband unwind over a round of golf in Land Park. "Pheng's really good," she says. "It's too humiliating to keep score."

Ly returns home to a hysterical phone call from another relative whose husband has just tossed out all her clothes and told her to leave.

It's time to get out of the marriage, Ly tells her.

"She got married at 14, and her husband had an affair that lasted five years. When she found out, she was a veggie...The clan leaders lectured (him) for 2 1/2 days that he had shamed the family, yada yada yada, and told him if he left, he would be disowned by the clan."

Ly had already spent two sleepless nights at their house, making sure they didn't shoot each other. She even tried to slap some sense into the husband.

"He said 'It's none of your business.' I said, 'If your wife blows your brains out and her brains out, too, your kids become my kids.' "

Then Ly confronted the husband's mistress. "She said, 'I'm not a b____ who sleeps with other people's husbands.' I said, 'Hel-lo...' "

Saturday, after honing her medical interpreting skills at a workshop in Oakland, Ly takes her daughter Mercedes shopping for the latest teen foot fashion—black platform heels. Then the family dines out at a Vietnamese-Chinese restaurant.

After spending Sunday morning at her Mormon church, Ly plays her favorite song, "I Walk By Faith," on the piano. She and her daughter have been taking lessons, free of charge, from Sister Catherine Coleman, a member of Ly's church.

"I just play for myself when I feel really down," Ly says. It's not easy being a mom, a wife, a mentor, a marital counselor and a Hmong maverick. "I'm just afraid I might be doing too much."

Pheng Ly, a taciturn fellow, jokes that he's the *man* behind Hmong Women. A modern Hmong man, he takes pride in his wife's activism. "I love it," he says.

"I tell her, 'You do it, then I'll back you up.' "

As May Ying has evolved, so too has Pheng. "He said, 'I thought I was marrying somebody who was just going to be my wife and cook for me and my children— instead, you are *everything*!' " she says. "Having the respect of my husband is fuel for what I do."

Hmong teen builds future in two conflicting worlds

SEPTEMBER 12, 2000

Julie Chang showed off her moves at her first-ever teen dance, causing her first-ever breakup—all on the same wild night.

"This was the first time I went to a party in my whole life," says Chang, 16, her fingers combing raven locks that flow past her waist. "It was so fun."

She boogied to "Larger Than Life" by the Backstreet Boys that fateful May night, then was confronted by her jealous boyfriend, who didn't know how to fast dance.

"He said it's over. His friend was saying that I was dancing with other guys—those were my girlfriends! I was so mad, too. I didn't cry—I'm not the one who broke up, I didn't do anything wrong…I was saying forget it, he's too old anyway. He's 21."

Her words pour out like a mountain stream in May. It's all part of Julie Chang's grand American adventure. She's 4-foot-11 without her high-heeled Soda shoes, but larger than life—a diminutive dynamo who honors her ancient culture while embracing the raft of opportunities that have come her way in Sacramento.

Things other American teens take for granted are landmarks in Julie's life: She recently saw her first movie and dined at her first all-you-can-eat buffet.

The future of the Hmong will fall on the shoulders of hundreds of young people like her who straddle two worlds often at odds.

Balancing those worlds will challenge Julie in ways she can't imagine.

It's 5:30 a.m. in her family's mildewed Meadowview apartment. The aroma of fried hot dogs, green beans and fresh-steamed rice wafts from the kitchen. Even her father's prize fighting cock is asleep, but Julie has already showered, dressed and made breakfast for her family—14 in all, including nine younger brothers and a baby sister.

For her grandmother, afflicted with dizzy spells and high blood pressure, she has prepared a medicinal chicken soup. "It's part of my job," she says. "I'm proud of it."

She was up past midnight studying for a history test, but there's not a crease on her eager face, not a shadow under her mahogany eyes. She hems her black bell bottoms while a parade of bleary-eyed brothers emerges from the bedroom.

One by one, they hop onto giant 50-gallon water jars—left over from Y2K, when many Hmong thought the world would end—surrounding a small oval kitchen table, and devour breakfast.

Also in the kitchen are two 40-pound bags of rice, a neatly stacked pile of clean dishes Julie washed the night before, and a list of 50 phone numbers—all for members of the Chang clan.

Soon, the three-bedroom house returns to its normal chaos: children bouncing on the sofa and chasing one another around the living room, babies bawling, the phone ringing.

Gliding through this kinetic sea is Julie Chang, Burbank High sophomore, big sister, chief cook and wok washer, laundress, textile artist, tutor, interpreter and the shining hope of the Chang family.

"Sometimes I have so much to do, I don't have time to go to sleep," says Julie, who shares a bedroom with her five oldest brothers. "Last night, I slept on the sofa."

At 7:20 a.m., Julie's mom begins ferrying children to school in her red pickup. She drops Julie and her brother Meng, 15, at Luther Burbank High School.

More than 500 Hmong attend Burbank, making them the school's largest ethnic group. They shine on the chess team, the volleyball team, in student government and the math/science engineering academy. Burbank has its share of ethnic tension, but most Hmong mix easily with other kids.

Miraculously, Julie is managing a 3.5 GPA. She's also president of an Asian-American girls club, a regular at the Friday afternoon Hmong forum and the star of Xavier Young's "All Hmong, All The Time" language class.

A few months ago her father, who earns $900 a month washing rental cars at Sacramento International Airport, paid her the ultimate compliment: He bought her a computer.

The computer, now squeezed into her bedroom, "is helping a lot," Julie says. But she still has to wait for her brothers to fall asleep before she can concentrate. "They're so annoying, talking talking talking...

"I love my life and I'm very happy, but I wish I was a boy," she confides. "Girls do so much more work. I've been cooking since I was a little girl in the refugee camp."

CULTURE SHOCK

Until she came to Sacramento six years ago, Julie had never been beyond the barbed wire of the Thai refugee camp where she was born.

From the time she was 6, she and her mom embroidered Hmong story cloths known as *pa ndao* that tell the Hmong odyssey through pictures. Julie stitched stories of a war she'd never seen in a country she'd never visited, then sold them in the camp.

Her family was among the last wave of Hmong refugees to leave the camps. Her grandparents held out hope of returning to Laos to the last.

In 1994, armed only with her ABCs and 1-2-3's, she was thrust into the fifth grade at Freeport Elementary School. Her initial excitement turned to sorrow when the other Hmong girls in her class tired of translating for her. "I understood what they were talking about, but I couldn't say it back."

Her parents were struggling, too. They felt abandoned by her aunt, who had sponsored them in Sacramento, then moved to Minnesota. "My parents said, 'Why is she going over there? We came over here because of her.'"

Julie's a fast learner. She taught herself to read and write Hmong in two months and she's steadily mastering English. When her grandmother had surgery to remove a fist-sized growth on her back, Julie went to the hospital—a place she'd never been before—to translate.

"I cannot really translate from English to Hmong," she says. "There's no word for 'complicated' in Hmong."

And that, in a word, describes the Hmong predicament: America is a land of many belief systems, cultures and lifestyles, confusing newcomers who have lived by the same rules for centuries.

As the eldest daughter in a Hmong family, Julie

rarely has time for fun.

"Fun?" she does a double take. "I never have time to go play my sport, volleyball." In six years here, she has seen one movie, *Godzilla*, and then only on a field trip. She does watch Hmong videos and catches snatches of *Friends* on TV.

The other night, she awoke at 4 a.m. to finish *Sweet Valley High*, the latest in her diet of teen romance novels.

Even then, the house isn't always peaceful. Sometimes Julie can hear her 75-year-old grandmother, recently widowed, crying in the next room or listening to sad Hmong songs. Sometimes Julie reads while brushing her teeth.

Julie's brains, looks and work ethic have already generated several marriage proposals, including one from the guy who broke up with her at the dance.

"He still calls me every day," she says. "He says he's sorry, he wants another chance because it's hard to find a girl like me."

He comes over Saturday nights and talks of love, "but I'm not taking it seriously," she says. "I don't have time to date. Education is more important."

Her mother, Cheng Thao, begs Julie, "Don't get married early. You're the only one who can help me." It's Julie who helps her mom shop, Julie who helps her grandmother cash her SSI (Supplemental Security Income) check, Julie who explains the notes from school, Julie who plans her siblings' birthday parties.

But Julie and her mom both know that when a traditional Hmong girl marries is often beyond her control.

ORPHANS REBORN

Cheng Thao, 33, met her husband in the refugee camp in 1983. She was brushing her teeth when he claimed her. He softened her up with love talk, and three weeks later, they married.

She still waits for him to come home at 11:30 p.m. after eight hours of washing cars.

At 34, Chang Lor is a handsome, practical man in a black Nike cap. His family adores him. "My dad caught a sturgeon in the river," brags son Meng. "He can wash 30 cars in an hour."

Chang's a firm believer in shamanism, but he allows his sons to hedge their spiritual bets: They go to Christian Sunday school.

Still, he values his Hmong heritage enough to set aside $15 a week for flute lessons for his eldest sons, Meng and Tou.

Meng finds it boring, but Tou, 13, enjoys feeling the music vibrate through him. He takes his flute off the wall and plays one of the 11 tunes he's mastered, a song about orphans being reborn. It's a fitting metaphor for the Hmong, orphans of history being reborn in America.

Chang also has enrolled Meng and Tou in Hmong 2000, a paramilitary youth group that meets Tuesday and Thursday nights. He sent Julie, too, but she quit to concentrate on school.

Chang's father, Choua Neng Chang, was a soldier for 20 years and mayor of a mountaintop county of 20,000. He was renowned as a mediator, investigator and judge.

After Laos fell to the communists in 1975, Choua Neng Chang moved his family into the highlands and fought with the Hmong guerrillas.

In April 1981, the Changs and about 1,000 other Hmong lashed bamboo trees into rafts and fled across the Mekong River into Thailand. About half drowned in the crossing.

Julie's dad studied English for two years in Sacramento but still finds the language frustrating. He dreams of buying a home and seeing his children through college. He expects Julie to lead the way.

HMONG GIRLS DOING WELL

Like Julie, half of the Hmong girls at Burbank have B averages or better, compared with 40 percent of the boys, says principal Kathleen Whelan. Only 25 girls—10 percent—have less than C averages, compared with 23 percent of the boys.

The disparity can be traced to the culture—while boys are often allowed to go out and play with their friends and roam the streets, Hmong parents keep a much tighter rein on their daughters, says Mai Xi Lee, a Hmong counselor at Burbank. "For a lot of girls, school is their only outlet."

Still, the girls' success is remarkable given their responsibilities at home, Lee says.

Julie's brother Meng, who also maintains a B-plus average, does vacuum, wash some dishes and make a few meals. But little is expected of their younger brothers.

Lee calls Julie "your typical Hmong girl but more so. Not only is she an obedient daughter who knows her duties quite well, she also knows American culture well enough to do well in school so she can be successful at whatever she wants to do."

Julie handles her many roles with grace and pride, partly because she was raised in an all-Hmong environment that offered no choice, and because her parents are wise enough to nourish her dreams.

But some of Julie's Hmong peers at Burbank, especially those born in America, find it harder to balance both worlds.

"I'm going through the struggle right now," says Mary Xiong, a freckle-faced senior who won a scholarship to St. Mary's College in Moraga. She says that when she becomes the Hmong Oprah, her first talk show topic will be "Double Lives of Hmong Youth."

Sometimes her parents support her desire to pursue a career. "Then, they'll give me lectures: 'You're getting old. You'll be 18 soon. When are you going to marry your boyfriend?'"

Traditional Hmong girls aren't allowed to date, partly because some Hmong parents believe their daughters will be kidnapped into marriage or their suitors will spike their drinks with a magic potion to turn them into love slaves.

If a Hmong boy breaks up with a Hmong girl after several months, he may have to pay her parents a fine, even if there was no physical contact.

Mary, yearbook editor and president of the Hmong club, says at 13 she was ready to marry her first crush, but thankfully he backed off. She says her aunt wasn't so lucky: "She got married last summer at 18...Now she's pregnant and divorced."

Mary swears she won't get married until she's 30 or 40. Julie says she wants to wait at least until she has finished college. But despite the pitfalls of early marriage, counselor Lee estimates as many as 60 Hmong girls at

Burbank—more than one in five—are already married. Some became wives at 14.

JULIE'S DREAMS

At the Friday afternoon Hmong Forum led by Hmong teacher Xavier Young, Julie and other students open up about how hard it is to reconcile their modern American dreams with the expectations of their old world parents.

"The only time I can talk to my dad is when we're eating dinner," says one girl. "I'd like to talk to him about education, but I'm just embarrassed."

Yee Xiong, 17, lost two older brothers in the secret war in Laos. But when he asks about the war, "My dad just walks away or turns the TV louder...it's just too painful to talk about."

Young, one of nearly 40 Hmong teachers who have been hired by the Sacramento City Unified School District in recent years, appreciates how hard it is for Hmong kids and parents to know one another.

"A lot of our students are hitting the same wall over and over again," he says, "but at the same time, a lot of these students are going to come back and lead us whether they like it or not."

He's counting on Julie to become one of those leaders.

After a long day of French adjectives, Bolshevik history, probability, anatomy and Hmong language, Julie presides over a meeting of the all-girl She Club.

Today the club, which deals with everything from leadership skills to breast cancer, is preparing a dance performance.

Julie shows a sextet of Asian-American girls how to gracefully twirl their hands and move their feet to a haunting Hmong love song. The song is about the first stages of a breakup (moral: You'll feel the heartache later).

At 5 p.m., her mother drives her home, where anarchy reigns. Meng has pulled out a hunk of frozen mystery meat from the freezer. He's hacking it up for dinner, stopping now and then to attend to a crying baby. The other kids draw with colored markers, watch TV or chase one another around the house.

Julie takes over, cooking a dinner that's not unlike the breakfast she made 14 hours earlier.

It's not until Saturday afternoon that she's able to steal a few moments for herself in the cool confines of the library a few blocks from her home. She asks the librarians to help her research how to become a registered nurse, a teacher, a scientist.

Tears shine in Julie's eyes when she thinks of Laos, the country that has shaped so much of her life, even though she has never even been there. "We don't have a country of our own," she laments.

But she's making America her own and says she's impatient to join the new wave of Hmong leaders. "I feel like I want to be in college, right there, right now," she says. "It seems so incredible to make my dreams come true."

But Julie's blueprint for life in America was about to change dramatically.

'IT'S TOO LATE'

After Julie came home from summer school at the end of July, her cousin showed up to fix her computer. He brought with him Kou Vue, a 17-year-old boy Julie met about a year ago at a meeting of Hmong 2000, the paramilitary youth group.

The computer fixed, the three of them got into Kou's car. But Kou dropped off Julie's cousin first, then told Julie he planned to marry her.

She was shocked: "We never went out; he just came to visit me. We never actually talked about love."

What happened next was even more of a shock.

Kou, a junior at Florin High, took Julie to his home, where all his relatives were waiting for her. As they walked through the front door, a shaman swirled a live chicken over their heads—a traditional Hmong ceremony marking the start of the marriage.

The next day, Julie's mother called and offered to take her home.

"No," said Julie. "It's too late." In Hmong culture, she knows, leaving once you've been claimed by a boy can ruin your reputation for life.

"He's a nice guy, you'll have a nice future," her mother responded.

Julie felt scared, confused and excited all at once. She likes Kou, and says she went with him of her own free will. Yet she knows little about him except that he gets good grades and everybody thinks he's nice. And, she says, he has promised to support her dream of going to college.

A bride price was set—$6,400—and the wedding took place Aug. 4 at her parents' home.

"I feel so bad for myself," Julie said during her third day in Kou's house—the day the Hmong believe a bride's fate is sealed. "I shouldn't have come with him that day. Before this, I told the whole world I didn't want to get married."

But, like a million Hmong girls before her, she's resigned to her fate: "Everyone regrets it after we get married," she says. "But I think he loves me, so I will stay with him."

Hmong refugee makes bittersweet pilgrimage

DECEMBER 31, 2000

VIENTIANE, Laos—Conflicting images burn through T.T. Vang's brain as he flies over the mountains of his native Laos.

He sees the land where he was born and raised, the land where his father bled to death, unable to get help while his village was under communist siege.

He sees himself riding horses "like a little Mongol, a little cowboy," carefree and wild. He sees a handmade bomb wrapped in barbed wire explode in his face, leaving him deaf for a year. He sees his nephew blown in half by a communist rocket barely two yards away.

"From the sky, my country looks beautiful, but 25 years ago it was destroyed by something terrible," he says.

Tsong Tong Vang, T.T. for short, is one of an estimated 10,000 American Hmong who returned home this year flush with hard-earned dollars and visions of a pre-war Shangri-La.

He's carrying a dozen envelopes containing $5,000 from friends in Sacramento, to dispense to their relatives in Laos who make as little as $50 a year.

Like most Hmong refugees, severed from their roots and relatives when the communist Pathet Lao took over in 1975, Vang has unfinished business in Laos. Eight years ago, he was denied permission to visit his father's grave and his birthplace, a village that grazes the sky.

This time, he hopes to make it home.

In Sacramento, Vang is a man accustomed to success: travel agent by day, security guard by night, chairman of his Hmong Catholic Church and host of a daily radio show, *Hmong New Life*, whose callers reveal how life in America has changed them.

He also is a husband and father of nine bilingual children—two sons and seven daughters.

Vang looks older than his 46 years, his face creased with laugh lines that overlay wrinkles of hardship and tragedy. He fled Laos in September 1975. His memory is still seared by images of a hellish eight-day trek across leech-infested mountains and jungles into Thailand.

As his plane descends toward the capital of Vientiane, Vang gazes down on the murky, mercurial Mekong River—where thousands of Hmong drowned trying to escape to Thailand—and wonders whether he will be treated like a spy.

He knows his clan name, Vang, is the most distrusted of all. The legendary Gen. Vang Pao led the CIA's secret Hmong army against the communists from 1961 to 1975. He remains on the Lao government's "Most Wanted" list for heading the Hmong resistance from his Southern California headquarters.

T.T. Vang knows his name could get him kicked out of the country. That's what happened to Nhia Chou Vang, a West Sacramento security guard who saved for years to visit his sister in 1999, only to be booted out the day after his arrival by Lao police for serving in Vang Pao's army 25 years ago.

The name Vang might also get you killed. That's presumably what happened to Michael Vang of Fresno, who mysteriously vanished while crossing the Mekong into Laos in February 1999. His disappearance triggered congressional investigations, stalled the appointment of a new U.S. ambassador to Vientiane, and delayed most-favored-nation status for Laos.

This year has been particularly tense for any visitors to Laos. Bombs have gone off at a restaurant, a hotel, and at the Vientiane airport.

* * *

As soon as his feet touch Lao soil, T.T. Vang wonders whether he's finally welcome. He muses about running for office in Laos someday, and certainly looks the part in his white dress shirt, pleated French pants, smooth leather jacket and tasseled loafers. His fine reddish-blond hair—a trait of a full-blooded Hmong—is perfectly coifed.

"I could become a congressman, but I'd have to move back to Laos and be reborn again," he says, adding that he's been reborn three times already: first, as a Catholic student in the ancient royal capital of Luang Prabang; then, as a medic and translator in Thailand after the war; and again, as a U.S. citizen.

Vang's pro-Lao reverie is shattered by customs officials, who detain him and about 20 other Hmong and Mien Americans for an hour, rummaging through every piece of their luggage.

While white Americans breeze through unquestioned, Vang must fork over $100 to Lao customs for his still camera and video camera. He angrily blames the discrimination on jealousy and suspicion.

He acknowledges, however, that plenty of Hmong in America do support the Hmong resistance in Laos. In March, Thai border agents arrested two gun-toting Hmong brothers from Sacramento who were trying to cross the Mekong into Laos.

In Vientiane, a city of some 540,000 with Internet cafes alongside ancient temples, Vang pays $6.50 to broadcast on Hmong radio. He lets relatives in the north know of his impending arrival.

Then, he visits an old Hmong friend, whose husband was killed in 1975 when his shovel hit a cluster bomb the size of a tennis ball. It was one of thousands of UXOs (unexploded ordnance) dropped by U.S. planes on Laos.

That bomb made his friend a widow and a hard-core communist. Dozens of Lao still lose limbs and lives to the UXOs every year.

A talkative, worldly man, Vang seems no more than three degrees of separation from any Hmong in the United States or in Laos. Hmong communists, royalists, rebels, shamans, priests—Vang knows them all, including some who have given up on America and moved back to Southeast Asia.

Vang's first cousin fled Merced with several other Hmong families for Hmong villages in Thailand because they were having trouble with their teenagers and thought America would be destroyed in Y2K. They believe the Hmong messiah will lead them to Laos, Vang says.

So far, few American Hmong have returned to Laos permanently. Among those are outcasts, outlaws or lotharios searching for second wives or mistresses, said one United Nations observer.

Even law-abiding American Hmong in Laos keep

low profiles to minimize "the death threats (from anti-communist Hmong in the U.S.) that surface any time someone has anything to do with Laos," said the observer.

But some younger Hmong Americans enjoy being in the spotlight in Laos. At his hotel, Vang meets the Twin Stars, a touring Hmong soccer team from Minneapolis-St. Paul.

Soccer has long been the national sport, and in the morning market in Vientiane, Vang sees a Hmong boy crying and begging his mother for a soccer ball. Vang buys him the ball for $6—more than a week's pay in Laos, one of the poorest places on the planet.

The largest unit of currency, the 5,000-kip note, is worth 60 cents, and the government's stated goal is to raise per-capita income to $400 a year.

The typical Hmong family makes only about $50 a year if they're farmers, maybe $120 if their wives and daughters make *pa ndao*, the colorful needlework for which the Hmong are famous.

* * *

Travel in Laos is dicey at best. Lao Aviation, the only airline, doesn't meet international safety standards. Accidents are so frequent that its motto is "Every Passenger Insured."

Driving can be dangerous, too. The Japanese government, for instance, won't let its employees make the seven-hour drive north from Vientiane to the old capital of Luang Prabang for fear they'll be kidnapped or robbed.

Vang chooses to fly to Luang Prabang, tucked between two rivers and the mountains of north-central Laos. Except for some clouds literally hovering inside the cabin, the 45-minute flight is smooth.

He is greeted at the airport by his cousin, Li Phone Vang, who heard Vang's radio message and rode his motorbike for eight hours over decaying roads to see him.

Vang gets a far chillier reception at his hotel in Luang Prabang: The desk clerk immediately takes his passport to the police station.

"What about my fellow Americans?" Vang asks, referring to *The Bee* reporter and photographer. He's told police require returning Hmong to register "for security reasons."

He's visibly stung, but soon he's strolling through "Luang'bang," as the city is known, reliving the good times. He passes the old downtown theater where he saw his first movies—Chinese kung fu flicks and Indian romances. He saw his first textbooks as a 12-year-old first-grader at a nearby public boarding school.

It was in 1965, two years after his father's death, that Vang's older brother moved the family to Luang'bang.

"If we'd stayed in my father's village, I'd be dead," Vang says. Four of his brothers died there of cholera, malaria or yellow fever.

* * *

Hiring taxis, Vang visits a series of Hmong villages south of Luang'bang, where he lived as a teenager.

At the first village, he hands out 10 envelopes, each containing at least $100, sent by his deacon in Sacramento.

Ten women weep for joy—the money will buy clothes, furniture and cookware. It's obvious which Hmong have relatives in America—they're the families with new homes, TVs and meat on the table.

The deacon's mother-in-law asks about her daughter in Sacramento, who she's heard has lost interest in her marriage. She asks about her grandson, whose wife took their infant son and ran away with another man.

In village after village, the Hmong never tire of hearing about marital problems in America.

Ancient Hmong marriage customs have changed in Laos, too. Vang's cousin, a city councilman, says that in 1995 the Lao government passed laws restricting the Hmong to one wife and outlawing "wifenapping," the practice of kidnapping a future wife.

The anti-bigamy law has improved Hmong marriages, the councilman says, because wives "don't worry about being replaced."

Vang also gets an earful about the government crackdown on opium, a cash crop that nets Hmong farmers as much as $1,000 a year.

The government has promised to help the Hmong grow replacement crops, but too often that help does not materialize.

Vang meets a Hmong *tuk tuk* (taxi) driver who studied economics in Russia only to see all the good jobs go to his lowland Lao classmates.

"Lao democracy is a total fraud," the driver says. "They use the Hmong name to get international funding, but the funding doesn't get to the Hmong."

Still, the roughly 400,000 Hmong in Laos, population 5.4 million, are better off than the other ethnic tribes. Besides help from the States and opium sales, they sell their traditional *pa ndao* needlework. At one market, Vang sees a Lao woman sewing *pa ndao*. It turns out she's working for the Hmong.

One of T.T. Vang's relatives, 13-year-old Tia Yang, sews *pa ndao* from dawn to dusk.

"I really want to go to school—I'd like to become a nurse someday—but my parents won't let me," she confides. "Uniforms and schoolbooks cost too much."

Before 1975, more than 90 percent of the Hmong were illiterate, says Ministry of Foreign Affairs official Sisavath Khamsaly, who like other Hmong in government has taken a lowland Lao name. Now, Khamsaly says, 60 percent can read and write.

But few Hmong make it past the third grade, Vang says. And many parents would rather put their daughters to work than send them to school.

Vang went to elementary school in a city 20 miles south of Luang'bang, walking six miles home every weekend to help work on his family's farm.

He attended school with his nephew Yeng Pao Vang, who at 16 was the pride of the Hmong—"He was better than the Lao students. He wanted to be a doctor or a pilot," Vang says.

But by 1973, the Hmong general, Vang Pao, was arming schoolboys.

"We were playing soldier—we didn't realize the danger. That's why so many got wiped out," T.T. Vang recalls.

At a hill just south of Xieng Ngeun city, Vang asks the driver to stop. "I was wounded right here," he says. "The communists attacked at 3 a.m. Dec. 3, 1973. My nephew was killed right there—his body was buried next to that tree."

Vang fled to a Buddhist temple, his head bleeding badly, his hearing gone. Thanks to a French doctor, he regained his hearing after a year.

* * *

Vang heads to the provincial capital of Udomxai, where in 1992 officials turned him back, telling him it was "unsafe" to visit his old village.

About 45 minutes outside the town, Vang's driver lurches around a mountain curve and nearly runs into a rogue elephant. Later they learn that the elephant had attacked its master that morning, putting him in the hospital.

The elephant is an apt metaphor for Laos, which for centuries called itself the "Kingdom of a Million Elephants."

Elephants, like the Lao government, are hard to figure. Laotians joke that the Lao PDR stands for "please don't rush," not Peoples' Democratic Republic. This may explain why Laos isn't brutally totalitarian, but it also explains why it takes years to build roads, schools and health facilities.

At breakfast the next morning, Vang's hands shake so much he can barely drink his coffee as he steels himself for the visit to the provincial authorities. After a tense, two-hour wait, they give him the necessary papers, and the bumpy, six-hour odyssey to his village begins.

Each pockmarked mile brings Vang closer to his traditional Hmong youth.

He points out the value of plants along the road: Elephant grass is used to make pillows and mattresses, mountain grass makes the best roof, and French grass is good medicine. A few years ago, when his daughter's menstrual flow wouldn't stop, a relative sent him some French grass roots to make a tea that cured her.

Though a devout Catholic, Vang swears by the saga of Chou Xia Lor, the Hmong Tiger Man. In the 1950s Lor, a magician, would change from a man to a tiger and back by putting a bamboo basket over his head.

"This Tiger Man kidnapped shamans, beautiful ladies and children and turned them into followers," Vang says, adding that two of his childhood friends were taken by the Tiger Man.

The pickup truck Vang has hired hits a rock and stops. Vang and four relatives jump out and disappear down an overgrown jungle path.

"I've waited almost 36 years for this," says Vang, his voice full of excitement and sadness. He leads the way through briars and branches to a large, overgrown earthen mound.

This is the final resting place of Wa Chia Vang, farmer, horseman, humanitarian and T.T.'s dad.

Wa Chia, founder of the village of Ban Mai where T.T. was born, taught his people how to farm, build and treat each other kindly. He grew opium, like other Hmong, but never smoked or drank. He raised village orphans as his own.

T.T. Vang stands by the grave and weeps.

"My dad picked this place out. He asked to face the rising sun—the Hmong feel the rising sun has the power to raise the dead," Vang says.

Vang places wild French grass flowers and a photo of his mother, who died in 1998, on his father's grave. "She's the best flower of all," he says.

* * *

Finally, Vang arrives in Ban Mai, a village time forgot until two years ago, when an international labor organization paid 150 villagers $1.80 a day to shovel out a crude road.

The village is a collection of 72 thatched huts between mountains planted with rice and purple and white opium poppies. It has no school, no plumbing, no electricity, no medical or dental care. Old superstitions died hard: A snake or a bird in the house is bad luck, but a cockroach is welcome because it means there's plenty of food.

Vang is received like a returning hero.

Several villagers his age burst into sobs at the sight of him, then nestle in his arms like small children. They are some of the orphans Vang's father took in. Everyone calls him grandfather, out of respect.

Still, they can't resist testing him. They hand him a stick of sugar cane and a Hmong knife to see if he can still handle himself. Vang skins the cane beautifully.

Vang stays in his village for three days, grousing about the cold nights and the hard bamboo bed. Two soldiers shadow him, and a police officer sleeps by his side.

One afternoon, after a feast of buffalo and wild pig, Vang seems to forget these hardships and more: the year a plague of grasshoppers destroyed the rice crop, or the year the rats devoured it.

"If you work hard, God provides everything—water from the spring, firewood, roofing, fresh air, and night music from the owls, birds and insects," he says.

"Let my wife know I'm not coming back. I'll just build a house on top of the mountain. Each of my children will send me $50 a month, and I'll have a good life. If democracy comes here, I'm pretty sure I'm going to run for Congress."

But his wristwatch gives him away—he hasn't reset it since he left Sacramento. "I'm never going to change my watch to Lao time," he says with a faint smile.

A week later, Vang is back in Sacramento.

Writers' Workshop

Talking Point:

1) Magagnini says he has the green light to write with authority about Sacramento's many cultures. How does that help his storytelling? What are the risks of assuming that kind of voice?

2) Quotes should move a story from one place to another, reveal personality and character, add spice or punctuation to a point, or otherwise advance what the reader knows and understands. Do the quotes in these stories measure up? How?

3) Note the way Magagnini shows while he tells, rarely allowing generalities to suffice. Where are those details most effective in helping the reader see what he sees?

4) Conflicting images woven together can create a powerful force to move the reader through a story. Read the first three paragraphs of "Hmong Refugee Makes Bittersweet Pilgrimage." Talk about how those images affect your interest in T.T. Vang's story.

5) It's important in reporting on undercovered groups, especially immigrants, that journalists tell their stories in the context of history. What have you learned about Hmong who have been displaced?

6) "Orphans of History," like many projects centering on immigrant cultures, highlights difference. In the story about Julie Chang, for example, Magagnini sheds light on the practice of kidnapping girls for marriage. How does a journalist avoid making cultures seem weird while reporting on traits very different from the American experience? Do you think Magagnini accomplished this feat?

Assignment Desk

1) To gain access to his stories, Magagnini builds sources and uses "guides" to lead him through the Hmong community. Identify an immigrant group in your community that has not received much media attention. Make a list of places you might go to begin building sources for reporting on that group.

2) Build a history of the newest immigrant groups in your area. What brought them to the United States? How long have they been in the community? What are the current issues in their homeland?

3) Find a "listening post" in an undercovered community, a place where a journalist might go to meet people and learn about the issues affecting those who live there. Read the walls. Talk to people. Then write about what you notice, using the sorts of details Magagnini employs in his stories.

4) Magagnini uses similes to help the reader relate to what he is seeing, hearing, touching, or experiencing. He says, for example, that Julie Chang's "words pour out like a mountain stream." Write a series of similes that capture what you find at the listening post.

5) After your visit, write a personal essay reflecting on the place, the people, the culture, and the ways it all might be different from your life.

A conversation with
Stephen Magagnini

KEITH WOODS: Let me start by asking you what kind of access you were able to establish for getting into a community that is culturally closed and has the additional obstacle of language as a barrier.

STEPHEN MAGAGNINI: This, like many things I work on, was a long incubation process. I became interested in the Hmong as far back as 1992 and started writing some stories dealing with Hmong refugees as early as '93. My philosophy on the beat has been to tell stories that explain and, perhaps, entertain rather than focusing on what we call the "minority bad news story of the week." After writing many of these stories, I knew the time was coming to address some of the very, very hard problems in the Hmong community that were not going away over time, such as the gang problem and the consequences of early marriage. So I had my antenna out for a vehicle to delve into those sensitive areas. I would go to a range of Hmong events. I heard about the Hmong Women's Heritage Association, for example, shortly after they began to really crank up, and I started going to a few of their meetings more than a year before this series was published. I didn't know what I wanted to do with that story, but I knew that sooner or later I wanted to write about this revolutionary organization.

Also, about 15 months before publication, my mentor, K.W. Lee, told me about this family who had three sons who were in prison for separate gang murders. It sounded like such a tragedy, but also such a powerful vehicle to tell the consequences of kids who start dropping out of school and drifting into gangs. And so he and I went out and met that family, and there was a college-aged young woman there who served as the translator between me and her parents and some of her other relatives.

So Lee has access himself?

He had met this family and he told me about it. Once I meet a Hmong family, I know enough about the culture and the history that it becomes quickly apparent and it helps put people at ease. And what I've found is in almost every family there is going to be a teen-ager or a young adult who is bilingual and can serve as a translator between himself/herself and the parents and myself. Now if that's not the case, I know enough Hmong advocates in the community who are willing to come with me to conduct interviews in folks' homes, and I never count on getting all my information in just one interview. I interviewed the Thao family that had three sons in prison. After that initial interview through their daughter, Pai, I returned numerous times with several different Hmong advocates I know from community service organizations and just folks I know in town who were very competent in both English and Hmong. Sometimes I'd come by without anybody and just chat and try to make do with the dad who spoke a little broken English. I must have gone to their home at least 15 or 20 times over the course of that 15 months from the initial interview.

The interview follows a period when you were attending the meetings of the women's association?

I had already attended one of those meetings and I continued to attend them up until the time the story was published. And I would do Hmong stories along the way, so I had a very large bank of Hmong sources.

What sorts of stories were you doing?

In '94 I did a project on Hmong and Iu-mien shamans and the conflict that they were coming into with Western medicine. That project was well-received. In the year previous to the series, I wrote a piece about Hmong who had turned to Christianity and how that was affecting the culture, because Christianity is pretty much directly at odds with traditional shamanism. I tried very hard to do balanced stories so that everybody felt they were getting a fair shake in the paper. I also wrote about Hmong who had been displaced from a fairly hazardous enclave called Nedra Court, where conditions were very unsanitary and the wiring was faulty. The refugees who arrived there had come not in the late '70s or early '80s like most Hmong refugees, but had come in the mid-'90s and really did not have a clue about how to adjust to American culture. They were burning wood right in their fireplaces to keep warm because they didn't know how to turn the heat on, or there wasn't any heat left in these apartments. The other thing that had been happening in the Hmong community, both in Sacramento and nationwide, was family tragedies where husbands and wives became increasingly frustrated with their lives here and committed acts of violence. In Sacramento there was a Hmong man who had seven children, and I guess the level of frustration with his life and his relationship with his wife got to the point where he snapped, and he killed five of his children and himself.

This happened when, Steve?

That happened in late 1999. So knowing the Hmong Women's Heritage Association, I was able to go with May Ying, who was the head of the association, to a home in Stockton where the widow and the two surviving sons were living and conduct a very long and gut-wrenching interview with her. These sorts of acts of violence have happened in Hmong communities around America. They've happened in Minnesota. I believe it's happened in the South where Hmong have resettled, and there are certainly episodes along those lines in Fresno. So as I got deeper into it, I saw that there were a lot of different things going on that needed to be looked at besides law enforcement and gangs, and so that's how the general idea for the series began to take shape.

Who were you working in collaboration with and what is the task of selling these ideas and this coverage structure to your editor?

Well, to get the dispensation to go and spend time with the Thao family and to look at the whole gang issue, I went to my editor, at that time Deborah Anderluh, and she was able to persuade the managing editor, Joyce Terhaar, that this was an important undertaking. And as

I got deeper into this, I gave Anderluh the head's up that there was more to this story than just a gang story. I guess they trusted me enough based on my conversation with them to let me look at the big picture. Getting permission to look into something and getting permission to take up acres in the newspaper are often two different things.

So what happened was I knew the first day was going to be the Thao family. Then in my search for teens I went to Burbank High School. I'd been to Burbank High School anyway because Jer Thao, the youngest Thao brother who was the kid I called the "Where's Waldo" of the Sacramento Unified School District, had supposedly been at that school. While there, I found out that there was a Hmong forum that was held on Friday afternoons, and so I went. While I was there, the kids were talking about their struggles with their parents and assimilation, and one girl said, "Well, you know, I didn't get any sleep last night because I was up all night doing homework. And I got to get up in the morning and do this and that and the other thing." That was Julie. So I began to develop a relationship with her and her family, and it turned out her younger brothers were going about a half a mile away to take flute lessons from this Hmong flute teacher. And so I thought to myself, that sounds kind of interesting. Maybe it'll be just a sidebar, a 15- or 20-inch sidebar for this story.

I went over to the flute teacher's house. He had a son who had a radio program and he was well-educated. As I got to know that family, I saw that this flute teacher and shaman was a really exceptional person and he would be the best person to tell the story of the elders. He had made adjustments in his world view and approach to meet the changing needs of Hmong in America. And for all the Hmong parents who by the dozens told me they couldn't discipline their kids without hitting them, and therefore had lost control, here was a guy who managed to raise his children pretty much in the heart of gang territory, with guns going off on the street outside his home, without ever laying a hand on them. So he was the perfect person to honor the elders and honor the culture, while at the same time, serving as an example for other elders who may have been resistant to the realities of life

in America. As far as the man-woman thing, I finally settled upon May Ying, whom I'd known for years.

You've known her how, Steve?

Well, I owe my wife for that. This goes way back to
1993 when Colleen was at the farmer's market and she
came across an old Hmong woman selling *pa ndao*,
which are the Hmong embroideries, and she said, "Can
we see some of your other work?" So we made an appointment to go meet her at her daughter's house and
her daughter turned out to be May Ying, who I could tell
was this dynamic individual. She was in the process of
helping New York writer Ann Fadiman write a book
about a Hmong child who was born with various birth
defects. The book is *The Spirit Catches You and You
Fall Down*. May Ying at that point was familiar with
journalists and she was pretty much fully bilingual and
bicultural. And what's intriguing about this is I could
tell that she was a special person. I did not know that
much about Hmong culture when I first met her. I knew
things, but every time I go to another Hmong event, I
learn something new. There are so many layers to this
onion.

**Beyond this serendipitous web that you've followed
through the years, what other ways did you get to
know things?**

Well, prior to this series, I would say that I'd written 70
stories, large and small, about the Hmong. Almost every
time I'd do a story, I would go to people's homes and I
would have them tell me their own stories. This is a very
basic interviewing tool. Whenever I'm going to get involved in sensitive personal questions, I always start out
chronologically and get people to tell me their life story.
And I've learned that if you're going to do an interview
with somebody about very personal stuff, very often
none of the good stuff comes out until you've been there
for at least 45 minutes or an hour. So I would go in these
homes and I would have the parents tell me their life
story, and often the teen-age kids would be hearing
these stories for the first time. By having them tell me

their story, I would learn their experiences and I would also honor them.

By listening?

By listening and by taking it down. Often they would tell me these stories that their own kids either had never asked them about or they'd never volunteered to tell, and that was a wonderful springboard into more sensitive subjects. Early on, I began to read books about the Secret War, and I kept hearing about the legendary Hmong general Vang Pao, who's sort of the Hmong George Washington, and so I wanted to do a profile of Vang Pao. I spent about six or seven months tracking Vang Pao. Finally, again through my various Hmong sources—in this case sources at Lao Family Community Center, which is a group whose board includes Hmong elders and veterans from the Secret War—I was able to get an invitation to a Hmong wedding in Sacramento where Vang Pao and one of his wives showed up. I got my chance to talk to him for about 15 or 20 minutes at that wedding. And then he came through town again to solve some of the Hmongs' insurance problems.

What happens is the Hmong are so poor that they have their own community insurance people who would collect money and then, if somebody died, the money would help pay for these very, very expensive funerals they had. One of the stories I had done was about the funeral of the father of one of my very first Hmong sources, whom I'd met at the trial of a Cambodian guy who had killed a Cambodian businessman. The translator at the trial was this very smart Hmong guy who spoke Cambodian and Hmong and some Vietnamese. His father, predictably, was a major Hmong leader in California, and when his father died, I covered that funeral. The funeral lasted for about four days and I began to see the importance of the flute player in the culture, so all these things get etched in my brain.

You are frequently turning relationships from "guide" and "source" to the subject of a story. Is that tricky?

That's an interesting point. In the case of the translator whose father died, clearly the father was someone who was honored by Hmong throughout America. I felt that on the merits, this man's father was a worthwhile story. And I think it was important for the readers of *The Sacramento Bee* to see what a Hmong funeral was like. There were issues about how this huge funeral home in the south area was taken over by refugees who had slaughtered animals for their ceremonies, so that was a story that needed to be done. All I can say is that when I chose to write about May Ying, whom I'd known for a long time, in my heart I knew that I was approaching these stories as fairly and as thoroughly as possible. So I think that I can say that the people I chose to write about were legitimate stories in their own right.

I'm wondering if you have to explain yourself to people? Take May Ying, for example, who went from being someone who was talking to you constantly but didn't wind up in a story to suddenly being the subject of the story.

That was sensitive, and May Ying had mixed feelings about that. Not because of any personal relationship she had with me. She was conflicted between wanting these critical issues to be aired, such as the consequences of early marriage, and not wanting to step on toes in the community by becoming the spotlight herself. Presciently, that's what happened, and the first reaction to the series was, "Who does May Ying think she is?" and "She's airing our dirty laundry, and she got this guy to write this story or she wrote the story herself." She became this lightning rod for many Hmong who don't read or speak English but had heard about the story through word of mouth and were calling into Hmong radio shows and basically threatening her in some cases.

Well, in the Hmong culture there is a price to be paid for stepping out and appearing to turn against the clan or against the culture, isn't there?

There is, and I guess the saving grace for May Ying was that even her most fervent critics who had read the series acknowledged that everything she said was true and everything in the series was true, but "we didn't like the way it came out and it should have been presented more diplomatically."

You talked about reading the books on the Secret War. There was a day, I imagine, back in 1993 or before, when you didn't know anything about the Hmong. Take me through the earliest learning. What did you do to bone up?

I had heard a little bit about the Hmong and maybe we had one or two stories in the late '80s, and it just struck me as this fascinating culture that was very complex and rich and yet was at odds with American mainstream culture. There was a case in the late '80s of a young Caucasian girl named Candi Talarico who was kidnapped with a little Iu-mien girl, Meuy Han Saefong, and all the stories focused on Candi. But after Candi and Meuy were finally freed by this abductor who was caught, Meuy's family sacrificed a cow to the spirits, thanking them for the return of their daughter. That was part of the bargain: The shaman called up the ancestral spirits and said, "If you return this little girl, we will sacrifice a cow to you." Another reporter wrote that story, and I found that fascinating.

Then I went off on an Asian studies fellowship in Hawaii through the Freedom Forum. I made a point of going to the library, where I found a videotape about a Hmong family in Chicago, and I remember watching that. And so as far back as early '92, I subconsciously knew I was going to start writing stories about this culture and these new Americans.

What's your beat called?

It's the ethnic affairs and race relations beat. I sometimes refer to myself as the "Rainbow Writer." My mentor, K.W. Lee, calls me Marco Polo. I kind of like that. But what happened was that after I had done this for about a year or so, they pretty much let me set the tone. So the good news is that 98 percent of what I do is self-generated. The bad news is every time I go out there,

I'm pretty much operating without a net, since it's not the editor's idea. I would say that at least several days each week are spent laying groundwork.

And is the newspaper patient with you when you are doing that kind of thing?

Yes, they are, because on my beat there is very little breaking news. Now if there is some breaking news, fortunately I'm well enough sourced so that I can deliver the goods, and I'll give you an example: There was a young Korean woman, about 25, an immigrant who was gunned down in front of her father's auto mechanic shop one night. We had our predictable police story on it, but I knew enough Korean Americans in their community that I was able to find out what church she belonged to. I went to the church service for her that night, and the next day was the memorial service. I went back to the church, and the Korean immigrant priest gave a powerful speech in Korean, and I was able to get a transcript. Then I sat down with a Korean-American college professor, who happened to be there, to translate it. There were some very powerful revelations about "How could this happen in this country?" and "How can America call itself free when it allows this to happen?" I was able to get a very, very poignant story about a family of immigrants who had basically left Los Angeles after the riots to find a more peaceful life in Sacramento, only to lose their daughter in this act of violence.

Then it turns out that a couple of Ukrainian refugees were arrested in the murder, and through my source in the Ukrainian community I was able to go out and interview the family of one of the young men who was arrested and get that story. And so after seven years on this beat, if there's any sort of crime or tragedy or breaking news involving virtually any ethnic community in Sacramento, there are people who I have a pre-existing relationship with.

Throughout the story there are sentences where you say, "In Hmong culture…," and "Like many Hmong fathers…," and "Like many Hmong, they became Christians." You state with some voice of authority

that there is something Hmong about this. Talk to me about using an authoritative voice.

Well, my editors very much wanted me to do that because I guess they trust my knowledge of this subject. Every declarative statement that you read in that series probably comes from the result of 100 or 200 interviews that support those declarations. The two things that my editors wanted me to do—and they want me to do this with whatever I'm writing about if they think I know what I'm talking about—is to write with an authoritative voice and, in the case of this series, to tell narratives. I guess I'm lucky in that respect. I don't know how many other reporters are given the green light to tell it like it is—or like we think it is.

One concern that I would have as a writer making those kinds of statements would be that somehow I would make something Hmong that's male or that's female or something Hmong that's American or universal or human. Did that worry you at any point?

Sometimes there are things that are both Hmong and American. That happens at various points in the series where there are issues among Hmong that are not just Hmong issues and have happened in other cultures. I think what makes it more acute is this: I don't know too many other immigrant cultures where men or women are killing themselves or each other or their children as a result of those issues. And that's what made it important to focus on. Not that the gender struggle or even the generation gap is unique to the Hmong. But in terms of the consequences on a culture, I have never quite seen these consequences. Because you've got, again, universal immigrant and refugee issues combined with very specific and unique cultural issues, and those two things together form this incredibly powerful and sometimes deadly brew that has made their assimilation so singularly tough.

You make really wonderful use of detail in the stories, specifics that really helped to take an idea and turn it into something very concrete for the reader.

You say, "Three days after he landed in America in 1976, he went to work on an Alabama assembly line, making lawn mowers for $2.75 an hour. He processed chickens in Arkansas, stitched upholstery in Kansas and cut mushrooms in Utah." In another place, you say, "Most came here with no idea how to turn on a faucet, a thermostat or a stove, no notion of the joy of soaking in a hot bath."

How does that work as you're thinking about the writing?

I want you to feel the reality of these people's lives, so when I talk to people, I want to try as best as I can to put myself in their minds and their experiences. So much of this is cumulative knowledge from six or seven years of reporting, where I've seen case after case of folks who were just paralyzed by the smallest detail of American culture. And that's probably why my heart goes out to them so much. I have talked to Hmong families who have lived in apartments and never taken a bath because nobody ever showed them how to take a bath, even if there was a bath. So I try to have my eyes open and I try to make a point of writing down the details while I'm there, which is why I had 17 notebooks for this project.

How do you tell a story like this that includes girls getting married off at 13 and 14, a mother who uses magic water to try to keep her son in line, the inclusion of shamans in the culture, all without appearing to laugh at the culture?

I've been very conscious about not bringing some sort of paternalistic bias to my stories. This goes back to something that happened in '94. I met a young Hmong woman who was a college student at Sacramento State. She had been married at 15. She was now 21, divorced, had a 6-year-old kid, and was in college. I met her through the Hmong Club at Sac State. She came down to the *Bee* one day and she was complaining about a story that had been in the *Los Angeles Times* that dealt with early marriage. So I called up the story and she sat next to me and we scrolled through the *L.A. Times* story and she ripped this story apart, paragraph by paragraph.

Now, I was not predisposed to writing the way this reporter was writing to begin with, but she underscored various phrases and things that tended to portray the culture as this oddity, as this freak show. "Look at the funny refugees" kind of thing. And although I was intuitively sensitive about that to begin with, having her take apart this other reporter's story really hit home for me the importance of tone and approach. My whole deal is—and that's why K.W. calls me Marco Polo—that I am just fascinated with these different cultures and their belief systems that have worked for centuries and millennia, long before America was ever discovered by the Europeans. And there must have been aspects about this culture and belief system that were working for it to have survived through all the Diaspora and the holocaust over the centuries, and so that's pretty much the tone that I take.

Steve, I don't find a wasted quote in any story, and I want to know what you're thinking about when you're trying to decide which ones to use and what role you're asking the quotes to take in the stories?

I very much want to let people of different cultures, immigrants, and refugees speak in their own words, and a lot of these words are translations, although a lot of them aren't. So when there are quotes that I feel really ring true to the bone, then I want to go with those quotes.

What does that mean when you say "ring true to the bone"?

That it basically is their authentic voice from their heart. When I'm writing about people whose voices never appear in the newspaper, I want to give them the benefit of the doubt and try to let them say it.

What has surprised you about putting together this package?

I'll tell you what shocked the hell out of me is what happened to Julie Chang. This is where the gods conspire to make something happen. Julie Chang was supposed to be my uplifting end of the series. Here's this young woman of 16 who basically is the perfect bridge between American culture and Hmong culture. She honors her culture. She's proud of her family. She's proud of her role in the family. She respects her parents. She does all this work, and yet she embraces American culture and all that it has to offer, and she's in these clubs and she's just kind of doing it all—a great beacon of hope and inspiration for the coming generation. And throughout my time with her—both at her home and at school—she talked repeatedly about how she's got this guy, and they broke up, but she doesn't really want to get married anyway right now because she wants to go to college. I called her up—this must have been in late July—just to see how she was doing, and she said, "Oh, everything's fine."

So on Tuesday morning (photojournalist) Ann Williams comes up to me and says, "I just called Julie's house and Julie got married." I said, "Well, that's impossible. I just talked to Julie Sunday night. She didn't say anything about any marriage coming up." The whole newsroom is kind of watching this conversation. And so I get on the phone right away and I called Julie's younger brother Ming and I said, "What's this? Did Julie get married?" Yeah, well, Julie sort of got married. "Sort of got married?"

So we drove out to Julie's house and she explained to me all of what had happened. It was a very, very dicey interview 'cause it's taking place at her fiancé's home. And here I am trying to stay within the bounds of being a reporter, but at one point I couldn't help myself, and I said, "Well, you say you don't really know this guy and you know that if you wait till you're 18 and finish school —and you still love him—it'd be okay to get married then," which ended up getting us disinvited from the wedding, basically.

I'll tell you the most powerful thing it did was underscore why we were doing this whole series in the first place. The pull of the culture is just so strong that even a young woman who has resolved not to follow in the footsteps of a million Hmong women before her and jeopardize her future and her self-development fell into the same thing.

Your description of people throughout the series was spare. You describe someone as cherub-faced, for example. You describe someone as having long hair and someone else as having the "reddish-blond hair—a trait of a full-blooded Hmong."

Any thinking going on about how you're going to handle the descriptive pieces?

Well, this goes to the fundamental rule of good journalism, which is: Don't describe someone or an aspect of someone unless there's a very good reason to do so. And that pretty much ruled my writing in this. The other thing is, the less description you provide, the more you can allow the reader to get into the souls and the hearts and the minds of the people you're writing about. I think too much description diminishes the spiritual and internal aspects of a person. On the other hand, there are times when a description is just so apt in describing a person's character. When I describe May Ying as cherub-faced and you see the picture, she is kind of cherub-faced. But it also talks about how—maybe this is my own subjective judgment—she's kind of this angel in the community.

You sprinkle history throughout the story. When you're including history, is there anything conscious about why you're doing it and how you're doing it?

One of the most important things that we need to do as journalists is explain to our readers why things happen and what consequences have brought the new Americans here. When the Hmong—and the Iu-mien as well—first arrived here, they were killing and roasting animals in their yards and they were banging on gongs and they were living in filth, by our standards. They couldn't really communicate. They couldn't read. They had huge welfare rates. They had kids who were in gangs. And there was a lot of negative reaction. "Who the hell are these people? What the hell are they doing here? And can't they learn the language? And can't they get a job? And why do we have to support them and why don't they go back to where they came from?"

It has been really important for me to explain that they really are orphans of history, and we have played a role in that. We have cost them in large part their home-land, certainly the ones who fought with the CIA. The readers need to understand that a lot of times these folks are very heroic and have sacrificed their lives and their families for an American cause, for our self-imposed view of what is right, of justice. And they are the ones paying the price. I think that when readers, even those who tend to be more conservative and tend to maybe have some bias against immigrants, read that, they are able to view the Hmong and the Iu-mien in a new light with a new level of respect and, hopefully, compassion. So in every Hmong or Iu-mien story I do, I make a reference to their role in history.

Did your editors need to know anything about this group in order to help you?

(Editor) Amy Pyle had been a reporter in Fresno and had been to a Hmong refugee camp, so she did know about the group and was excited about it, and that was helpful. Deborah Anderluh, who has been my editor for several years and has edited quite a few Hmong stories, also knew a fair amount about the group.

Mostly from you?

From me and, in Anderluh's case, totally from me. This project could not have happened had the *Bee* not allowed me to pursue it over 15 months and literally hundreds of interviews. Fortunately, I was able to write 50 or 60 or 80 or 90 stories a year while I was reporting this. But the editors were supportive of this project and my vision for the project. And when I told them this was more than just a gang story and was about a whole society imploding, and how this was emblematic of the problems the Hmong were having throughout America, they said, "Go for it."

The Atlanta Journal-Constitution

Mark Bixler

Finalist, Diversity Writing

Mark Bixler has reported for *The Atlanta Journal-Constitution* since 1997.
He covered crime in suburban Atlanta
before beginning to write about immigrants and immigration in 1999. He got an English degree from the University
of Georgia and began his career in 1992 in a one-person
bureau of the *Winston-Salem Journal* in the North Carolina
mountains. He covered county government and crime in
Winston-Salem before moving to Atlanta.

Bixler combines exhaustive reporting and cinematic
detail to portray the largely invisible world of immigrants from the same hometowns who cluster in apartment buildings and trailer parks in Georgia. His portrait
introduces readers to people facing tough choices on
both sides of the border.

Coming to Georgia, Day 2:
The village left behind

NOVEMBER 20, 2000

VILLA JUAREZ, Mexico—Sofia Izaguirre steps out of the shade of her grocery store and into the sunlight of a September afternoon. She puts her hands on her hips and stares at vacant houses with low-slung roofs on Zaragoza Street. Then she turns her head to the left and squints down another street to see three teen-age girls on bicycles, far off, cycling toward her like figures in a silent film.

It's so quiet she can hear herself breathe, so quiet she can hear the distant clank of a hammer striking metal blocks away. The echo ricochets off crumbling adobe walls and shoots down dirt roads the color of coffee with too much milk. Then it fades and silence returns.

Here in Villa Juarez, a town like a thousand others in the middle of Mexico, the strongest impulse is the urge to leave. More than half the town—about 5,000 people—has left over the years to go to the United States.

Especially eager to leave are young and middle-age men who say they can't find jobs in their hometown that pay enough to support a family.

"People in every house have relatives in the United States," says Izaguirre, 43.

Immigrants from Villa Juarez used to go to California, Illinois or Texas.

Now many of them go to metro Atlanta.

They share houses and apartments and shop at a Hispanic grocery store on Roswell Road where the owner is from Villa Juarez and the cashier once led the town's government.

The store is named *La Carreta*—the Cart—after the wooden carts that almost every townsperson's grandfather drove into corn fields years ago, before drought and recession made Villa Juarez a place to escape.

Izaguirre's husband, Fernando, has lived in Marietta since 1989.

It is his telephone call that summons her back into the shade of her store on this September afternoon. They talk on the phone several times a week but see each other only in December and January, when Fernando returns to celebrate Christmas and New Year's with his family. They've lived apart like this, connected only by telephone lines, for 12 of their 21 years of marriage.

Sofia inquires after him politely and picks up a pen. Fernando has wired money to a nearby bank and he is telling her how to pick it up.

"How much?" she asks.

A pause.

"Two hundred thirteen?"

This is a weekly ritual for hundreds of women in Villa Juarez with husbands, brothers or fathers in the United States. They depend on money sent from what they call *El Otro Lado*—the Other Side—to put food on the table and shoes on the children. They also use it for luxuries like pickup trucks or satellite TVs.

Sofia—pronounce her last name "Eee - sa - gyere"—runs a store that is smaller than most two-car garages in metro Atlanta. She sells sweet bread, tostadas and Modelo beer along with Gatorade, Coca-Cola and Tang, but has so few customers that she spends huge chunks of her day in her house, which adjoins the store. She'll watch television, wash clothes or cook dinner while listening for the footsteps of an approaching customer.

Izaguirre says the store earns about $2,600 a year, hardly enough to support the three children at home—a fourth got married and moved to Houston. There's no way on her salary alone that she could have bought the light gray sofa and matching chair in her living room or the satellite dish that brings 102 channels into the house. No way she could have built a green concrete house and stocked it with six televisions and four VCRs, a glass coffee table and a ceiling fan and a grandfather clock.

"We have bought all this purely with money from over there," she says.

Look around Villa Juarez and you see she's not alone.

Across Independence Street from Izaguirre's store is a parked blue van with Georgia license plates, one of dozens of cars or trucks in Villa Juarez with plates from metro Atlanta. Most of the owners have made the 26-hour drive from Georgia to visit friends and relatives.

Others visit in cars with plates from California, Texas and Illinois. You also see plates from Iowa, Nebraska and North Carolina, places that, like Georgia, began attracting thousands of Hispanics in the 1990s.

Young men in Villa Juarez look with envy at the visitors. Several dozen leave town each year, sometimes before they finish high school, to work in an American city where friends or relatives from Villa Juarez give them a place to live and help them find a job.

It's a classic immigration pattern that has transplanted thousands of villages and towns from five or six states in the middle of Mexico to places around the United States.

There were a few job openings in Villa Juarez this year, when the local government built a highway, but work is winding down and the pay was not so great to begin with. Some men still work the fields, but not nearly as many as decades ago, and fewer still since machines made the harvest that much easier for farmers.

Workers earn up to $8 a day in the fields, compared with at least $80 a day in Marietta, said Jose Manuel Rosas Garcia, a 28-year-old who runs the Villa Juarez government. He spent two years working in a garage in Chicago, and six of his eight siblings live in the United States, including one in Decatur.

About 150 jobs will come to Villa Juarez when a clothes factory opens soon, but Garcia said it won't be enough to stem the annual flow north. The population of Villa Juarez and surrounding villages has gone down 16 percent since 1995, from 12,734 to 10,951, according to the Mexican government.

It's a place where one in five people is illiterate and 45 percent of people older than 15 did not finish elementary school. Two in five houses have dirt floors and lack electricity. Some of the poorest live on a patch of dirt surrounded by vast fields of corn about 10 miles from Sofia Izaguirre's house. She goes there on a Tuesday afternoon tour of the land around her hometown.

STRUGGLING TO SURVIVE

She rides in her father's pickup truck down a straight, flat, dusty road that ends just beyond empty corn silos and a railroad track that bisects the fields like a river.

She steps out of her truck and walks toward a ramshackle hut where 35-year-old Apalonia Asua sweeps dirt floors with a broom made of twigs tied together. The hut has two bedrooms and an open-air kitchen. A double bed with a sagging mattress dominates one room. An 8-inch black-and-white television wired to a car battery takes up a shelf on the wall near a shrine of candles and flowers to St. Gertrudis, patron saint of Villa Juarez.

The walls are made of sticks and concrete blocks and corrugated tin. A thatched roof blocks sunlight but cannot keep out the water when it rains.

"Sometimes they eat and sometimes they don't because there isn't enough money," Izaguirre says.

Asua's children, dressed in rags and caked in dirt, drift past the tub where she soaks clothes in muddy water. They amble toward an outhouse with walls of cactus and rotting wooden planks. Two mangy dogs bark and growl, but most keep quiet in beds of dust they have made for themselves in the shade.

Camilo Vasquez, a 12-year-old who shares this desolate corner of Mexico with about 50 relatives, dreams of crossing to the Other Side "to maintain the family."

"I don't have anything," he says.

Macario Vasquez also thinks about leaving. He is a 23-year-old father of three who makes bricks for about $7 a day. "The passage costs a lot," he says.

By which he means that many men from Villa Juarez pay about $1,500 to a guide to lead them across the American border in violation of U.S. immigration law. Immigrants already in the United States often lend money that friends and relatives need to make the trip, a practice that is draining Villa Juarez of its youth. "The majority of the young people are over there," Garcia, the Villa Juarez official, says.

Many of them return one month a year.

"Right now it's a ghost town, it's very quiet, but during December, there's a lot of people," says Raquel Perales, 25, a Villa Juarez native who lives in Decatur and returned to her hometown for a visit in September. "It's like a custom, you know? That all the people from Villa Juarez come here in December."

DECEMBER WEDDINGS

For men who have saved money in Marietta, December in Villa Juarez is the ideal time and place to find a bride. So many men and women get married then that the town's only reception hall is booked most days of the month. Some of the new wives stay in Villa Juarez when their husbands venture north. Others move to the United States.

"Every day you're down at the hall because there's a wedding almost every day," says Perales, who came to Atlanta after she married her husband, Francisco.

December also is one of only two months that Sofia Izaguirre's children, ages 8, 15 and 18, see their father. January is the other month.

"At first it was hard," she says. "Now I'm used to living alone."

She and her husband have lived apart since Fernando Izaguirre decided in 1988 to stake his family's future on work in the United States. One neighbor told him about husbands and cousins who earned $5 an hour working restaurant and landscaping jobs in Dallas and Chicago. Another said her relatives earned $6 an hour in metro Atlanta. Izaguirre's cousin was in Atlanta, too, and that settled it.

Douglas Massey, a sociologist at the University of Pennsylvania who has studied migration between Mexico and the United States for 20 years, says immigrants like Izaguirre typically go where a friend or relative can help them find a job and a place to live.

"They go where he is," Massey says. "That's where he can provide housing and an entrée into the community."

Izaguirre, a portly 41-year-old with the mischievous grin of a boy, got settled in metro Atlanta in 1988 with the help of a cousin who grew up in a house on Zaragoza Street, within sight of the house where his wife still lives. Izaguirre moved into a house in Grant Park with his cousin, and a friend from Villa Juarez helped him get a job framing houses.

A year later, he moved into an apartment on Lake Drive in Marietta with six other men from his hometown. He got a job at Los Reyes, a Mexican restaurant near U.S. 41 and Roswell Road. The owner is one of the seven men from Villa Juarez who discovered Marietta after the Chicago container company where they worked transferred them to an Atlanta factory 30 years ago.

HELPING FRIENDS

Marcelo Reyes opened the restaurant in 1979 and brought friends and relatives to Marietta to staff it and other restaurants he later opened. So many relatives from Villa Juarez followed him into business that they now employ 1,500 people in several businesses. They own 11 Mexican restaurants in metro Atlanta and three in North Carolina and Virginia. They also own a tortilla factory in Marietta with warehouses in Alabama, North Carolina and Indiana.

For a year or so, Izaguirre bused tables at Los Reyes for $300 a week until a friend from his hometown lined him up with a landscaping job that paid $350 a week. He got his current job thanks to a fellow from Villa Juarez whose uncle was one of the seven men transferred from Chicago. He makes $450 a week tending to New Jersey mustard greens and Washington state rhubarb in the produce section of a Marietta supermarket.

About half his paycheck goes home to Sofia and the children, but he has set aside several thousand dollars over the years to lift townsmen out of poverty just as his cousin helped him. Izaguirre said the men were eager to join him after they heard him talk about the "magnificent" salaries that await men who are willing to work.

"I told them that there was a lot of work here in Marietta," he said.

He lent each man about $1,500 to help pay the costs of getting to the United States. He also helped them get jobs at Reyes' tortilla factory, in an industrial park two miles north of the Big Chicken. Each man repaid Izaguirre. Then they encouraged people back home to come to Marietta.

"You bring someone and then they bring someone else. That's how it works," says Jose Ramirez Reyes, son of Marcelo Reyes.

Meanwhile, some of the men who inspired a culture of emigration by leaving Villa Juarez in the '50s and '60s have finally come home. They are elderly men with faces of leather who pass their days staring out onto empty streets. Some survive on pensions sent from former employers on the Other Side, but it's unclear how many of the sons and grandsons who followed them north will also follow them back.

Fernando Izaguirre is vague about the future.

He talks half-heartedly about wanting his wife and children to join him in Marietta. In the next breath he says he's thinking about returning to Villa Juarez to open a second grocery store. Maybe he'll do that in two or three years. Then again, he says, the store his wife runs isn't doing so well. Maybe he'll stay in Marietta a few more years.

Lessons Learned

BY MARK BIXLER

The idea for a series on Latinos coming to Georgia first took shape in the booth of a restaurant near Atlanta. I went there one day with an immigrant from the middle of Mexico and nodded as he sketched a map on a place-mat between us. He said immigrants from his home-town used to go to California, Illinois, or Texas. Now they follow brothers and cousins to specific neighbor-hoods in Georgia, creating transplanted Latin American towns in the heart of the American South.

Penetrating those worlds would require lots of re-search and help from people like the man who drew that map. It also would require time and support from my editor.

First I read some academic studies about immigration and a book or two about Latinos in the United States. Then for the next two months, I asked dozens of Hispan-ics whether they knew of places where immigrants from the same town had clustered in a mobile-home park or apartment complex. They did. After several weeks of nosing around, I typed up a proposal and showed it to my editor. She gave me the go-ahead for a three-day series so long as I kept writing daily stories.

It was a long-term project that came together only with help from two behind-the-scenes guides—informal experts who showed me around and provided entrée into communities that might otherwise remain largely invisi-ble. One guide was a Hispanic preacher. He let me at-tend Thursday night Bible study in a trailer park that is home to 200 people from the same corner of Mexico. He introduced me to a young man who became the focus of the first installment of my series.

The other guide was the restaurant mapmaker, a man who led the local government in Villa Juarez, Mexico, population 4,000 and falling fast, before moving to Georgia to work as a grocery store clerk. He introduced me to several of about 500 townsmen in a city north of Atlanta. And I coordinated my travel plans so I would be in Villa Juarez the same week he was there. He introduced me to person after person whose dreams of a better life involved relatives in a place called Georgia.

By the time the reporting was done, I had interviewed about 100 people in nine or 10 months. Beat reporters rarely get so much time unless they tackle a project in chunks—one interview here, another there. My editors did not come up with the idea for these stories, so they were not clamoring for copy. That gave me time to produce something of substance. It also reminded me that reporters can find time for meaningful stories by taking a long-term, low-key approach. Work on your big idea a few hours at a time and your editors might not lump it with all your other stories and demand it for the next day's paper.

As for the writing, it is hard to overstate the importance of revision. Few writers nail it the first time around, and the best ones share drafts with writers they trust and keep themselves open to suggestions. I rewrote the story reprinted here three or four times because the first few drafts just did not convey a sense of place. At my editor's urging, I rearranged the story to tell it through the eyes of a woman whose husband works in metro Atlanta. We focused on the wife even though a photographer and I had spent hours and hours with her husband in Georgia.

Her story opens like a movie. If the approach worked, readers should see her stepping from shade into sunlight. They should squint with her down dirt roads the color of coffee with too much milk and hear the clank of a hammer striking metal several blocks away. And they should gain an understanding of the distant forces that are suddenly diversifying neighborhoods around Georgia.

Stephen Henderson
Editorial Writing

Stephen Henderson, 29, is a Detroit native and a 1992 graduate of the University of Michigan, where he served as editorial page editor of the *Michigan Daily*.

Henderson has worked as an editorial writer for the *Lexington Herald-Leader* and the *Detroit Free Press* and as a reporter for the *Free Press*, the *Chicago Tribune,* and the Baltimore *Sun*. Since July 1999, he has served as associate editor of *The Sun*'s editorial page.

Henderson's journalistic endeavors have almost always inspired positive change in the communities where he has worked. A 1993 editorial series in Lexington forced local schools to confront (and subsequently alter) policies that denied equal educational opportunities to black and poor children. His investigations into corruption in the Detroit schools won the removal of the school board president and the resignations of two other board members, and helped lay the groundwork for massive reforms. And his yearlong chronicle of 27 Baltimore first-graders learning to read brought citywide changes in classroom instruction.

His current editorial project on Maryland's death penalty has already inspired the removal of one inmate from death row, and aspires to force a re-examination of capital punishment statewide.

Henderson's work has been honored with more than 10 national awards, including National Headliner awards for editorial writing and public service; the Education Writers Association's first prize for editorial writing and grand prize for distinguished reporting; the Sigma Delta Chi Award for public service; and the Pew Charitable Trust's James K. Batten Award for public service.

Henderson lives in Baltimore with his wife, Christine Kloostra.

—Karen Dunlap

O'Malley's pettiness shines through again

JANUARY 5, 2000

Now comes Martin O'Malley, taking his place in the pitiful queue of Baltimore mayors who have thought small and acted smaller with regard to city schools.

Mr. O'Malley has wasted no time using his school board appointive power to exact petty political revenge. He booted board member Edward J. Brody last week— basically because Mr. Brody worked vigorously on the mayoral campaign of Carl Stokes, one of Mr. O'Malley's chief rivals.

It wasn't possible to work with Mr. Brody, Mr. O'Malley said. Too much political history. Too many bad feelings.

Huh? Are we back in third grade on the playground?

Some advice for His Honor: Grow up. There's a reason they don't let kids be mayors.

The mayor's action might be more defensible if Mr. Brody were a slouch on the board. He's not.

On a board where everyone boasts some expertise and shoulders the work of five people (pro bono), Mr. Brody is a standout.

Mr. Brody, founder of one of the city's largest trucking companies, brings a business sense to school matters. He engineered many of the labor negotiations that yielded concessions from city teachers. He led the search for the schools' chief executive.

It wasn't uncommon for Mr. Brody—like other members—to spend upward of 30 hours a week working on school matters. Even if Mr. O'Malley finds an executive with Mr. Brody's experience to replace him, how likely is he to unearth one who will give so freely of his or her time?

Mr. O'Malley made his tantrum even more juvenile by leveling absurd accusations that Mr. Brody had something to do with literature on zero tolerance that called him a racist during the campaign.

Of course, Mr. O'Malley offers no proof. But on the playground, who needs proof? The bully always gets his way.

This isn't the first time Mr. O'Malley has shown himself to be more petulant than mayoral. He offered departing police Commissioner Thomas C. Frazier a foot in the rear on his way out. And as a member of the City Council, he built a reputation for making sure his "enemies" got what he thought was coming to them.

The school system doesn't need a mayor like that. Neither does the rest of the city. If Mr. O'Malley can't see past political vendettas and act in the best interests of the people and institutions that can help save Baltimore, we're in for a rocky administration.

Taking over
Baltimore schools

FEBRUARY 3, 2000

It's not the children. It never was.

Years of low test scores, hopelessness and frustration in Baltimore's public schools aren't the product of defective or dumb kids. They're about principals and teachers who don't do their jobs, and a system that has repeatedly adopted and ditched curricula. They're the fruit of a community that has woven a pitiful tapestry of excuses for its refusal to gird and nurture public education.

It's not the children who are failing; it's everyone else.

So getting everyone else out of the way to "reconstitute" the three worst city elementary schools makes sense. Drastic as it may seem to clean house and turn these schools over to private companies, the State Board of Education had no obvious alternatives.

The three schools that will be re-made—Furman L. Templeton, Montebello and Gilmore elementaries—have been on the state's list of low performers for four years. They've had a measure of help from the state's reconstitution program and, more important, they've benefitted like every other city school from the system-wide reforms of the last three years.

But where are their test scores? No fifth-graders at Templeton posted satisfactory scores on the Maryland School Performance and Assessment tests last year, capping a three-year decline in that school's scores. Only a handful of third- or fifth-graders at the other two schools met the standard.

No one should believe these schools haven't had sufficient time to show improvement. And the state—already under fire for not making good on its threats to reconstitute persistently failing schools—had no more time to waste.

The trick will be to make sure that the three private interests that want to run these elementaries can actually deliver on their promises. Two of them—Edison and

Mosaica Inc.—have decent track records running schools elsewhere. The third, Kennedy Krieger Institute, has only managed a special education school before.

No private operator should be let off a tight leash. Results—not excuses—are what the state should accept from these companies.

It's not the children who are failing. It never was. Now that state officials are taking responsibility for the three worst city schools, any future failures will be theirs.

A silence that kills

MARCH 19, 2000

Keep quiet, Baltimore.

Keep quiet about the 4,000 recidivists who run city streets, committing crimes with increasing bravado and little fear of punishment. Keep quiet when probable murderers slap hands and embrace in court after they walk free.

Say nothing about a police department that can't solve more than half the 300 city murders each year. Or homicide detectives who trash important evidence before trials. Or prosecutors and judges who can't or won't stop the delays that so often set criminals free.

Keep quiet, Baltimore, because you've got other things to think about. Like the upcoming baseball season. Or which weekends you'll spend in Ocean City this summer.

Keep quiet if you will, but know that your silence and your lack of outrage over the pathetic state of this city's criminal justice system make you an accomplice to the mayhem. Your silence kills.

These are *your* courts. They're *your* cops. They're *your* judges and *your* prosecutors. Until you stand up, tell them you've had enough and demand a system that works for citizens instead of criminals, the nonsense will continue.

Thugs will walk the streets undeterred—maybe in your neighborhood. They'll rob and rape and kill—maybe they'll do it to people you know. And the slow rot that's eating at this city's core will become a ravenous decay, leaving no neighborhood untouched, no life unscarred.

How much more will it take for the city to raise its collective voice in protest?

When will Baltimoreans shout, like the television anchor in the 1976 movie *Network* suggested: "We're mad as hell and we're not going to take it anymore!"

At *The Sun*, we're already there. For more than a year, we've been writing (in editorials and news stories) about the continuing violence and how screwed up justice has become in Baltimore. We've pleaded with the governor, the mayor, the state's attorney, the chief judge of the Court of Appeals and others to fix it.

We've advocated changes in the city prosecutor's office, which is overworked and understaffed but also suffers from a lack of direction and an unacceptable level of incompetence.

We've pushed for reform at the city's Central Booking and Intake Center, where the absence of a judge to hear bail reviews has helped to clog the system with frivolous cases.

We've asked city and state officials to shelve their turf squabbles in favor of a unified approach to curbing the city's crime epidemic.

Some of what we've suggested has been enacted: The prosecutor's office will get more attorneys, prosecutors took over charging of criminals from the police department and the police department's rotation policy has ended, among other developments. A Criminal Justice Coordinating Council has been resurrected.

But much more has to be done. State's Attorney Patricia C. Jessamy still offers more excuses than answers or solutions to her office's pitiful performance. Judges who make upwards of $103,000 (some as much as $110,000) a year still roll their eyes at the mere suggestion of weekend or holiday duty at the clogged Central Booking facility. And despite Mayor Martin O'Malley's election on a platform of "zero-tolerance" of criminals, thugs still know that justice is a joke in Baltimore.

Just ask Jay Anderson, William Harrison and Stacey Wilson. That trio walked last week—for the second time —on charges they murdered Shawn L. Suggs in 1995.

The case against them seemed promising when it was filed five years ago, but what happened in the intervening time made it easy for the defendants to beat the charges.

Prosecutors, judges and defense attorneys delayed the trial 12 times between 1995 and 1999, which violated the defendants' right to speedy justice. So in 1999, a Circuit Court judge threw out the charges.

An appellate court later reinstated the charges and ordered the defendants to stand trial. But by then one

key witness was dead and another—a heroin addict—
had changed her story. Moreover, homicide detectives
admitted that they had destroyed key evidence against
the defendants. (Just Friday, *The Sun* released details of
a report on the homicide squad suggesting that lost evidence, incomplete case folders and other inexcusable
dysfunctions may be the norm.)

Not surprisingly, a jury returned not-guilty verdicts
for all three in the Suggs case, and they walked out of
court free men. But is that justice? Did the process fairly
serve either the defendants or the victim's family?

These kinds of screw-ups should make Baltimore
want to scream with anger and frustration. Judges' and
prosecutors' phones should ring off the hooks and the
mayor should be bombarded with complaints. But do
you think that happened? Want to bet that it didn't?

This week's judicial miscarriage was only the latest
example of what goes on every day in Baltimore, the
most recent in a long line of debacles that allow criminals to do whatever they want and not fear reprisal. But
there's still no palpable outrage, no sense that city residents are gut-sick about what's going on.

Something has to change. There must be a ground-
swell of public opinion that forces the important fixes
we need in the criminal justice system. It would be no
less important than was the civil rights struggle or the
push for women's suffrage at the beginning of the early
20th century.

Anyone can lead this movement. Mayor O'Malley
has a perfect platform from which to do so. Gov. Parris
Glendening—an influential two-term governor with
fewer than two years left in office—also has a position
of advantage.

But you, Baltimore, must do your part. Your anger
and persistence could be the fuel that feeds this effort.
Phone your leaders. Pressure them to change. Do something.

No one in this city can afford to keep quiet any more.

Capital case filled with doubt

JUNE 4, 2000

No evidence proves Eugene Colvin-el ever held the knife used to kill 82-year-old Lena Buckman at her daughter's Pikesville residence 20 years ago.

No fingerprints matching Colvin-el's were found in the room where Buckman was stabbed 28 times, in the bedroom ransacked after the murder or anywhere else in the house.

But Colvin-el is sentenced to death because his prints were found on broken glass outside the home.

He is going to die because he pawned two watches that could have been found among jewelry strewn across the lawn.

He is a condemned man, awaiting execution at the Maryland Correctional Adjustment Center in Baltimore, because he had a lawyer who put on no defense at trial, and because his appeals never adequately remedied that injustice.

Sometime during the week of June 12, state officials plan to strap Colvin-el to a gurney and fill his veins with drugs to stop his heart, making him the fourth Maryland prisoner executed since the death penalty was reinstated in 1978.

But to let him die would sanction the worst kind of premeditated killing.

The facts of Colvin-el's case simply don't lead to a moral certainty that he was Buckman's principal murderer, or that he received the "especially vigilant" attention to due process that the Supreme Court expects in capital cases.

His case doesn't meet the common-sense standard that death is reserved for the worst of the worst, convicted by the strongest evidence.

It's not even close.

The moral arc of Colvin-el's case bends toward injustice. It bends toward unfairness and a perilously low standard for state-sanctioned killings. Whether Colvin-el is "innocent" is not at issue. Whether the state has established his guilt as a killer with unwavering affirmation and probity is.

Gov. Parris N. Glendening—who has a petition for Colvin-el's clemency awaiting his attention—must stop Maryland from passing final judgment on Colvin-el. He should commute his sentence to life in prison.

* * *

It's thin.

Dig through the reams of paper that constitute Eugene Colvin-el's 20-year case file, and this is the conclusion that jumps out regarding the prosecution's case.

Overwhelmingly circumstantial, with a distressingly small amount of evidence to connect Colvin-el with the murder, the file makes for unsettling reading.

Prosecutors say most criminal trials turn largely on circumstantial evidence—though Colvin-el's case sets a new low in that regard.

Prosecutors also say jurors were able to draw "reasonable inferences" from the evidence to conclude that Colvin-el wielded the knife. But those "inferences" seem more like great leaps.

The state says it happened like this:

On Sept. 9, 1980, between 1 p.m. and 2:45 p.m., Colvin-el broke into the house on Cherokee Drive in Pikesville where Lena Buckman was visiting her daughter, Marjorie Surrell, and her family.

They say he broke a pane of glass in an exterior basement door, entered and stabbed Buckman 28 times with a knife he found in the kitchen. He wiped his hands and the knife with a kitchen towel. Then he rummaged through the master bedroom and stole several thousand dollars' worth of jewelry.

At trial in 1981, the prosecution presented evidence that fingerprints found on the broken glass near the basement door matched Colvin-el's. Evidence was also presented that showed Colvin-el pawned two watches reported stolen from the Surrell home on Sept. 9.

The state's case raised more doubts than it erased:

■ Investigators were unable to find any "comparison value" fingerprints (prints complete enough to use for identification) on the knife used to kill Buckman. Did Colvin-el handle it? Prosecutors could not say conclusively that he did. They asserted—without any supporting evidence—that the presence of the bloody towel proved Colvin-el wiped his prints off the knife.

■ Of the three comparison-quality fingerprints found inside the house—including a bloody partial palm print on the refrigerator—not one matched Colvin-el's. Police found the broken glass with Colvin-el's fingerprints outside the home.

Was Colvin-el in the house or just at the scene? Prosecutors offered no conclusive evidence. Were there other people in the house at the time of the robbery and murder? The unidentified bloody palm print on the refrigerator suggests that's possible.

■ In written reports, Baltimore County police investigators said the basement door Colvin-el used to gain access would only open "approximately four inches," because a cabinet placed against the basement wall blocked part of the door.

Colvin-el was approximately 5 feet 7 inches tall and 140 pounds at the time of the murder. Could he have slipped through such a small opening? Prosecutors did not offer conclusive evidence.

They found no fingerprints on the door or on items in the basement. The cabinet that partially blocked the door had not been moved.

■ Pieces of jewelry were found on the driveway outside the Surrell home after the crime. Did Colvin-el obtain the watches he pawned from somewhere other than inside the home? The prosecution's evidence did not rule out that possibility.

Colvin-el's lawyer should have had an easy time challenging the evidence.

Even if he did not question the idea that Colvin-el was present at the scene, he had several avenues for assailing the prosecution's assertion that Colvin-el murdered Buckman. Only that assertion made the defendant eligible for the death penalty under Maryland law.

Questioning this assertion was especially critical in a case that dealt with a crime in Baltimore County, where prosecutors seek death in any eligible case, regardless of the circumstances or the weight of the evidence.

So what went wrong?

Enter the shortcomings of the legal system.

Let's start with Colvin-el's first lawyer, Robert W.

Payne, a private-practice attorney appointed by the public defender's office to represent Colvin-el at trial in 1981. Payne, who is now deceased, had handled only two murder cases before being assigned Colvin-el's case. He had never dealt with a death-penalty defense.

Baltimore County prosecutors and Colvin-el's current attorneys have different views about how well Payne represented Colvin-el. But certain things are clear in the court records.

Payne did very little pretrial preparation because he was "frustrated" by Colvin-el's refusal to cooperate. Colvin-el wouldn't allow Payne to put on the case he wanted, according to Payne's testimony in a 1985 post-conviction hearing. He wouldn't answer Payne's questions or respond to his requests.

In turn, Payne didn't inspect the prosecution's evidence until a month before trial. He didn't interview any witnesses Colvin-el asked him to interview, including at least one who Colvin-el said might offer an alibi.

Colvin-el himself entered pretrial motions, including one at the case's first hearing that got the trial moved from Baltimore County to Anne Arundel County.

At the same hearing, he filed a motion for a change of attorney; Payne concurred with an oral motion to remove himself from the case.

Both said Colvin-el was dissatisfied with Payne's work and that, because this was a death-penalty case, attorney and client needed a close working relationship. These motions were denied. The judge said there was insufficient cause to change attorneys.

Payne's poor preparation hobbled his performance at trial. He called no witnesses and introduced no evidence.

He put no questions to prosecution witnesses that exposed the lack of identifiable fingerprints on the knife or the absence of Colvin-el's fingerprints inside the house.

The trial lasted two days. The jury deliberated three hours and returned a guilty verdict.

At sentencing, the jury was asked to answer two questions: whether Colvin-el was the "principal" in the murder—the knife-wielder—and whether his crimes warranted death.

Lacking strong evidence, prosecutors attempted to prove Colvin-el was the knife-wielder by detailing his past convictions. Especially damaging was testimony about an eerily similar 1972 robbery incident, during which he threatened a woman with a knife while stealing jewelry from her home.

On the witness stand, Colvin-el testified that he was a drug addict who committed burglaries for money for his wife and two children. He said he never hurt anyone and offered wandering statements about everything from his faith to the prosecutor's nationality.

The entire sentencing phase lasted less than a day. By sundown, the jurors had deliberated again and returned a sentence of death.

* * *

In all of Colvin-el's appeals, his lawyers have focused—with good reason—on the inadequacy of his representation at trial and the grave doubts about Colvin-el's role in the murder. Those are the primary issues that make his planned execution indefensible.

Five judges in three proceedings found these problems significant enough to lodge serious objections to Colvin-el's execution. But the courts never saw fit to remedy either problem with a new trial: in essence, to start again from the beginning, presuming Colvin-el's innocence and introducing all of the evidence before deciding his guilt.

The closest he came was in 1992, when he was granted a resentencing after the Supreme Court found fault with Maryland's death penalty procedure. However, at the hearing, his guilt in a felony murder was not the issue. This was not a new trial, although it is often inaccurately referred to that way.

Even worse, problems arose at the resentencing over how evidence was presented.

Jurors first were supposed to decide if Colvin-el was the "principal" in the Buckman murder. If they found he was the killer, only then could they decide his punishment.

But the prosecution presented evidence for both questions at the same time. Thus, jurors heard damaging testimony about Colvin-el that they weren't supposed to hear unless they decided he was the principal killer.

The prosecutor talked about Colvin-el's prior convictions in his opening statement. Yet those records had nothing to do with establishing what did or did not happen on Sept. 9, 1980.

After opening statements, the prosecutor called Buckman's relatives to the stand and had them talk about the impact of her death on their lives. None of that evidence could be used by the jury to ascertain Colvin-el's role in the killing.

The judge told the jurors to disregard statements about Colvin-el's record and from the relatives in deciding if he was the primary murderer. The judge instructed them to stick to the prosecution's evidence against Colvin-el, as required by law.

But that's like telling someone to forget an elephant in the room and concentrate on a mouse instead. It was unreasonable.

A federal district judge said as much when he ruled that the resentencing violated Colvin-el's constitutional rights. But even he didn't find legal grounds to grant a new trial. He only ordered another sentencing hearing that separated the two questions and the evidence the jury heard.

His ruling was overturned by the federal Court of Appeals in Richmond, which determined that Maryland law didn't require separation of the proceedings. The Supreme Court refused to hear an appeal.

Prosecutors say they have met the legal standard for execution. They say Colvin-el has had his day in court, and has been condemned by two juries. His appeals were rejected on the basis of the laws of this state and this country.

But do technical legal judgments assure that "especially vigilant" attention to due process and fairness was given? Do they assure that Colvin-el actually did what he is accused of doing?

No.

Gov. Glendening, with whom Colvin-el's fate now rests, has an obligation to look beyond legal arguments to moral issues: Can the state end his life while serious doubts remain about his role in the murder and the fairness of his trials?

This process must be stopped before the state imposes the ultimate—and irreversible—penalty on Eugene Colvin-el.

Bill Struever,
Marylander of year

DECEMBER 17, 2000

Four walls and a foundation are all he needs.

Carl William Struever (everyone calls him Bill) adopts buildings that others have discarded, neglected or marked for destruction. He sees what they want to be, what purpose these abandoned hulks might serve in the communities that surround them. And with single-minded resolve, he helps them fulfill that potential.

You can spot Mr. Struever's work all around Balti-more—almost anywhere an old warehouse or industrial plant is thriving as a home or an office, a bookstore or a restaurant.

And if you take a step back, you can see his impact. By restoring hope to buildings that everyone else has given up on, he's also helping to restore hope to a city that many people have forsaken.

This year, Mr. Struever's plans to create a "Digital Harbor" started to pay off, bringing high-tech jobs to both sides of Baltimore's harbor, from the American Can Co. in Canton to the newly restored Tide Point, site of the old Procter & Gamble plant.

His achievement has significant implications for Bal-timore's waterfront, and by extension, the city. And it is the primary reason we've chosen Mr. Struever, 48, as our Marylander of the Year.

* * *

It might be easy to view Mr. Struever as just another of Baltimore's many developers—a rich guy who makes himself richer by putting up office complexes, stores or housing units.

But that view understates the development chal-lenges Mr. Struever and his partners at Struever Bros., Eccles & Rouse confront without blinking, and the gambles they take in the name of urban revitalization. What they do is all about risks. It's about fighting through setbacks, headaches and environmental and financial constraints to make something work where others have failed.

Anyone can put up an office building on a pristine patch of open land in the suburbs. Not just anyone can bring life to rejected urban relics.

The American Can Co. in Canton is a good example.

It sat unused for nearly three decades and was slated for demolition twice before Mr. Struever got involved.

The site was polluted with lead and oil. The buildings had odd footprints that didn't lend themselves cleanly to modern needs for office space or commercial ventures.

But Mr. Struever saw possibilities. Taking care of the pollution was just a matter of patience and money. And he knew if he could secure historic tax credits for the property—again, with patience and money—he could make the numbers work.

Design was a matter of vision: finding virtue in concrete industrial-grade columns and old shop-floor layouts. Retail outlets and restaurants quickly bought in. Mr. Struever got office tenants by targeting high-tech companies whose employees might appreciate the site's quirkiness. (He also persuaded DAP, an old-line caulk company looking to jazz-up its image, to move in.)

When the Can Co. opened in 1998, it was a rousing success. It has since become an anchor for Canton and helped produce a thriving real estate and commercial market in the neighborhood. Across the harbor at Tide Point is Mr. Struever's newest effort. The abandoned Procter & Gamble plant had been bought by Korean investors who planned to make sake there, but their financing fell through, and Mr. Struever stepped in.

After conquering similar challenges to those he faced at the Can Co., Mr. Struever has turned the 400,000-square-foot complex into the centerpiece of his Digital Harbor venture.

He has already attracted some big-name dot.coms to inhabit the office spaces. And he has some non-technology tenants, too: architectural firm Ayers Saint Gross and ad agency Gray Kirk/VanSant will soon move in. When Tide Point is finished, about 2,200 people will work there. In its heyday, Procter & Gamble never had more than 550 workers at that site.

There's little doubt the Can Co. and Tide Point would be empty or demolished if Mr. Struever had not revived them. The risks were too great for others, and the vision wouldn't have been there for many.

The communities these developments serve—Canton and Locust Point—might still be groping for ways to turn a neighborhood drag into a catalyst if not for Mr. Struever.

The same is true of other Struever developments: the old Bagby Furniture building at Inner Harbor East; Tindeco Wharf and Canton Cove in Canton; the planned redevelopment of the once badly polluted Allied Signal site near Fells Point. He also has plans under way to turn the long-closed National Brewery plant in East Baltimore and the Munsey Building at Baltimore and Calvert streets into apartments.

Mr. Struever also lends his extraordinary vision to other people's projects.

He's trying to resurrect the Belvedere Square retail complex on York Road.

When the old Camden Yards warehouse was being redone to complement the baseball park, it was Mr. Struever who found a way to have office space on every floor of the gargantuan building, rather than mechanical equipment on half of them.

When the Children's Museum was looking for a new home, it was Mr. Struever who suggested the former Fish Market on the edge of downtown and helped inspire the idea for Port Discovery—one of the most cutting-edge experiential museums in the country.

When the city school board was reconfigured in 1997 in the hope of massive education reform, it was Mr. Struever—the only retained member of the old school board—who took the lead early in defining what was achievable.

That school board involvement is just one aspect of his civic life: He has served on more than 20 civic boards and committees over the past two decades and has been honored numerous times for his volunteer work.

His associates say he is driven to all of these things by an unswerving commitment to rebuilding communities by capitalizing on what's already there, and an equally strong belief that this city should aspire to greatness.

He believes in Baltimore's promise. He works tirelessly to help realize it.

Maybe those are qualities that come with being the Brown University-educated son of a Johns Hopkins professor. Or maybe they come from studying development at the knee of James Rouse.

Whatever the reason, this much is clear: Baltimore would be worse off without Mr. Struever. To see how true that is, you need only look at the many thriving places around town that were once no more than four walls and a foundation.

Writers' Workshop

Talking Points

1) What makes a good editorial writer? What are the qualities required?

2) How can an editorial page staff show affection for a community and still take it to task for community shortcomings?

3) Stephen Henderson said he was drawn to the editorial page from his youth. What might young readers find to attract them to these pages? What could editorial pages offer to attract more young people?

4) The editorial "A Silence That Kills" asks readers to take specific steps in addressing a problem. Should most editorials call for a reader response? What were the different types of responses sought in Henderson's collection of work?

5) Should editorial writers have bylines? How would a signed editorial differ from a column?

Assignment Desk

1) Report on a story, then present it as a news story and as an editorial. What skills are needed for both tasks? What other skills are needed for each?

2) Read several editorials and describe the voice of each. Now write two editorials on the same topic, but using different voices. What does it take to bring voice to your writing?

3) Write editorials on opposing sides of a heated debate. How do you generate lively prose when writing something that you don't believe?

4) Try to sit in on an editorial board meeting. Note how arguments are presented to move toward a position.

5) Study letters to the editor for a month. What issues seem to draw the greatest response? What can you learn about the readers/writers of these letters?

A conversation with
Stephen Henderson

KAREN DUNLAP: Stephen, I think it's fair to say that the common editorial voice is that of an erudite scold. How would you describe your editorial voice?

STEPHEN HENDERSON: Well, I think my editorial voice is a lot like my speaking voice, or at least that's how I try to approach it. I definitely agree with your description of the typical editorial. My first editor told me that reading an editorial is a lot like eating a dried-out broom. He always encouraged me to write an editorial in the same voice you'd have in a conversation with your family over dinner or the way you talked to a friend at the bar.

Lately I have been interested in trying more of a feature-writing style with literary devices, but generally I write the way I talk. It's harder to do that with more serious topics, but that's certainly what I'm striving to do.

Who are your readers? How do you imagine them as you write?

I think our readers are just normal, average people in Baltimore. I don't necessarily write for politicians or other kinds of decision-makers, mostly because those are the people whose conversations I'm most bored by. Some of the pieces that we submitted were pleas to politicians to do something or to think differently, but certainly when I'm sitting and writing I'm not thinking of them. I'm thinking of my neighbor or my wife or my mother, just normal people.

Your voice is distinctive, but you are also distinctive because of your age. You were 29 when you wrote some of the winning editorials. That's well below the median age of editorial writers. How should editorial page editors weigh the balance between seasoned writers who have thought through issues over time, and younger writers with different perspectives?

The word you used is the right word: balance. That balance is what's missing. Most boards have tons of people who have done unbelievably diverse things in their long careers. What they're missing are younger people who maybe aren't as experienced and maybe don't know quite as much about everything, but really have something to contribute and have something to say. It's an incredible gamble for an editorial page editor to hire somebody who doesn't have that experience. Maybe it won't work out, and you could be setting that person up for a failure that would affect him pretty deeply. At the same time, the potential payoff is pretty high, too. Sometimes younger journalists are more energetic or they think of things differently. So it makes sense to try to get that balance, but there's not a lot of effort on the part of most editorial page editors to achieve that balance.

How did you become interested in editorial writing and how did you get started so young?

When I first started reading the newspaper, the editorial page fascinated me. I grew up in Detroit reading the *Detroit Free Press*. It was delivered to our house. I started writing letters to the editor when I was about 14 or 15. I'd write two or three a week responding to the editorials or trying to mimic things I saw in the editorials, and you know, they never printed one of my letters. From the time I was 15 to the time I left to go to college, I never saw my name in the paper. And so when I got to college and began working at the college newspaper, the editorial page was where I started.

Do you remember what fascinated you about the *Detroit Free Press* editorial page?

Keep in mind that this was in the late '80s. Editorial pages were stodgier then than they are now, if that's possible, but there was a point of view to the stuff. It made you think more. The editorial page really was about politics, which I was interested in. It was about policy. There were lots of parts of the *Free Press* that I just loved, but the editorial page drew me. There were writers there at the time who I still imitate.

Who were your favorite writers then and now?

When I was a kid, Bill McGraw and Barbara Stanton, who is now retired, were my favorite writers at the *Free Press* along with Patricia Montemurri. I got to work with them in the mid-'90s when I was at the *Free Press*. As for editorial writers now, I'd say Richard Aregood impresses me, and Paul Greenberg is a huge, huge idol of mine.

Mr. Aregood of the Newark *Star-Ledger*, and Mr. Greenberg of the *Arkansas Democrat-Gazette*, both past winners of this award.

Yeah, and Bailey Thomson. When I found out I'd won this award, I had Bailey's project from *Best Newspaper Writing 1999* sitting on my desk and I was reading it thinking, "God, I hope he didn't enter this contest because he's going to beat me."

Those are the editorial writers I look up to. I also look up to a lot of feature writers. Tom French (of the *St. Petersburg Times*) is one of my favorites. His "South of Heaven" series was just phenomenal. And Lisa Pollak, who works here at *The Sun*, is one of my favorite writers. She is a very close friend of mine from the University of Michigan. I am always emulating her.

What do you learn from the feature writers?

Mostly I get ideas pertaining to structure and pacing. They help me think about how a piece begins, how it sustains itself through the guts of the material, and how it ends. These are people who I think have really perfected voice and really perfected style, and they're distinctive. You can spot their stuff anywhere, even without the name on it, and that's what I try to do.

Is it important to have readers of the Baltimore *Sun* editorial page recognize your voice?

Yes. It's real important to me that my friends know which ones I've written, and they usually do.

Should newspapers carry bylined or signed editorials

instead of printing them as anonymous, institutional statements?

I like signed editorials the same way I like a feature story or a news story that has a byline. I like to know who wrote that wonderful story I read on the front page. I shouldn't have to call up and ask who wrote the editorial. It's also about accountability. There should be a name there, and I don't think it diminishes the idea that the opinion is from *The Sun*. People identify with other people. They identify with voice, but an institution doesn't have a voice. People do. So I think readers would appreciate signed editorials.

Let's talk about the Baltimore *Sun* editorial process. How do you come to decisions there?

There are 15 people on the board, including six writers, a page designer, an editorial page editor, and various other editors. I'm the associate editor. The way we come to decisions is pretty typical. Every morning at 9:30 we have a meeting of all the writers and some of the others. We just sit around and talk about what's going on that day, the big topic that we think everybody's thinking about, and maybe wondering what we think. That meeting usually lasts about an hour, hour and a half, and at the end of it we have a pretty good idea of what topics will appear on the next day's page, and how we're going to approach them. Then the writers go and write, and by 1:30 we've got the copy and we're putting the page together.

Do you have beats?

We don't have beats per se. We all have things that we know more about than the other people on the board. We have three writers who are assigned to suburban bureaus, and so they are experts on those areas. One of my specialties is education. That's what I've been writing about most of my career, as an education reporter in Detroit and here in Baltimore. And so I do most of the schools editorials. We have people on our board who were foreign correspondents before they came here to the editorial page, and so they write about foreign policy. All of us dabble in lots of different things and sometimes you've got to pick up the slack for somebody else, but each of us has sort of a specialty area.

Although you've written quite a bit about public schools, you attended Quaker and Jesuit schools. Does that affect the way you view public schools?

I went to Quaker and Jesuit schools essentially because my parents had no faith in the public school system in Detroit, and because they wanted some sort of values-based education for my sister and me. I think both of those school philosophies, which are at the same time very different and very similar, show up in my work. I see an inherent value in all life and all people, and strive to make others see that. And I have a strong mind for justice. Inequalities of any kind make me gut-sick.

I don't think that background ever conflicts with my efforts to write about public education, because most of those values are the ones the public schools *should* embody, though they fall quite short.

You write with such passion. What is it like to write an editorial when you don't wholeheartedly share the opinion?

That's really tough. I try not to have to do that. One of the things that we're conscious of here is almost never making the staff writers do that. Sometimes we must write an opinion that we don't embrace, because, say the publisher thinks differently from the board. Certainly the publisher has the last say. When that happens, we try not to get the writers involved, and either the editor or I write it.

You know, I would say that I don't think those are the best editorials I write. I don't think I can carry that off, because I do have to feel something in order to do what I do. My writing's not based just on what I think and it's not just reasoning. There's a lot of emotion that goes into my work. And if I don't have an emotion, I can't fake it.

I sense that you felt strongly about Mayor Martin O'Malley's school board appointments. You wrote: Martin O'Malley "thought small and acted smaller" with regard to city schools. Tell me a little bit about

your writing process in doing this piece.

That piece came up because I covered city schools here
for two years before I came to the editorial board. I know
the school board members well, and I know how the
board works, and I know how difficult it was to get that
board together. When, in probably the first two months
of his administration, the mayor decided to kick one of
these guys off, I got really angry. I kept thinking, here's a
mayor who doesn't know anything about this board.
He'd been in city council and was never involved in
school issues. He was removing a member largely because he had a political grudge against the guy, yet the
whole point of this reformed board was to get politics
out of schools.

I can remember thinking, in the shower the morning
that I wrote the editorial, this is not the first time this has
happened. The last mayor was a real small thinker in
terms of schools and just sort of let the whole thing deteriorate, and the mayor before him, William Donald
Schaefer, who's this great venerated politician around
Baltimore, really took a very poor and small-minded
attitude toward schools. And I said this is what O'Malley is doing. He's taking his place in this pitiful little line
of small thinkers.

**In the editorial you didn't call it a "pitiful little line,"
you called it a "pitiful queue." An interesting word
choice. It's a British term. How does that language fit
in with your friend-at-the-bar conversational tone?**

I don't like the word "line." I would never write that
someone was standing in a line. I like the idea of queue
and I think queue evokes a very different image than line
does. Queue to me is almost purposeful. In other words,
we really were trying to say that O'Malley is taking his
place. He's stepping in behind these guys, and to me
that's more of a queue. I think the person at the bar
would know what that means.

**And the context helps clarify it nicely. Any response
from the mayor?**

It drew a very funny reaction from the mayor. We equated his actions with those of a third-grader and told him to grow up. The day the editorial ran, he sent me a handwritten note that read: "Your editorial of today's date was unkind, unwarranted, and untrue; furthermore, my mother says none of you can come over anymore, and I'm not to go near you at recess."

I, of course, died laughing when I opened it. I still have it in my desk.

He was a good sport.

Your time as a reporter on the education beat was invaluable in this editorial. How important is it for an editorial writer to have had experience as a reporter?

I think it is really important. My first professional job was as an editorial writer, and I think I was pretty good at it then, but I'm a lot better now because I have been a reporter. You know, reporting is what we do in this business. It doesn't matter whether you're writing editorials or feature stories or news stories, it's the material that you have that allows you to apply your writing skills to make something really good. You've got to get the right material and know when you have enough. That's what you learn as a reporter.

Did you attend to the world differently as a reporter than you do as an editorial writer?

I don't think so. I don't think there's really any difference. I'm just doing something different with the material once I have it.

Your editorial, "Taking Over Baltimore Schools," is another look at the city's educational system. I am interested in the structure of the piece. The lead circles to the kicker with the repetition of the theme, "it's not the children." You present the characters who should not be blamed for poor performance, then follow with a list of those who should accept blame, and who should be held accountable. You start the editorial with short, powerful sentences followed by a longer

paragraph, then again punchy, shorter sentences. Do you write that way on first draft or does it come in your editing?

An awful lot of it comes just the first time I sit down because it is just the way I think of it. In this editorial, I got that first line from the state superintendent of schools. She was meeting to tell us that she was going to take over these three schools and that she had had it, that she'd given them every opportunity to get better, and she said, "I'm not going to wait any more." She was very emotional about this, and this is a woman who's not very emotional normally. She turned at one point and said, "I'm just sick of this. It's not the kids. I know it's not the kids. It's got to be something else." That just clicked in my mind. I thought that was such a simple, but really elegant statement about what's going on in schools. So when I sat down to write, that was the first line I had.

I always talk about the line. "Gotta get a line on the editorial." And once I have that, I'm pretty much done. I can sit down and do it very quickly.

You began "A Silence That Kills" with six imperative sentences. Five of them are "Keep quiet." The other one is "Say nothing." It's a powerful technique put to great effect, but when you use an innovative technique, how do you know when you've gone too far?

I think you know you've gone too far when the editor says, "You know, this is too much of this and we've got to get rid of some of them."

Is there much conversation among the board members about writing?

There's more than there used to be, and certainly the editor and I think there ought to be even more. Writing ought to be a part of what we talk about all the time, and a lot of times that's not the focus. The focus is on the ideas, which it should be, or on the topics. Writing gets pushed off. I think one of the things that could help make editorial pages better would be if more editorial writers talked with one another about writing. It doesn't really matter what you're saying in an editorial if you're not sucking readers in to stay with the stuff.

This editorial really came down hard on Baltimore. Do you love your city?

I do. I think this is a great city. You know I've lived in Detroit and Lexington, Ky., and in Chicago and now Baltimore, and my wife and I really feel like this is home. We've been here four years and we've got no plans to leave, which for us is incredibly unusual. Everyone keeps asking us, "How long are you going to stay there?" We're going to stay a long time, because it's got big-city attractions and a very real urban grittiness, like Detroit. We also have all these wonderful parks in this city.

I really like this place and feel attached to it. I really feel this could be just a great place with wonderful schools and great parks. So, yeah, that piece was written largely because I do like it so much here, but we were so angry about what's going on with crime.

How important is it for a newspaper to show that it has an affection for its city?

Oh, I think that's everything. That's the foundation for your relationship with the community. Because it's really the only thing you have in common with them. Lots of people who work at the newspaper here are not from here. I think more so than in other industries, people in this business hop around and go from place to place. The newspaper institutionalizes its affection for the community that it serves by saying, "Look, we're part of this and we're here with you and we want this city to be good."

But I bet if you asked many people, they'd say *The Sun* hates Baltimore because we're real tough on our public officials. Right now some bad things are going on and nobody seems to be doing anything about it. So we are, almost on a daily basis, jumping up and down, waving our arms, saying, "Hey, we've got to do something about this." I don't think people see that that's out of a real desire for this to be a good place and real affection for it.

At the same time, I'd rather be criticized for being too

hard on the city than for being too easy on it. That is even more dangerous. We ought to be pushing for change, positive change, all the time. If you are pushing for positive change, sometimes that's going to mean writing an editorial that seems negative. But really the point is to make things better.

It's not unusual for an editorial to have a call to action. This one had a very specific call. It didn't just tell citizens that they should be concerned, or that they should contact someone. It went beyond that to include the names and numbers of public officials in a box. Near the end it said: "Phone your leaders. Pressure them to change. Do something." How much response did the editorial draw?

We got a lot of response. We had two full pages of letters in the next week talking about the editorial and the fact that people were also sick and tired of what was going on. Public officials were not going to tell us what kind of response they got. They were very upset with this editorial, by the way. I mean everyone who was named in that little box with numbers called to express outrage. They felt that they were doing everything they could and we were blaming them.

I don't know that we have that kind of influence over people to spur them to action with officials. I think there's a lot of complacency, feelings of helplessness. People don't know what they can do, and so they do nothing.

This editorial was part of a campaign, right?

Right. "Getting Away with Murder" is actually a project that's about two years old now. One of the writers on our staff, Antero Pietila, has written 98 percent of the editorials. Most of them have been investigative editorials about the sorry state of criminal justice in Baltimore, and occasionally there have been pieces like this, which are more emotional than investigative.

I sense you've had involvement with several editorial campaigns. How effective are editorial campaigns?

It really varies, and the real variable is the community. When I was working in Lexington, we had three different editorial crusades running at the same time. Each one led to incredible progress. One was about domestic abuse in Kentucky. It was written by Maria Henson and ultimately won the Pulitzer Prize. It changed every law on the books in Kentucky in terms of domestic violence.

Back at *The Sun*, you were also involved in a year-long reporting series following 27 Baltimore first-graders.

That was part of *The Sun*'s "Reading by Nine" project. Another reporter and I were in two really, really bad city schools, each in one classroom documenting how they taught the kids to read.

What's the difference, for the writer, between a reporting campaign and an editorial campaign?

Well, the two schools' reading project was probably the most different thing I've ever done. First of all, I defy you to find anyone who could spend a year in a classroom with 20 first-graders and not develop an emotional connection with the kids. That began to play a real role in how the series was written. It was written almost exclusively as a narrative. Every one of the pieces tried to put the reader in the classroom. The readers were just seeing what was happening and were left to draw their own conclusions.

Which is harder to write, an editorial or a feature?

Oh, gosh, that was much harder to write. I faced so many opinions and so many feelings about what was going on. Reading was the most important thing these kids needed to learn. If they don't get it, they were doomed, and we saw lots of kids who weren't going to get it. It was very difficult to show that while restraining yourself from telling what was happening. As an editorial writer, I just let loose on the whole thing.

Which gets back to "Keep Quiet, Baltimore."

Exactly. It can be much more blunt. When I'm writing editorials, I'm not really telling or showing, I'm interpreting. I'm presenting what I think, and saying, this is what you should think, too.

You were probably doing all of that in "Capital Case Filled with Doubt." How much reporting did you do on this one?

All of it. The news department was covering this as just another Maryland execution. We don't have that many, which is why the coverage surprised me. Capital punishment is one of my big issues. I had never lived in a state where they executed somebody, at least not while I was there. And so I went to the editor and said, "I think we ought to look into this. Maybe this guy did what they said he did. Maybe he got a fair trial, and under the law he deserves what he's about to get. But we ought to make sure that that's true in our eyes. But if it's not, then we ought to say that he shouldn't be executed." She said, "Fine."

So I dug up the case file, which at that point was 20 years old, and filled the floor of my office with evidence: hearings, all kinds of stuff. It was just a mess in my office. I read all of it and then started talking to the prosecutors and to the defense attorneys. There really wasn't any case. The evidence they presented was razor thin.

Some people on the editorial board didn't agree. Some doubted that my analysis of this evidence could be better than what all these lawyers and judges over 20 years had come up with. And to be quite honest, there were people who believed that capital punishment's a great idea and we ought to be doing more of it. So it took a little convincing in there, and I don't think everyone was in agreement when we published.

It's possible that he did it?

It's entirely possible that he did it. I don't know whether he did it, and that was one of the hardest things about writing that piece. I didn't want to make him look innocent, because I don't know that he's innocent. All I know is that the state has not proven that he did it, at least not beyond any sort of reasonable doubt. And the other thing that I know is true is this guy's trial was pretty much a sham. I think a little more attention to detail on the prosecutors' part, and they probably could have come up with some evidence that actually showed that he did do it.

Where do you find the confidence to take a stand like this?

Oh, God. Really, in this case it was just a deep-seated belief that, (a) capital punishment is wrong. That is a long-standing position that this editorial page holds. And (b) if a state uses capital punishment, every "i" ought to be dotted and every "t" ought to be crossed. If they aren't, then you haven't upheld the standard that the Supreme Court says you have to uphold in these cases. This is the most serious judgment you can render on another human being. You're taking somebody's life. You cannot cut corners.

Was he removed from death row?

Yes, the governor commuted his sentence to life in prison without parole. That was the appropriate sentence because the guy was obviously at the scene. His fingerprints were on the glass outside. He might not have been the killer, but he was there and, we think, that alone warrants a life sentence.

I think the governor acted three days after the editorial appeared, and we were very happy, obviously. The family of the victim was not happy and let us know that. In their own way, the prosecutors were very angry. We continue to deal with that because we've got some other cases coming up this year.

About how long did it take you to do the reporting and writing on the capital punishment editorial?

I want to say that it took about a week and a half, maybe two weeks. We were under some time pressure because the execution day was scheduled. I pretty much extracted myself from everything else around here and just dealt with that. It took me a day or so to write. I didn't want it to read like a dry retelling of the case. I wanted it—particularly the top part—to read like an impassioned plea to spare this guy's life, but I knew we had to have all of the evidence that we had found, too. So it took me a little while to come up with how to structure it.

Each of your winning pieces has a different tone. The piece on Mr. Struever is very different from the one on capital punishment. How difficult is it to shift tone?

I find profiles the hardest to write because you don't want to sound like you're fawning over the person even though you are. We've created this recognition called "Marylander of the Year," which is a great honor in the community. We're saying this person has made the most important contribution to the community over the last 12 months. That's so different from what we do normally, because we are often very critical. We try to write good things, but gosh, probably 75 percent of what we write is saying somebody's screwing something up or not thinking the right way. It's difficult to shift gears. I tried to talk about what he's done and why that's important. I actually spent a day with one of his vice presidents, going around the city, looking at and talking about the projects that he's done. And I really got a sense of why he was noteworthy and why his work was important. I tried to show, it's not just that he's a great guy, but look what he's done, and look how hard it was to do this, and look why most other people wouldn't bother.

Now I've talked about your leads and your endings in other pieces. I want to talk about the middles of stories. After you have set up this piece and made the theme clear, you introduce a gold coin. In the 10th paragraph you say: "The American Can Co. in Canton is a good example."

That picks up the piece and keeps it moving. Are you aware of avoiding sag in an editorial? What do you do when a piece needs something to keep it going?

On all of the longer pieces we do, I try to find something that sucks you back into the piece in the middle. Some-

times it's something that I've come across in the reporting or that I know about that I think is really interesting.
If I throw it in there, it picks the piece back up and sends
it running again. If you notice, all three of the longer
pieces begin with a very engaging section and then
there's a bullet or there's a line of bullets. Some people
think that stops the piece, but I think it pauses the piece
and says to the reader, "That was a complete thought you
just got there. Now we're going to do something a little
different." I think that keeps people from just putting it
down and saying, "I've had enough." It's better if you
can find something in the reporting, but sometimes
you've just got to write in a little different way or with a
little more flair so that you keep people's attention.

**We've talked about qualities of editorial writing, but
let's summarize. What makes good editorial writing?**

I think there are a few things. First the writing has to be
very clear thought. Second, the editorial has to have a
compelling opinion. Some writers want to say this, but
they sort of want to say that. I think you've got to get all
that out of your mind before you sit down at the key-
board.

**Then you're opposed to editorials that say, "On the
one hand…" and "On the other hand…"?**

That's the kiss of death. I also think very strong reporting
is important. An editorial writer ought to sit down and
know as much or more than a reporter writing a story.
You can't have a forceful, clear, well-thought-out opinion if you don't really know the details.
     The writing for an editorial shouldn't be monumental-
ly different from the writing for a great investigative story
or a great feature or a great sports column. Good writing
is good writing. I meet people who say, "You know, I've
thought about editorial writing, but I don't think I'd be
very good at it." They're some of the best feature writers,
sportswriters I know. I keep saying a good writer can
write about anything and can write in any form, can learn
any form. The mechanics are the same. I emphasize that
the most because I think that's the piece so many editorial

writers miss. They sit down and they think that this stilted institutional language is the way to do it. You don't see that kind of writing anywhere else in the newspaper and there's a reason. People don't like it. People don't identify with it. They can't relate to it.

This is my last question. When you've achieved so much so young, what do you look forward to doing?

That's a good question. I guess I think it's a good question because I don't think of it as achieving so much. I'm having a ball at what I'm doing. I'm having the time of my life in this job, and I've had a great time at every job I've had up until now. When I stop having fun at what I'm doing, I'll go find something else that's just as much fun. It's nice to get awards. That's important to me, but more important is that I'm having a good time.

Paul Greenberg

Finalist, Editorial Writing

Paul Greenberg was born in Shreveport, La., the youngest child of orthodox Jewish immigrants from Poland. He has a bachelor's degree in journalism and a master's in history from the University of Missouri.

Greenberg found his first newspaper job at the *Pine Bluff* (Ark.) *Commercial*, where he would spend the next 30 years (with the exception of a brief and frustrating year at the *Chicago Daily News*). He became editorial page editor of the *Arkansas Democrat-Gazette* in 1992. He would soon see the nickname he used for the state's governor—Slick Willie—become a national byword.

Greenberg won a Pulitzer Prize for his editorials in favor of civil rights and against George Wallace's presidential aspirations in 1968, and has also won various other awards including the William Allen White Award, the H.L. Mencken Award, and more than one award from ASNE for his editorials and newspaper columns, which are now syndicated by Tribune Media Services. Collections of Greenberg's columns have been published in three books: *Resonant Lives, Entirely Personal,* and *No Surprises*, a compilation of his writings about Bill and Hillary Clinton.

In 1964, Greenberg married the former Carolyn Levy of Waco, Texas, who died in 1995. She gave him two children who in turn have given him great satisfaction and unmerited devotion.

Whether urging readers to contact the Arkansas legislature about ethical matters (and providing a telephone number) or exposing the pettiness of the president of the United States in "Word to a Friend," Greenberg's editorials advocate without equivocation for the good of the people.

Word to a friend:
Was that a threat?

MAY 27, 2000

Skip Rutherford, director presumptive of the Clinton Library, is always a pleasure to see, and almost as great a pleasure to talk to. But sometimes our old friend may inadvertently say more than he means. Consider the Skipper's medium-wrought reaction to the news that a disciplinary committee of the state's Supreme Court had recommended that a lawyer friend of his be disbarred. That's always a shock, though it's become a more frequent one in Arkansas—another sign that standards are coming back.

Mr. Rutherford's lawyer friend is out of state at the moment—in Washington, D.C., though there's talk he might settle down in Chappaqua, N.Y. But wherever he is at the moment, The Hon. William J. Clinton, Esq., somehow manages to stay in trouble with the law.

And that, says Skip Rutherford, may mean trouble for those of us who had been looking forward to spending our declining years quietly researching the Clinton era and comedy at the nearest presidential library, the one rahtcheer in little ol' Little Rock, Ark.

What's the problem? Well, if folks down here keep giving Bill Clinton trouble, says the Skipper, that presidential park the City of Little Rock keeps talking about just might turn out to be only a park after all. Because the president and his friends might take their library and go home, wherever that is at the moment.

Mr. Rutherford says he's already fielded some phone calls from donors who are not at all happy with our Supreme Court's committee on professional conduct and its blatant, its extreme, its wholly unfair emphasis on, well, professional conduct. Mr. Rutherford doesn't sound all too happy about it himself. Indeed, he sounds a bit, well, extreme:

"Speaking independently here," he told the *Democrat-Gazette*'s Elisa Crouch, "if I were the president, I would now begin to question why I would want to put a library, a policy center and $125 million worth of ongoing private investment in Arkansas."

Is that supposed to be a threat, or does it only sound like it? Surely not. Not from Skip Rutherford, one of our own, a booster of every good cause that ever came down the pike, like this presidential library. He's got to know us better than that. Can he think that a court of law—*that the Supreme Court of this state*—is going to be swayed in the slightest by that kind of talk? Can he have confused our judges with the kind in Washington who somehow always direct the cases of Clinton cronies to Clinton appointees?

But just in case the Skipper thinks there's any percentage in making less than subtle threats—and surely he didn't realize how his words would sound when they came out in the paper—allow us to remind our old friend that this is Arkansas. Here the people rule. And despite any impression to the contrary left by the remnant of an old, one-party political elite, we here would not trade our honor (or our independent judiciary) for a presidential library no matter how grand. Some things are not buyable in these parts, however readily available they may be elsewhere in the more mercantile quarters of the American Union. Like the White House at fund-raising time.

Nor have we in these latitudes ever responded well to threats, however unintended. Arkansas is part of the South, Skip. (You'll find our geography impeccable.) You remember the South, don't you? She had many and grievous faults—who does not?—and was regularly seduced by her own passions, but she never sold herself. And certainly not for some fancy presidential library-policy center-*cum*-commercial development.

We hope we have made ourselves clear on this fine point.

We'd also like to think it won't be necessary to elaborate the point in the future. After all, the knowledgeable Dale Bumpers, the president's talented mouthpiece, has assured all that the presidential library is a Go for Little Rock. To quote the former senator and always advocate: "I know that Bill Clinton wouldn't change his mind where the library would go. It would be out of character for him."

Which leaves only one question: What character?

Lessons Learned

BY PAUL GREENBERG

Writing editorials for decades in a small town where the people you write about are likely to be in the same grocery line or maybe Sunday school teaches the writer some things. Writing this editorial helped me re-learn some of those lessons:

■ Be candid but firm, principled but friendly. Be tough on ideas, easy on people. Hence the headline, "Word to a Friend." And the subhead, too, which indicated that not even a friend should bully others: "Was That a Threat?" Remember that the headline is part of the editorial, too. Don't compose it hurriedly as an afterthought. Write it with care.

■ Address both reader and subject directly. Don't orate, but converse. We said the same things in this editorial that I would have said if I'd come across my friend Skip Rutherford of the Clinton Library at a coffee shop.

■ Let the reader in on the conversation. Reveal not only something about the subject but try to transmit something of your own values. Preferably subtly. Nobody likes to be hectored. Your most important audience is the next generation, and here was an opportunity to pass on some manners.

■ A newspaper is a persona; the *Democrat-Gazette* has a personality. It, or rather she, should speak in a human voice. In this case, it's the voice of an aunt who loves us, but isn't about to be quiet when she sees one of her favorites, ol' Skipper, walking up Fool's Hill. She even addresses him by his nickname.

■ Cultivate a sense of place. There can be no doubt that this editorial appeared in an Arkansas newspaper and appeals to Arkansas pride. The tone says: We are the kind of people who will help you any way we can, but who do not respond kindly to threats. The lesson: Identify with your community, speak for it, and exhibit its best qualities.

■ It shouldn't be necessary to note this lesson, but it is: Be completely accurate with the quotes and facts you're relying on to make your rhetorical point. Check and double-check. It's a strange but common occurrence: People don't mind being quoted in a news story, but let those quotes be used as the basis of a critical editorial, and they discover they've been misquoted.

■ Write with feeling, edit with reason. Feel, then think. I was outraged when I read Skip's remark in the paper, but by the time the editorial appeared, it was a proper, friendly, and restrained rebuke, almost more a word of advice. People in a temper tend to be less than convincing. Leave some room for the reader to react with anger; don't express it all for him. Let him participate. Don't rob the reader of a personal reaction by expressing it all for him. You may lead him to the brink, but don't jump for him. In short, be decorous. The essence of this business may be setting the right tone.

■ Go to a second level of interpetation. In this editorial, we didn't just criticize the threat being made, but we explained why it was particularly ill-suited in these circumstances and latitudes. We offered the reader some mental traction, not just a snap judgment that he might easily have reached on his own when skimming the news article. An editorial should go deeper than that. It's the news after somebody's had a day to think on it. This editorial spotlights the particularly interesting detail that may have been buried in the news article, but that sheds light on the times like this revealing quote from the Skipper. His ill-advised comment summed up a whole, baneful attitude.

■ If the editorial satisfies the writer, and this one did, it's a good sign that it will satisfy the reader.

■ Be fair, mercilessly fair.

■ Give local topics top priority, and write about them in a knowledgeable, local way.

■ And don't go on and on.

MOBILE REGISTER

Bailey Thomson

Finalist, Editorial Writing

Bailey Thomson is an associate professor of journalism at the University
of Alabama and coordinator of his
department's graduate studies. He joined Alabama's
faculty in August 1996. In 1999, the Society of Professional Journalists bestowed on him its National Excellence in Teaching Award.

Thomson grew up in Aliceville, Ala., and earned bachelor's, master's, and doctoral degrees from the University
of Alabama. After working at the *Orlando Sentinel* in
Florida as chief editorial writer, he returned to Alabama
in 1992 to become associate editor of the *Mobile Register.*
In 1994, he directed a special investigation of Alabama's
antiquated constitution, titled "Sin of the Fathers." He
and two colleagues were Pulitzer finalists for editorials
on that subject.

After joining the university's faculty, he continued to
write for the *Register*. His 1999 editorial series titled
"Dixie's Broken Heart" won the Distinguished Writing
Award from the American Society of Newspaper Edi-
tors. Meanwhile, Thomson writes a weekly column for
Alabama Public Radio.

He also writes frequently for other state newspapers,
has written articles for historical quarterlies, and recently
wrote an introduction for the reprint of Clarence Cason's
classic, *90° in the Shade.*

Thomson and his wife, Kristi, live in Tuscaloosa.
They have a daughter, Sarah, who attends high school.

"Let Us Convene," the leadoff piece of Thomson's editorial series "Century of Shame," is imaginative in more
than one way. But its message—strong, reasoned, and
deeply informed—is grounded in the real challenges facing Alabama.

Let us convene

OCTOBER 22, 2000

MONTGOMERY—They are a diverse bunch—old and young, white and black, male and female. These delegates to Alabama's first constitutional convention in a century look, well, pretty much like Alabama.

They have worked and debated here for months in the Statehouse building, drafting a modern charter of fundamental laws and human rights. They now will ask voters to ratify it.

Lobbyists and other capital regulars had warned that citizens could never do the work of politicians, but delegates surprised everyone with their mastery of details. Most of them rose above petty special interests—again, defying the insiders' predictions.

Newspaper editorials credit Gov. Don Siegelman for insisting that the Legislature call a citizens convention and for persuading voters to support such a move. Earlier, he had been coy about reform, but then he came alive to the prospects for changing Alabama forever. Many say the state has never had a governor of such vision and vigor.

Polls indicate voters will embrace this new constitution. Reformers expect a massive, last-minute ad blitz by offended interest groups, but supporters appear to be well-armed with facts to dispel scare tactics. They have crisscrossed the state to hammer their arguments that this new constitution would make life better for Alabamians.

Supporters say they have been helped by news coverage around the world that depicts their efforts as casting aside the racist, negative images from Alabama's past...

* * *

This touch of fiction presents a grand dream, to be sure, but certainly not an impossible one. Other Southern states, such as Georgia and Florida, have written modern constitutions, and they have prospered under them. Alabama can do the same.

A convention is the ideal way to proceed, but the present constitution also allows the Legislature to rewrite the document article by article for voters to consider. Regardless of the method, reformers face the same challenge: They first must persuade the Legislature to accept reform. And as sad as it sounds, many legislators refuse to surrender the power they enjoy, under the 1901 document, as lords of the manor over local affairs.

Thus citizens are compelled to organize and help their legislators see the light. In the process, Alabama can enjoy a revival of its civic life and begin reversing the tragic influence that the present constitution has exerted, beginning when it stripped the vote from African Americans and poor whites.

Many Alabama governors, beginning with Emmet O'Neal in 1915, have championed a new constitution. But for various reasons each attempt—however noble— failed.

These past reform efforts originated at the top of Alabama's political system. Lurking to destroy them were reactionary special interests, such as the Alabama Farmers Federation, jealously guarding their constitutional privileges.

But what if a new movement arose instead from the grass roots, gaining momentum as it grew? Could this crusade overpower the special interests?

Equally important, would such a movement help reverse citizens' alienation from public life? Could it become an antidote to the poisonous and divisive politics that regularly roil our state and confuse our people?

We often hear complaints that our citizens, if they show up at the polls at all, can be motivated more easily to vote "no" than "yes." The negative attack ad is widely reviled but remains crudely efficient.

Yet let us be careful to assign blame where it belongs. For almost a century, our state has endured a constitution written by industrialists—dubbed the "Big Mules" —and rich planters, who vested themselves with power and pushed citizens aside in the quest for cheap labor and tax advantages. This alliance and its political heirs denied people the education and economic opportunities they needed to be productive citizens.

Only a few political reformers rose to challenge the

oligarchy. Others, such as Gov. George Wallace, posed as popular champions, yet they practiced the familiar politics of hate, diverting public energy into an ugly reaction.

In Alabama, we simply don't know what an enlightened citizenry might produce. But times are changing.

The former plantation counties now cry for help to overcome the debilitating poverty that results from generations of enforced ignorance. Many corporate leaders join in calling for good schools and fair taxes.

Urban counties such as Mobile are ready to revolt against the Legislature's despotism, which denies them local control. Citizens resent the way that legislative delegations dictate how local taxes may be raised and spent. These citizens want local officials to be able to protect communities from runaway growth and other threats. The present constitution denies such lawmaking power to counties.

And across the state, a growing and diverse army of young new leaders is learning to work together for larger causes. They are the nucleus of the rallies and forums now demanding constitutional reform.

In coastal Alabama, for example, a broad coalition of citizens has organized a large event for this afternoon at Battleship Park on Mobile Bay. They have engaged many volunteers to make this rally a milestone in the march for a new constitution.

In fact, one would have to go all the way back to the 1890s to find a more fertile time for citizenship. The Populists from that depression-ridden era sent hundreds of speakers into the field, demanding honest elections, fair labor laws and other reforms. They organized study groups to educate citizens. No wonder the Big Mule alliance was determined to bury this movement under the 1901 constitution.

Self-styled "realists" of the present day, who often represent entrenched interests, dismiss any possibility that reform might bubble up from below. These cynics claim to see the world as it is, not as it might be or should be. Many of them are comfortable in the house the 1901 fathers built, where they know how to open the doors to power and influence.

Opponents' logic might sound impeccable, except

they ignore one important variable: the capacity of citizens to grow and change. What appears to be immutable reality today may be but curious history tomorrow.

Surely, Alabamians who came of age during the civil rights struggle understand the power of a great idea to transform society. A similarly idealistic movement sprang from the bloodstained earth in the 1960s to challenge and ultimately overthrow segregation. This experience suggests that an energized citizenry can create a new moral order.

It is true that we Alabamians have usually waited for Congress and the federal courts to save us from our constitution's worst features, such as its notorious voting restrictions. But many Alabamians believe in redemption, even in politics. Citizens can make things right if they can find the courage and the will to act for the common good.

They can join groups already forming around the state to demand a new constitution. They can write or call their legislators and urge them to act. Equally important, citizens can beseech Gov. Siegelman to lead this movement and become the champion of a new Alabama in a new South.

From the old must be born the new—*nova ex veteris,* as the Latin paradox says. Our challenge is no less than to transform Alabama's civic life so that an age of possibility succeeds a century of shame.

* * *

And someday we may read…

MONTGOMERY—A beaming Gov. Don Siegelman announced tonight that Alabama voters had ratified a new constitution. The unofficial count from the voting today showed overwhelming support, especially among urban counties, where citizens demanded more responsive local government.

Siegelman credited the victory to the careful work of the convention that wrote the document and the tireless support of citizens who campaigned for its approval.

"Let the word go out to the nation and the world," he declared "Alabamians on this day have blessed their state and prepared the way for generations to follow."

Lessons Learned

BY BAILEY THOMSON

My late friend Ron Casey, who won a Pulitzer Prize at *The Birmingham News* in 1991, used to say that if one wanted to be a wine critic, then go to France. But if one wanted to be a great editorialist, live in Alabama. There does seem to be a certain advantage to roosting in my native state and commenting upon its political culture. Alabama has a long and deep tradition of journalism devoted to exposing the ugly underside of politics, while holding aloft a vision of what might be under more progressive leadership.

I come to this tradition quite naturally, having grown up in Alabama during the violent resistance to civil rights. After college and my first jobs as a newspaperman, I left the state in 1977 and did not return until 1992. Many things had improved in the interim. Yet I was astounded at how certain old themes persisted, particularly race. In many instances, education and other services remained abysmally poor, in part because of an almost fanatical devotion to low property taxes. A closer reading revealed that certain interest groups pretty much ran things through their influence on the Legislature, while on the surface politicians mouthed populist clichés. By almost any objective standard, Alabama's effectiveness in self-government was miserably low.

But how does a writer, particularly an editorialist, get his arms around such a mighty subject? Yes, the material is ample and rich, as Ron suggested, but the writer must know what to do with it. Here is where my continuing education as an editorial writer intersects with each big project I undertake.

Some years ago, I discovered that an editorial could incorporate much of the literary power associated with great narratives. Although an editorialist must use language more compactly, he is still free to employ vivid details, anecdotes, scenes, digression, and other techniques. The editorialist makes his case by taking readers by the hand and pointing out the contours of the story, rather than simply by preaching the point. I also learned and continue to believe that writing a series of editorials, each addressing a different idea but within the same theme, allows a writer to magnify his influence. With "Century of Shame," I presented my case in seven pieces for why Alabama's failure to move forward can be traced to its racist and antiquated 1901 constitution.

Something else a good editorial shares with a strong narrative story is richness of fact. I am a ravenous collector of facts—all of which I carefully catalog in my computer. Most of these facts never appear in my pieces, but together they create the base upon which I write.

I also believe that a writer has to smell a story to understand it—something my recent experience illustrates. I spent about four weeks in the field collecting material for this series. My research carried me into the dusty bowels of the state archives to learn how an African American challenged the 1901 constitution all the way to the U.S. Supreme Court. And my reporting took me along rutted trails in rural Mobile County, where the constitutional failure to grant local home rule was encouraging trailer slums to sprout.

A final lesson reiterated by my recent work: A good series deserves a title that expresses the theme. "Century of Shame" came to me after I had completed most of the research and was poised to write. Those three words summarized what this constitution, forced upon citizens through a fraudulent ratification, had done to my beloved Alabama. Yes, a writer profits from studying history, especially when the villains and victims can be identified and the results are evident in the present. But a good editorialist also has to feel a slow burn toward the injustice contained in that history.

Steven Erlanger
Deadline News Reporting

The work of Steven Erlanger proves that there is nothing dead about deadline reporting. In his hands, it is a lively craft. The exercise of that craft depends not just on the hands, but on the feet, working hard day after day, month after month, fighting for access. Erlanger crosses borders closed to others. His goal is always to directly observe events, to be there when a government topples.

Erlanger's credentials are impeccable, his education, apprenticeship, and professional experiences all attached to the most prestigious institutions: Harvard. Oxford. *The New York Times*.

Born in Waterbury, Conn., in 1952, Erlanger had the benefit of an elite education, graduating with high honors from Harvard in 1974 with a degree in political philosophy. For the next eight years he taught at Harvard, first at the College and then at the Kennedy School of Government.

Before joining the staff of the *Times*, Erlanger worked at *The Boston Globe* for 11 years. He served as a foreign editor and correspondent, reporting from Eastern Europe, Canada, and revolutionary Iran. He received a Robert Livingston Award in 1981 for his work on Eastern Europe.

By 1987, Erlanger had not only academic credentials but impressive experience, a combination *The New York Times* could not resist. From 1988 to 1991, he reported out of Southeast Asia and then spent four years in the Moscow bureau. He prepared for this post by studying Russian for 10 months at Oxford University.

Erlanger became chief of the *Times*'s Prague bureau in 1999 and from that venue reported tirelessly on the political conflicts in the war-torn Balkans. To these dispatches from Serbia, Erlanger brings all his skills: an intellectual curiosity, an ambitious energy to get it first and get it right, an almost prescient instinct that a strike by Serbian miners marked the beginning of the end for the nation's dictator, Slobodan Milosevic.

—Roy Peter Clark

Serbian strikers, joined by 20,000, face down police

OCTOBER 5, 2000

KOLUBARA, Serbia—If the regime of Slobodan Milosevic breaks and Vojislav Kostunica takes office as Yugoslavia's president, it could be because of what happened at this gritty coal mine here today.

Hundreds of Interior Ministry policemen swooped in to break a protest strike at the Kolubara mine, which produces the coal for half of Serbia's electricity. The police ordered the workers, who have been on strike since Friday demanding Mr. Kostunica's inauguration as president, to leave.

But the strikers refused, calling for help. Confronted with up to 20,000 people pouring into the mine to defend the workers, some from as far away as the city of Cacak in central Serbia and Belgrade, the capital, 40 miles to the northeast, the police broke and stood aside.

One police commander said: "I'm fed up with this. After this, I'm throwing my hat away and going home. The police in Serbia are more democratic than you think."

The police watched as Mr. Kostunica himself arrived this evening, pushing through the crowd of miners and their families, to cheers and shouts of "President," coming closer to claiming the prize he says he won with an outright majority in elections on Sept. 24.

"I will be with you until we defend what we won on Sept. 24," Mr. Kostunica said. "Is there anything more honest than the miners of Kolubara rising to defend their votes?"

Some miners began to chant, some to cry. "I'm telling you, what you are doing here is not subversion," Mr. Kostunica shouted, his voice breaking up over the primitive sound system set up beside him on the steps of a single-story wooden office building. "You are defending the people's will, and those who step on the people's will and try to steal their votes are the ones committing subversion."

Mr. Kostunica has accused the government of steal-

ing votes and faking the election results. He is appealing
to Mr. Milosevic to recognize his defeat and step down
to spare the country. The opposition is planning a huge
rally in Belgrade on Thursday, which it hopes will be
decisive and push Mr. Milosevic out.

On Tuesday, the Serbian government issued a stern
warning to the organizers of this spreading strike, saying that they would be arrested for action that "threatens
citizens' lives, disrupts normal functioning of traffic,
prevents normal work of industry, schools, institutions
and health facilities."

The government has accused the strikers here of sub-
verting the national interest, and early Tuesday morning
sent the country's top general, Gen. Nebojsa Pavkovic,
to tell the workers to go back to work or face punishment. Blaming the miners, the government began power
cuts all over Serbia on Tuesday, a reminder of last year's
NATO bombing war over Kosovo. And a judge issued a
warrant for the arrest of 11 strike leaders, plus two opposition politicians.

But the police failed to make the arrests today. Miners asserted they had behaved correctly and, said Dragan Micandinovic, an electrical engineer, with "a sense
of shame." Mr. Micandinovic has remained here for
three days except for two brief visits home to see his
children.

"During the NATO war, we worked four shifts, including Sundays, and the government called us heroes,"
he said bitterly. "I was here and saw the missiles flying
over my head. Now the government calls us enemies."

"But we are victims," he said. "Their victims."

Slavoljub Sajic, a mechanical engineer, said, "This is
the heart of the protest, the heart of Serbia, and we're
not leaving until Milosevic leaves."

The police hung back while Mr. Kostunica spoke, but
did not immediately withdraw from the office buildings
and other facilities they had occupied earlier in the day.
Tonight, workers were negotiating with them about
whether they would withdraw altogether, but expressed
confidence that the police could not get the mine going
again.

The police, in camouflage uniforms and riot gear,
with helmets and batons, arrived about 11 a.m. when

only about 100 workers were gathered.

"They came from all directions," Mr. Micandinovic said. "They threatened us and told us to leave or they would drag us out. It was very risky."

"There are a lot of people here now," he said. "But it was pretty risky this morning."

The police set up a cordon around the mine with roadblocks and moved into offices, talking with a strike committee and the management, who are supporting the workers.

But Mr. Micandinovic and others began to telephone opposition politicians in nearby Lazarevac, 30 miles south of Belgrade, and independent Radio Lazarevac spread the news. Relatives, workers and ordinary people began to come toward the mine, some dodging the police roadblocks by crossing fields and streams.

By early afternoon about 1,000 people were trapped behind a police roadblock on a bridge just outside the mine itself. Two opposition politicians, Vuk Obradovic, a former general, and Dragoljub Micunovic, negotiated with the police, to no avail.

"This shows the weakness of the regime," Mr. Micunovic said as he stood at the bridge. "They are faking this campaign of an electricity shortage to frighten people and make them suffer and blame it on the opposition."

The Kolubara coal mine is critical, he said. "Copper mines are on strike, too, but people can live without copper, not without electricity."

But the police were clearly unhappy with their orders, Mr. Micunovic said, adding, "Both sides are being very patient."

One young policeman, accepting some water, said quietly, "This is a mess." He stopped, then said, "Don't worry, everything will be all right."

A bus full of protesters moved slowly through the crowd and, almost gently, shoved aside a police van blocking the bridge. The crowd surged forward; the police moved aside, looking sheepish. Some protesters gave them apples and clapped them on their shoulders.

The mood on the long walk from the bridge to the strike headquarters was that of exhilaration, even as opposition leaders sped by in cars and buses. Then more cars moved by, with license plates from Cacak and other towns, full of people who had come to defend the mine. People shouted, "Cacak! Cacak!" and the slogan of the student resistance movement, *"Otpor"* ("He's finished").

Nadia Ruegg, who is married to a Swiss, told the police to let her through to see her brother, Aleksandar Nikitic. "When I asked the guy, 'Do you have a brother?' he didn't answer," she said. "Then he told us, 'We won't beat you.' And we told them, 'Well, we won't beat you either.'"

In 1914, Kolubara was the site of one of the most famous Serbian victories, when the Serbs turned back the Austro-Hungarian Army. The *"Kolubarska bitka,"* or "Kolubara battle," became part of nationalist folklore, and the famous writer and later, briefly, Yugoslav president, Dobrica Cosic, featured it in his novel, *Time of Death*.

That part of the novel became a stage play in Belgrade in 1986, as Serbian nationalism was growing. At one point, the Serbs wait for ammunition from the French, but when it arrives it turns out to be the wrong caliber. As the soldiers start to wail and weep, the commander turns to the audience and says, "Don't cry, no one can do anything to us."

On the Kolubara coal field this evening, those words were echoed, unwittingly, by Milanko Bulatovic, a miner here for 26 years, who has been here every day of the strike from 6:30 in the morning until the evening.

"This is the end of him," he said. "This is the beginning of the new Serbia. Milosevic cannot do anything to us now."

Yugoslavs claim Belgrade for a new leader

OCTOBER 6, 2000

BELGRADE, Serbia—As the federal Parliament burned and tear gas wafted through chaotic streets, vast throngs of Serbs wrested their capital and key levers of power away from Slobodan Milosevic today, bringing his 13-year reign to the edge of collapse.

Vojislav Kostunica, the opposition leader who claimed victory in the presidential election on Sept. 24, moved through an ecstatic crowd of several hundred thousand and proclaimed, "Good evening, dear liberated Serbia!"

The crowd shouted his name, and he shouted back: "Big, beautiful Serbia has risen up just so one man, Slobodan Milosevic, will leave."

Behind the crowds, smoke from the burning Parliament building mingled with the blacker smoke from the burning state television and radio center—bombed by NATO during last year's war over Kosovo—and tear gas, all set loose as hundreds of thousands of Serbs roamed through the city to demand the exit of a leader who had brought them years of ethnic conflict, isolation and international contempt.

The whereabouts of Mr. Milosevic and his family were unknown, though he was believed to be in Serbia. Two main pillars of his regime, the state news media and many of his police, were gone. But though the army stayed out of the fray, the chiefs of the security forces had yet to formally shift their allegiance to Mr. Kostunica, and Mr. Milosevic had not relinquished power.

While the Belgrade police did not take serious action against the protesters and many joined them, Mr. Milosevic's interior minister, Vlajko Stoiljkovic, refused to meet Mr. Kostunica's representatives, instead asking them, "What have you done to Belgrade?"

Opposition leaders, including Momcilo Perisic, the chief of staff whom Mr. Milosevic fired in October 1998, were reportedly talking to the army to persuade them to recognize Mr. Kostunica as president.

For the time being, there were no contacts between Mr. Milosevic and Mr. Kostunica. The opposition leader told the crowd not to march on Mr. Milosevic's home and office in Dedinje, a suburb, saying: "Answer their violence with nonviolence. Answer their lies with the truth."

As Mr. Kostunica tried to call the new federal Parliament and city government into session, the mood was boisterous, ecstatic and proud. "All of us have simply had enough," said Petr Radosavljevic, a mechanical engineer. "All we want is a normal country, where there is a future for young people."

Damir Strahinjic, 25, waving his arm over the crowd, said: "This should be enough to see the end of him. But you never know in this country, with this guy." His fears were echoed by a senior member of Mr. Kostunica's staff tonight, who said, "I'm thinking Milosevic has one more trick up his sleeve."

Earlier, Mr. Milosevic's ruling Socialist Party attacked the opposition for causing unrest and violence and vowed to fight back with "all means to secure peaceful life." But faced with an uprising that has spread throughout much of Serbia, Mr. Milosevic may have run out of moves. Party members were talking to opposition leaders and even human rights lawyers.

The United States and European governments threw their support behind Mr. Kostunica. In Washington, President Clinton declared: "The people of Serbia have made their opinion clear. They did it when they voted peacefully and quietly, and now they're doing it in the streets."

With the massive outpouring in the streets, major bastions of state power defected to Mr. Kostunica. The state news agency Tanjug began referring to him as "the elected president of Yugoslavia" in a report signed, "Journalists of Liberated Tanjug." The state newspaper *Politika*, founded in 1904 and deeply degraded under the Milosevic regime, went over to the opposition. And on state television, a new slide appeared: "This is the new Radio Television Serbia broadcasting."

At 11:30 tonight, Mr. Kostunica appeared on the "liberated" state television, urging reconciliation on a nation used to a steady diet of government propaganda.

Speaking of the burning buildings and clashes, Mr. Kostunica said: "We hope that these sad incidents are behind us. My first hours started with pleasure, that a vision of Serbia I had all these years has started to be fulfilled." He promised that state television would remain "open to all views and all voices," including those of the coalition that has run this country.

He called for the lifting of international sanctions against Yugoslavia, which he said the European Union tonight promised him it would do as early as Monday. While he said "we cannot forget what some countries did to us last year during the NATO bombing, we can't live against the grain," and he promised normal relations with the world.

As thousands of people pressed into Belgrade from opposition strongholds, some were spoiling for a fight. They pushed aside police barricades on the roads to Belgrade, and some stripped police officers of their shields and weapons. Some were equipped with sticks and rocks, and they led the taking of the federal Parliament building, which was heavily guarded by police.

The building was soon on fire, its windows broken, and some demonstrators began to loot it for souvenirs, including chairs, hat racks and leather briefcases used by Parliament members. Portraits of Mr. Milosevic and ballot papers for the Sept. 24 elections were dumped from the second floor, all of them already circled to vote for Mr. Milosevic.

The police were lavish with their use of tear gas, which filled downtown Belgrade, but they did not charge the crowd. They used batons and stun grenades, but those who did were overwhelmed by the crowd, and some young men marched happily with their trophies: plastic police riot shields and helmets.

When crowds approached the back entrance of Radio Television Serbia, the police started to come out with their hands raised. The crowd greeted them with "*plavi, plavi,*" or blue, the color of their uniforms, and gave them opposition badges.

As people entered the building, some workers came out the side, including television anchors and personalities like Staka Novakovic, Simo Gajin and Tanja Lenard, who is a senior member of the Yugoslav United

Left party of Mr. Milosevic's wife. The crowd began to spit on them, and Ms. Lenard found refuge behind some garbage containers.

The crowd then looted the building.

There was a similar scene at a police station in nearby Majke Jevrosime Street. When the police left the building, some in the crowd gave them civilian clothes. But the building was then looted—with weapons taken—and was set afire with gasoline bombs.

In the skirmishing, at least one person died and 100 were injured today, according to independent radio B2-92, which also returned to its old frequency in Belgrade when its own headquarters were taken. The station had been seized by the government twice, and had been broadcasting by satellite. Belgrade Studio B television was also taken back from political control, and private stations affiliated with the Milosevic regime, like TV Palma and TV Pink, stopped broadcasting and put up slides that read, "This program is canceled because of the current situation in the country."

The day's vast uprising was the culmination of a campaign to defend Mr. Kostunica's victory in the presidential elections that Mr. Milosevic called in an effort to restore his own tattered legitimacy. It was a tactical mistake of the first order, because Serbs took the election as a referendum on Mr. Milosevic's 13 years of rule and misrule.

According to the opposition, Mr. Kostunica won at least 51.33 percent of the vote against four other candidates, an outright victory. But with electoral fraud, the Federal Election Commission reduced his percentage to just under 50 percent and called a runoff.

Mr. Kostunica called it theft and vowed that he would not accept a runoff for an election he had won. Strikes and protests on his behalf began to spread through Serbia this week.

The key moment may have come on Wednesday, when Mr. Milosevic's police failed to break a strike at a key coal mine in Kolubara. The workers, who had struck Friday to support Mr. Kostunica, refused to leave and called for help. Some 20,000 relatives and ordinary citizens from surrounding towns came to their aid, and the police let them go through, refusing to attack.

Tonight, the police withdrew entirely from the mine.

Later Wednesday night, Tanjug reported that the highest court had ruled that the presidential election was invalid because of irregularities. But the court's judgment, supposed to be published today, did not come, and Mr. Kostunica made it clear tonight that it was simply too late to think about any compromise over the election with the authorities.

Milosevic concedes defeat; Yugoslavs celebrate new era

OCTOBER 7, 2000

BELGRADE, Serbia—Bowing to a vast popular revolt against him, a pale Slobodan Milosevic resigned tonight as Yugoslavia's president, ending 13 years of rule that have brought his country four wars, international isolation, a NATO bombing campaign and his own indictment on war crimes charges.

Vojislav Kostunica, a 56-year-old constitutional lawyer of quiet habits and a firm belief in a future for Yugoslavia as a normal country within Europe, is expected to be inaugurated as president on Saturday.

An already exuberant and chaotic Belgrade, celebrating its extraordinary day of revolution on Thursday, exploded with noise as the news of Mr. Milosevic's resignation, made in a short speech on television, quickly spread. Cars blasted their horns; people banged on pots and pans from balconies, blew whistles and danced in the street.

Mr. Milosevic appeared on television about 11:20 p.m.—shortly after Mr. Kostunica announced, on a television phone-in program, that he had met Mr. Milosevic and the army chief of staff, Gen. Nebojsa Pavkovic, this evening, and that both had congratulated him on his election victory on Sept. 24.

The resignation deal was helped along by Foreign Minister Igor S. Ivanov of Russia, who met with Mr. Kostunica and Mr. Milosevic today. Mr. Ivanov was carrying assurances that if Mr. Milosevic gave up power now, the world would not press for his extradition to face war crimes charges in The Hague, senior Western officials said tonight.

"I've just received official information that Vojislav Kostunica won the elections," Mr. Milosevic said in his television address. "This decision was made by the body that was authorized to do so under the Constitution, and I consider that it has to be respected."

Mr. Milosevic spoke with a straight face after an extraordinary set of manipulations on his part—of the

Federal Election Commission and the highest court in
the land—to deny Mr. Kostunica outright victory.

Speaking of how important it is for political parties to
strengthen themselves in opposition, Mr. Milosevic said
he intended to continue as leader of the Socialist Party
of Serbia after taking a break "to spend more time with
my family, especially my grandson, Marko."

Despite his brave words, it is unlikely that the Socialist Party, with its own future to consider, will keep Mr.
Milosevic as its leader for long. The remarks seemed
part of a deal to save him a little bit of face.

There is deep resentment in this semi-reformed
Communist Party—Serbia's largest and best organized,
in power since World War II—of Mr. Milosevic's indul-
gence of his wife, Mirjana Markovic, who began her
own party, the Yugoslav United Left. Ruling in coalition, the Socialists saw more and more of their posi-
tions, powers and benefits going to the United Left.

The reaction in Belgrade was immediate and loud.

Tanja Radovic, a 23-year-old student blowing her
whistle furiously on Knez Mihailova Street, said: "He's
gone. It's finally true. We had too much of him, it's
enough. This is the end of him and all these thieves."

Dragana Kovac, 31, said: "I'm happy, and not just
because of him, but because of her. He should have
spent more time with his family starting 10 years ago."

Ilija Bobic said: "I wish all my family were alive to
see this. My father used to say that the Communists
would finish quickly. He was wrong, but it came true,
finally."

Mr. Bobic stopped, then said: "We all know it won't
be better quickly here. But now you can talk. You're not
afraid of the phone, of being an enemy inside, of having
to join the party to have a job."

The United States and Europe have promised a quick
lifting of international sanctions against Yugoslavia, as
well as aid, once Mr. Milosevic goes. The sanctions include a toothless oil embargo and a flight ban, currently
suspended. But financial sanctions and a visa ban aimed
at the Milosevic government are likely to remain in
place for now.

The United States and Britain have urged that Mr.
Milosevic be handed over to the war crimes tribunal,

and continued to do so publicly today. But Mr. Kostunica, who considers the tribunal a political instrument of Washington and not a neutral legal body, has made it clear that he will not arrest Mr. Milosevic or extradite him.

Mr. Kostunica's vow was also intended to give Mr. Milosevic the security to leave office, so that an electoral concession did not have to mean, as Mr. Kostunica said, "a matter of life or death."

Foreign Minister Ivanov came here today to deliver a similar message, Western officials said tonight.

If Mr. Milosevic conceded and renounced power, even after the pillars of his rule collapsed this week, he and his family would be allowed to remain in Serbia, they said. But no Western country would say so publicly, given the United Nations tribunal's indictment.

Mr. Kostunica has pointed out that if democratic and international stability is at stake, the requirement to pursue those indicted is secondary under international law.

The collapse of Mr. Milosevic's position came soon after Mr. Ivanov met him this morning in Belgrade. This afternoon, the Constitutional Court suddenly issued its ruling approving Mr. Kostunica's appeal of the election results.

The official press agency Tanjug said on Wednesday night that the court had decided to annul the main part of the Sept. 24 presidential vote, implying a repeat of the election. But then the court said that in fact Mr. Kostunica had won the first round outright, with more than 50 percent of the vote, precisely as he has insisted. It was another example of Mr. Milosevic's manipulation, but this time to others' ends.

Then the speaker of the Serbian Parliament, Dragan Tomic, one of Mr. Milosevic's closest allies, announced that he would convene that body on Monday to recognize Mr. Kostunica's election as federal president. He addressed a letter to Mr. Kostunica this way: "To the president of the Federal Republic of Yugoslavia."

The election of Mr. Kostunica—carried to power first by the votes of a majority of Serbs, and then by an uprising by even more of them—will present difficulties and opportunities for Montenegro and Kosovo, both parts of Yugoslavia.

The Western-leaning president of Montenegro, Milo Djukanovic, will find himself offered a new deal within Yugoslavia that will be aimed at blunting the effort toward independence. That may quickly undermine Mr. Djukanovic's governing coalition in Montenegro, which contains parties firmly backing independence.

Mr. Djukanovic boycotted the federal elections, allowing Milosevic allies to win all of Montenegro's seats in the federal Parliament. Those allies are now likely to make a deal with Mr. Kostunica, abandoning Mr. Milosevic, and leaving Mr. Djukanovic in effect powerless in a Belgrade that could quickly become the center for democratic life in the Balkans.

Mr. Kostunica will also offer Kosovo a high degree of autonomy. While outside powers recognize Yugoslav sovereignty over Kosovo, Mr. Milosevic was a perfect foil for Kosovo Albanian desires for independence, which have only grown stronger since NATO intervened on the Albanians' behalf in the 1999 bombing war.

Mr. Kostunica says he will live within United Nations Security Council Resolution 1244, governing Kosovo, but will insist on the return of Serbs who fled during the war.

In his television appearance, Mr. Milosevic thanked those who voted for him and even those who voted against him, "because they lifted from my soul a heavy burden I have borne for 10 years," he said. He also said a time in opposition would be good for the left coalition, to allow them to purge those who got into the party "to feed some personal interest," an extraordinary comment for a leader who allowed a form of state-sanctioned mafia to develop.

"I congratulate Mr. Kostunica on his election victory and wish for all citizens of Yugoslavia great success during the new presidency," he concluded.

In his own television appearance, Mr. Kostunica described his meeting with Mr. Milosevic. "It was ordinary communication, and it's good that we met, because there was a lot of fear over the peaceful transfer of power, especially last night," Mr. Kostunica said.

"This is the first time for many years in this country that power has been transferred normally, in a civilized manner," he said.

And he said he pointed out a lesson to Mr. Milosevic: "I talked about how power, once lost, is not power lost forever. You can regain it. This is something that all my experience taught me. The other side couldn't even imagine something like this, but now the other side has accepted this, and it is getting used to this lesson."

Writers' Workshop

Talking Points

1) Erlanger says that he likes to use quotations in his story to let key people speak for themselves. Study and discuss how quotes are used in "Serbian Strikers Face Down Police": how many there are, where they are placed, what leads up to them, what follows, where the attribution is placed, and the identity of the speakers.

2) Near the end of the story about the Serbian strikers, Erlanger includes some history of Kolubara, citing a novel titled *Time of Death*. Discuss the effect of this cultural detail, its placement in the story, and what it adds to the credibility and authority of the writer.

3) The way a writer uses language reflects not only his or her own voice, but the writer's sense of the audience, its interest, educational level, and seriousness. In his lead for "Yugoslavs Claim Belgrade for a New Leader" Erlanger uses the following words: *wafted, chaotic, throngs, wrested, levers, collapse.* Discuss which of these words seem familiar in the context of a news story, and which seem strange. Underline words in the story that surprised you.

4) In the story about Milosevic's concession, Erlanger records an important moment in European history, a daunting task for any reporter, especially one working for a newspaper with the standards of *The New York Times*. Discuss the reporting and writing strategies that make this story seem "big." Obviously, its position in the newspaper, the display of photography, the size of the headline all contribute to the effect. But focus your discussion on the use of language, the structure of sentences, the organization of the whole, and the quality of the reporting.

5) Canadian scholar Stuart Adam judges newspapers stories by these standards: a) news judgment; b) quality of the evidence gathered; c) language use appropriate to the content; d) effective narrative strategies; e) quality of analysis and interpretation. Grade Erlanger's work against each of these standards.

Assignment Desk

1) One technique for fast writing is to "find your focus in the field." If you find it back in the office, you may not have the material in your notebook to back it up. Think about when you tend to "find" your focus or your lead. On your next story be more self-conscious about this process.

2) Erlanger is a strong believer in eyewitness reporting. Study all his stories and mark the passages that seem to be the result of direct observation. Now read some of your own stories and apply the same test.

3) Erlanger says that a key to writing stories like this on deadline is to move all over the place. Different perspectives add depth and texture to the reporting and the writing. Try this technique on your next story. Find vantage points that may be unusual to you, but that are key to the characters in the story.

4) When journalists want to emphasize something, they often place it at the beginning: of a sentence, paragraph, or story. But the best journalists also use the place before the period as a point of special emphasis. After studying Erlanger's use of this technique, read your own work. Circle the ends of paragraphs. Are you using these places to their full advantage?

5) A classic journalistic technique is the "man on the street" interview. Notice how Erlanger employs it in "Milosevic Concedes Defeat" to capture efficiently the jubilation of the crowd. Think about using this technique in similar ways. Be aware of why you pick certain people in a crowd but not others. Consider whether or not you're approaching the "safest" people or the "most outrageous." Are you leaving some folks out?

6) Erlanger writes, "Cars blasted their horns; people banged on pots and pans from balconies, blew whistles and danced in the street." This appeal to our sense of both sight and sound transports us from our chairs to the scene in Belgrade. Look for opportunities in your stories to appeal to the reader's sense of sight—but also of sound and smell.

A conversation with
Steven Erlanger

ROY PETER CLARK: Do you have to be a fast writer to write well on deadline?

STEVEN ERLANGER: Yes, I think you do. But you also need to know what you want to write. I think most people are like this: You struggle with the first couple of paragraphs; you want to get those right, and then everything else seems to flow pretty well from there. I think everyone also knows a deadline is a great aid to production because the adrenaline rushes to meet the time that's left. The advantage of being abroad is that you have a few more hours, but it also means you've got to be more complete; one always tries to give people a considered picture of the day despite the rush of adrenaline. That's one of the strengths of my newspaper. The best news writing has at least some context, some touch, particularly on a big story, that you're covering something that matters and that may resonate beyond the day.

When you write your lead, if it has to be just right, doesn't that slow you down?

Well, you think about it all day. I used to work for *The Boston Globe* where you often understood that you were writing a second-day story for people who'd seen the news already. But at the *Times*, one of its tenets is you write the story from the day that it happened, not presuming that people know everything. So in the end what you're trying to do is tell people the most important thing that happened, but do it when the writing's going well, and God knows, I don't always do it well. You do it with a degree of weight and grace that brings someone into the story and gives them a sense that it's important. That's the ideal, anyway.

Do you have to get your lead just right or do you have to just be on target, as opposed to hitting the bull's-eye, before you can move forward?

I think you can move forward, but at the same time, I think like most journalists, we're all a little bit privately arrogant, and I'm always happiest when editors don't mess around with my copy. I try to send copy that's clean and that can go right into the paper. Sometimes on a breaking story there are elements from different places, Washington or something, and they have to maneuver them in. So lead stories are a kind of work in progress. You know you can change them for different editions. But I do try to write them as a complete text with a narrative pull if possible, and some logical progression from the beginning to the end.

You made reference to the fact that you would think about the lead all day. Can you tell me a little bit more about that? Are you rehearsing it? Are you looking for it? Are you searching for it?

Sometimes when you're in the middle of a big story, the daily story can seem like a penance because things keep shifting. As Milosevic was falling and the election was going on, the events were going on late into the night, so that you were never quite sure what your lead was going to be. You knew at some point you were going to have to sit down and do one, and you knew even if you did it badly, it would be on page one because it mattered. But this is where you really do want to get it right. I'm always writing two stories a day and sometimes, nicely enough, they were both on the front page. So you're thinking about that, too. What do you have and how do you want to parse it up? And what do you have that gives added value to the news story that makes it more than just a wire story, because you're there and you're writing for a newspaper that allows you a certain leeway? But also what do you have to add in terms of a feature or an analysis or a scene that would get lost in the main story?

So one of the things I think a lot about—and you know in the end you have to do this, editors can't do this for you—is how you divide up what you've seen and what you've heard and what you've talked to people about into stories that are ideally coherent and different, each of them compelling in its own way. There are certain stories you know you're going to write as soon as you've reported

them. I mean they're just obvious to you. And then the
lead story depends on what finally happens: You end up
writing it the very last thing when you're the most tired
because you can't really judge it. You may have ideas for
leads and they get simply overrun.

Overrun?

This so-called revolution happened on a Thursday, and
Milosevic resigned on the Friday, and on the Tuesday
and the Wednesday there had been a great drama at a
coal mine outside Belgrade where workers were on
strike. I'd gone down there for two days, and by the second day it was clear that the police were not going to
fight the strikers. And I remember writing a lead that appeared in the *International Herald Tribune* as I wrote it
but got a little altered in the *Times*, that said something
like if Vojislav Kostunica becomes president, it will be
because of what happened at this gritty coal mine today.
    And then the *Times* got *Times*-like and changed it to
"could" or something. They made it conditional. And I
thought, well, that's fine but I'm glad the *Tribune* ran it
as I wrote it because that's what happened. And then we
had this debate because, later that night when I got back
to Belgrade and was writing this, there was a news story
that the highest courts came down with a very mixed decision about the election. I had to write that as well as a
second story, and the *Times* was going to put that story
on the front page, and I argued that it was the mine story
that should be on the front page. And I think we looked
good because of that. Not because I was so prescient,
but because the editors listened, and I think that matters
tremendously. Even though in strict news terms perhaps
the court decision might have seemed more important,
the real story was what happened at the mine and the
paper went along with that. So that's where it works
very well. You end up doing two stories. One of them is
a traditional news story, but in fact the real news is in the
other story.

**You just reminded me that the deadline writing
strategy you're talking about is something that often
falls on the shoulders of sports writers.**

American Greg Lemond won the Tour de France bicycle race twice. And the second time he was behind a Frenchman on the last day, and through some amazing sprint he won by a matter of seconds. *Sports Illustrated* reported that the French sports writers were throwing down their notepads in disgust at the finish line, and most people thought it was an act of chauvinism because the Frenchman had lost. But it's actually because they had already written their leads and then had to rewrite the story.

In the end you've got to think about what's happening around you. I'll never forget Syd Schanberg who used to work for us and did this wonderful work in Cambodia. There was an Italian journalist named Tiziano Terzani who was with Schanberg during the American involvement in Cambodia, and Tiziano would say to Sydney, "Sydney, take your head out of your notebook and look around." And in the end I think that's really what you have to do. It's not just the news; it's what you think the news is.

When events pile on, they seem like a curse, but in the end, you're catching a rolling wave. But that's what a deadline is, right? You've got to capture where it is when you have to file it. But if you're lucky, you understand where it's going and can shape your story to account for what's *likely* to happen as well as what *has* happened.

That's well said. One of the things I try to tell all my students is that to write fast, it really helps if you can find your lead in the field rather than back in the office. Because if you find it in the field, you have the opportunity to get what you need to support it. Does this make sense to you?

Well, it does, and often on the way back from a place, I scribble a few paragraphs that I can refine and think about later. But it is helpful to get it down when it's really fresh in your head. First, because good journalism is tactile, and also it helps to have a few moments to think about all the things you've seen and heard, the people you've talked to, and what sticks in your head. The best way to do that is not by looking at your notebook. It's by thinking about what you've been through and what was the most interesting, most astonishing, most important thing that you heard. Then you can always go back to your notebook and find it. I tend to take a lot of notes because I never know what I'm going to end up using. But I also find the process a great aid to my memory. Oftentimes I find that when I stop and think about what I find most interesting, it was something I didn't really understand when I was writing things down.

So you didn't understand when you were writing the things down in your notebook, but upon reflection you begin to understand. As you think, are you scribbling some ideas to yourself?

I'm mostly thinking to myself—in a car on the way back—about what was most striking. Very often it wasn't the thing that struck me as I was just jotting things down quickly or just taking notes. So that's why I often take a lot of notes, because I can then go back and find what, upon reflection, seems most striking or interesting or compelling.

Do you have a protocol for going through your notebook and highlighting anything you know you're going to use?

It's taken me a long time just to be able to read my own handwriting. That I can now do. You know, you develop your own little codes. On newswriting you tend to deal with a fairly concrete number of pages in your notebook. So it's not so hard. But I've been a grateful fan of the Post-it® note because then you can stick them all over your notebook pages when you go to find something.

So you index your notes?

I wouldn't say "index" them. When I go over them, I will use a different ink and then sometimes will use Post-it® notes to remind myself of what is on a particular page so I can find things. I tend to use big notebooks and I get a lot of stuff in them.

It's consoling to writers who read this that at some point you can reduce your reporting to Post-it® notes and spiral notebooks.

Well, you know what's in front of you and you know whether you've done it well or not. I've written a lot of stories, and I tend to know when I finish them whether they're good or bad.

How do you know? What would be a definition? What would be some of the words you would use to describe a story that you think was good?

Well, if it has the right cadence, if it has some grace notes, some color. If it's got a good kicker, if it catches the moment, if it has good quotes. I like to write with a lot of quotes. I like letting people speak in my stories. I don't know. I mean, it's so hard to tell, but I think in general everybody knows when they've written something well or badly.

Do you know a kicker when you hear it or see it? Or do you have to find it?

Usually you know it. I mean you don't always use it because it doesn't always work. I tend not to do much rewriting, particularly on deadline. I tend to type cleanly and I know how to spell. Sometimes you don't have room for the kicker, or it doesn't fit the story you end up writing, but very often if it's really in your mind, you move toward it quite consciously because you know before you start that that's how you want to end.

That's the destination, so you've got to get yourself from here to there.

I often have an idea that this is the lead and this is the end and this is where I roughly want to be in the middle. Everything else, I don't tend to worry too much about.

Is it fair to say that you know or you can see the global structure of the piece, the big architecture, before you start writing?

Only in the sense that you have an idea of a beginning, an idea of a middle, and an idea of an end. Journalists are a little formulaic. One hopes to stretch the formula, but at some point news stories are news stories. So you want to write them well, but there are certain things your stories need and they're unavoidable. They need leads and they need explanatory paragraphs—particularly in American journalism, we pretend everybody's an idiot so you have to explain everything, every time—and there's a way of doing that gracefully. And you've got to have some quotes, and you've got to back up what you're saying. But I think you can also—particularly in the heat of an important moment when the paper's really with you—push it, too. You can be a little more interpretive, you can write as well as you can. But in the heat of a big story, a paper like mine lets you write as well as you can more often than it does during ordinary moments.

I want to talk about the stories more directly. One of the things that impresses me is that it seems as if you're omnipresent. You not only see the things that are happening before your own eyes, but there are things being announced on television. Can you tell me how that magic is worked?

I don't know if there's much magic to it. I mean there's a lot of running around, you know? Oftentimes you can be a little lazy, and there are the news wires, and you can kind of poke around the wires and report a little bit and write it your own way. But not when this sort of thing is happening. You just can't do it. There's no time. You need to be ahead of the wires. You need to see things in real time. That's more exciting. So in these days you're running around all afternoon, and here you have the benefit of the six-hour time difference from Belgrade to New York, which the European paper doesn't have, and so you can spend all day running around or you can go to the mine and then you can come back and catch up with the news and watch the news on television and also when Milosevic breaks in to give a live speech, you're there for that, too. The great advantage is having colleagues: If you are out somewhere and you miss something, you can catch up with it. You have friends and you talk to them, particularly when it's in a different language that I only imperfectly understand. You are reliant on local translators and local journalists and local people. They can say, look, this happened on the news tonight and so that's really part of it. But what I loved about covering the war in Serbia and Kosovo last year is that you don't pay attention to what anyone else is doing. I mean I never cared what *The Washington Post* was doing or the *Los Angeles Times* was doing or what the wires were doing. It was all right in front of you. I mean it was liberating and also very satisfying.

You were an eyewitness. That's the most powerful kind of reporting.

Absolutely. Then, of course, you can write eyewitness material very badly. You can overwrite it and you can be dull about it and you can write with clichés, or you can try to write it so you actually bring it home to people. That's something I hope one learns to do. You need to care about the impact of your writing. There are lots of ways to describe blown-up bodies, and I've always felt a kind of discretion and understatement with strong quotes is much more powerful. And so I've always tried to write that way.

Does this sound like a guideline that other writers might think about—that where there is inherent drama, the temptation to overwrite is great, and must be resisted?

Yes. The writer should get out of the way. The writer's always there, the reporter's always there, you're in the middle of an event. That's when Tiziano's advice is very good: Get your eyes out of your notebook and look around. What does the air smell like and what's the color of the charred flesh? Listen to what people are *not* telling you. Let them speak. Don't interrupt them. Let them fill the silence. Sometimes the best quotes come when someone you're talking to is made uncomfortable by silence.

One of the things that impressed me about these sto-

**ries, and it's obviously the result of strategic think-
ing and writing, is that in the Kolubara mine story
there are moments when I'm actually experiencing
things vicariously. I'm seeing what you saw.**

Good.

**Such as "A bus full of protesters moved slowly
through the crowd and, almost gently, shoved aside a
police van blocking the bridge. The crowd surged
forward; the police moved aside, looking sheepish.
Some protesters gave them apples and clapped them
on their shoulders." But at other times you stopped
the narrative and moved the camera—I'm using
metaphors here—back from the action to see something larger or to understand something. So you're
zooming in and out from narrative to explanation or
narrative to background. Does this seem true to
what you try to do? Am I reading too much into it?**

I think this is right. It's not always conscious. You know
when you're writing a story that you want to bring people where you are, otherwise there's no point in being
there. Not everybody's where you are, so that you have
a kind of precious treasure that you want to get across to
people. At the same time you really have to let people
know why you're there and why it matters in the context
of the larger story that you're doing, the one that's been
going on for weeks. I mean it began with the Kosovo
war, it began with Bosnia, it began with the secretary of
state thinking she understood the Balkans. So all these
things are part of the story. But how one moves from
paragraph to paragraph, I couldn't tell you.

You discover that through the writing?

Yeah. You write a story to pull the reader through and
get done what needs to be done. I do think of a good
news story as somehow—the word "didactic" sounds
wrong, but there is something didactic about it. You're
showing people, but you also have to put what you're
showing into a context and in some sense you have to
do that for people who haven't been paying attention.

So is it fair to say that part of what you're trying to do is help people experience something and then part of what you're trying to do is to help them understand something?

Oh, yes. And I think one needs to do both in the same piece. That's really one of the great burdens. At least for a good newspaper you have the room to do both, and if your editors trust you, you have the leeway to write it pretty much as you'd like and what you see in the story is what you bring to the table as well as what you know.

In addition to keeping your eyes open, being there, gaining access, using your powers of observation, you're also bringing in some other things. You make reference to a story about the place where the miners went on strike.

This place was an important historic place. There was an important battle there, and there had been a play written about this place and what had happened there, and I thought it worked well with the events of the day because what had happened there mattered very much. So for the second time in this century, this place would be very important for serving history.

And where did that come from? How did you know that?

I brought it to the table because I had called local friends and was talking to them about what I'd seen and the importance of the day at the mine, and one of them brought this up and so I grabbed it.

David Von Drehle once said that when he knows he has to write on deadline quickly, he gets a little scared and the more scared he gets, the more prepared he gets. He's saying that he tries to store up his reservoir with knowledge and understanding as much as he can ahead of time so that when he hits the ground running, he'll bring something to the story that he's going to be able to use. Does that make any sense to you?

Well, it does. One of the reasons I took this job was to watch Milosevic fall. I had spent most of the previous year in Serbia and Kosovo because of the war. I got to know a lot of people and I had access to things that most journalists didn't because they weren't there. And I worked very hard to keep up access to Serbia, even after the war.

Like all Balkan places, you need to find people in the government you can call when you're being held up at the airport by the police and who will say to somebody, "It's okay, let him in." They know that you're not on their side, but on some level they make a judgment that you're at least going to try to get their point of view across in a relatively straight way. And so I was there through a lot of this when other people had trouble getting in, and I got there to cover this election which was September 23.

So you cashed in on the equity of that experience?

Yes, and I arrived in Serbia at the end of August to cover this election on September 23 partly because I knew it'd be better to get in early and also because I knew it was going to be important, and that in a free vote Milosevic would lose. I tried to get that across in the paper, and we were one of the few papers who took the election seriously. But it's because I'd been there for six weeks— that's what I was also bringing to the table.

Now I want to talk briefly about some technical aspects of the writing, if I may. Let me start with vocabulary. One of the things that interests me is that these stories contain words that are in most people's working vocabulary but that tend not to find their way into news stories. Words like "gritty" and "wafted" and "wrested." Those are some interesting words in a single sentence. Is this something you're conscious of, encouraged by your editors?

I try to write as well as I can, and people disagree about what good writing is. The problem with news stories is you're always skating on the edge of cliché. And the only way to avoid it sometimes is through original language or metaphor or cadence or something. I don't want to write a news story that reads like every other news story if I can help it. But a good news story has to do certain things that we're all agreed upon, and a lead news story has to be pretty declarative. I mean you can't start a lead news story with a vignette—at least not in my paper. But you try to be a little surprising and bring people face to face with what is there and to recognize that you're not a TV camera but you can appeal to people's senses of sight and smell and sound, and that description matters.

The other thing I notice about this story—and I want to see how much of this is you and how much of this is *The New York Times*—is that these sentences are so filled up that they barely hold together. That's a compliment.

I think that's me, actually.

There's a kind of lead that doesn't work. People call it a "suitcase lead" where you cram everything in and if it doesn't close, you sit on it until it closes. But yours doesn't work that way. Yours holds the reader right to the end.

Sometimes I tend to try to cram in too much, but it's important to me that the sentences parse. I think sometimes it's good in an important story to slow the reader down. To say to the reader, this matters and this is interesting and this may be worth putting down the coffee cup for a second and reading it. I mean certainly that was the way I felt about a lot of the war coverage.

Another thing that you do technically: Even when you have these longer leads that contain a lot, they seem to arrive at an important place. In journalism, most writers think about the beginnings of sentences and leads as being points of emphasis. But you know that the period is where things tend to come together, where the sentence resolves itself. Is that fair?

I think it is fair. I've been doing this a certain amount of time. I read a lot of fiction. I like writing. I think about writing. I don't always do it as well as I would like, but it matters to me. Writing well matters to me, and I think it matters to my newspaper, and sometimes we, like all newspapers, print writing we think is good that I think is bad. It happens, right? That's overwritten or calls too much attention to itself as opposed to what it's describing. But we're telling stories. They're true stories, but we owe it to readers to try to pull them in and pull them along, and what works in narrative works in journalism, too.

The Virgin Islands
Daily⊕News
A Pulitzer Prize-winning newspaper

Darrin Mortenson

Finalist, Deadline Reporting

Darrin Mortenson came to *The Virgin Islands Daily News* in January 2000 to lead the development of the paper's coverage of the growing local Hispanic population. Relatively new to newspaper reporting, Mortenson, 33, joined *The Daily News* after earning a master's degree at the University of Arizona. He is a veteran of the U.S. Army and has worked and traveled extensively in Latin America.

His writing experience includes monitoring political news in South America, translating news articles, and writing synopses of events for the Foreign Broadcast Information Service. He also wrote for the U.S. State Department in Nicaragua, as well as for the Nature Conservancy and the University of Arizona on U.S.-Mexico border issues. His awards include the National Headliner Award for a news series and the Society of Professional Journalists Sigma Delta Chi Award for non-deadline writing.

In reporting on the Navy's efforts to thwart an aquatic protest off the coast of Vieques, Puerto Rico, Mortenson takes readers through a tense, high-speed cat-and-mouse game with high political stakes fueled by the passions of ordinary people.

Navy unleashes force
on protesters

JUNE 28, 2000

VIEQUES, Puerto Rico—Two Navy boats crashed into reefs and ran aground while pursuing five local fishing boats just after sunrise Tuesday in waters within the Navy's bombing-range impact zone. Two Marines were injured in the accident.

The Navy has denied that the boats ran aground and instead has said the fishermen attacked the vessels.

Navy spokesman Lt. Jeff Gordon told reporters at midday Tuesday that the five fishing boats entered the waters of the range and surrounded a Navy vessel, which he said was having mechanical problems. He said the fishermen pelted the two shield-wielding Marines with 12-inch-long metal bars, injuring both servicemen in the neck and chest.

The Navy report differs markedly from what the local fishermen experienced and from what *The Daily News* reporter, the only journalist accompanying the fishermen, observed.

Gordon recounted the Navy's version of events to *The Daily News* based on a videotape taken from a Navy helicopter that had hovered over the fishing boats. He said the Navy will turn over the tape to the FBI for investigation.

"I haven't actually viewed it personally. I was briefed on its content. But I have no doubts about what it contains," Gordon said.

The dramatic, high-speed boat chase in the early daylight occurred just hours after approximately 150 protesters had infiltrated, on foot, the Navy's restricted bombing range. The protesters entered the range in the dark at numerous points along a four-mile-long fence-line.

Many who penetrated the range by land were arrested immediately, but protesters who keep watch at the range gate said a number were still on the range when the Navy resumed bombing about 9 a.m.

One of those still on the range was a protester that

The Daily News reporter had seen being dropped off by a fishing boat and going into the range from the water.

Tuesday afternoon, Gordon said that 164 people had been arrested and taken to Roosevelt Roads Naval Station on the main island of Puerto Rico to be processed.

Protesters said that Tuesday's incursion into the range by land and water was an attempt to test the willingness of the Navy to risk injuring or killing Puerto Ricans to sustain the Navy's first military exercises in more than 14 months.

As reports of Tuesday's boat chase and the Navy boat groundings began circulating around midday, Vieques residents celebrated what they viewed as a successful mission—eluding the most powerful Navy in the world—but said they were saddened by the Navy's accusation that the fishermen had used violence.

"It just shows they completely disregard the safety of people of Vieques," said Robert Rabin, leader of the Committee for the Rescue and Development of Vieques. "The fact that they would lie about it is nothing new. The people of Vieques have experienced one-half century of lies and deceit."

Tuesday's boat chase began shortly after five small fishing boats quietly launched, under the cover of pre-dawn darkness, from the southern port of Esperanza. Their mission was to block the Navy from bombing and to drop off a small group of protesters on beaches they had occupied for more than a year before the Navy forced them off the range in May.

The tiny fishing armada moved eastward into open water, plunging through 4-foot and 5-foot swells. Heavy spray pelted the crews, and a strong headwind nearly flipped the light boats as they bounced over and through the swells and raced on.

The rising sun gradually illuminated their destination: a series of southeastern points and beaches below the Navy observation post where civilian worker David Sanes was accidentally killed by errant bombs on April 19, 1999.

In the lead boat was Fishermen Association leader and veteran anti-Navy protester Carlos Zenon, accompanied by *The Daily News*.

At approximately 5:30 a.m. a small, inflatable Navy

boat and a 30-foot federal patrol boat—a whaler marked "Harbor Patrol"—intercepted the fishing boats at high speed.

No one on the fishing boats had seen them coming.

Faster than the fishermen's small boats, the patrol boat, crewed by two Marines, raced ahead with its blue lights flashing and made zigzagging sweeps to slow the fishing boats and cut them off when they tried to escape.

The smaller of the two military boats charged at the fishing boats from the left and then from the right, nearly ramming them and forcing them to turn sideways into the swells and risk capsizing.

Using well-orchestrated interdiction maneuvers, the patrol boat broke up the fishermen's formation while the two-man inflatable trapped the slowest of the fishing boats by cutting it off from the others.

Zenon's boat and two other craft carrying his sons Pedro, Cacimar and Yabureibo, turned to give assistance to the trapped boat. The fifth fishing boat headed around a point and out of sight, to drop off a protester on the beach.

The Zenon boats bolted toward the shallow, reef-filled waters, which most of the fishermen have sailed all their lives—often in the dark. The patrol boat followed the fishermen. A Navy helicopter joined the chase, swooping about 12 feet over the fishermen's heads and nearly swamping their small craft with heavy spray.

Just after 6 a.m., the two military boats and four fishing boats had reached the shallow turquoise waters of Bahia Allende, a bay in the middle of the Navy's bombing impact zone.

Clearly visible on the long, horseshoe-shaped Carrucho beach, about 20 Marines in brown T-shirts stood about 50 feet apart, guarding the white, bomb-littered sands against a landing by protesters.

"Watch this," Carlos Zenon said as he saw a fishing boat and the patrol boat pass dangerously close to each other—no farther than five feet apart. As the fishermen and the two Marines aboard the patrol boat exchanged one-fingered salutations, the patrol boat jolted to a halt.

With the wild smiles of underdogs, the fishermen cheered as the patrol boat sat perched atop the jagged coral and rocks of Cayo Conejo—Rabbit Reef.

Laughing, wrinkling his dark leathery face with a wide, satisfied smile, Zenon told *The Daily News*, "This is how we did it in '78—only then we had 30 or 40 boats. They need to read their history." Zenon was referring to the intensive protest period when he led armadas of fishing boats against Navy warships off the Vieques coast.

As the grounded patrol boat languished on the reef, maneuvering continued out in the bay, where the Navy helicopter controlled the action.

To conserve gasoline, the three Zenon boats halted temporarily in various spots, trying to stall until the slow boat that had been cut off from them earlier could join them.

They took turns being chased by the low-flying helicopter. The fishermen believed the helicopter would not jeopardize one of the Navy's own boats with the same blast of spray it was inflicting on them with the churning of the chopper blades, so they also took turns taking shelter close to the grounded patrol boat where they could frantically bail water.

When finally the fishing boat that had gone around the point rejoined them and the slow boat that had been cut off from them was within sight and shouting distance, the armada began moving out of the impact zone.

Once again, a military patrol boat appeared and intercepted them, then attempted to impede their return to Esperanza.

As the new patrol boat chased the fleeing fishing boats—cutting them off while the helicopter flew just above them and pelted them with spray—the fishermen sped toward Cayo Gracioso, a shallow reef barely visible on the choppy horizon.

Within minutes, the second patrol boat fell victim to the same ploy as the first: When it accelerated to pursue one of the fishing boats, it stopped suddenly in its path.

Four of the fishing boats were able to speed away and wait about a quarter-mile ahead while the fifth boat caught up to the formation. Fishermen on the boat closest to the patrol boat said they saw it strike the reef of Cayo Gracioso at full sped, then tilt to one side.

"With all their technology, all their money, they can't

drive a damned boat," one of the fishermen shouted to Carlos Zenon.

Zenon waved for the other four to form a tight victory formation, and they slowly made their way back to Esperanza.

As they approached the port, Zenon turned and told *The Daily News*: "This is very important, very important. Tell this to the people of St. Croix. Tell this to everybody."

Tuesday afternoon, Navy spokesman Gordon said that all of the occupants of the fishing boats were "involved in an assault on federal officers in the charge of their duties."

He said they would be charged accordingly.

Gordon said he could neither confirm nor deny that the two boats had grounded themselves on reefs.

A picture snapped by one of the fishermen during the chase and later distributed around the island clearly showed one of the patrol boats stuck on the rocks, and another snapshot showed the helicopter nearly on top of one of the fishermen's boats, inundating it with spray.

Lessons Learned

BY DARRIN MORTENSON

Reporters are witnesses. We are trusted by the public to observe events as they occur and immediately record them for history and all who were not there.

Writing "Navy Unleashes Force on Protesters," I learned what happens when a reporter is the only disinterested witness on the scene who can tell the story. I inadvertently participated in the events of the story, and to many people my experience of the event became almost as important as the event itself. I was suddenly thrust into the story, testing my professional mettle, my skills, my editors' confidence, and my readers' trust.

I stood subject to scrutiny from everyone. It was my word against the Navy's. I was the only reporter to go with the fishermen that morning. Most Puerto Rican reporters were prohibited by their news organizations from entering the range to document the civil disobedience.

That prohibition effectively allowed the Navy to deny claims that protesters were on the range, because the only non-Navy witnesses were protesters themselves.

As a reporter for *The Virgin Islands Daily News*—the main daily published from the island of St. Thomas, which is 20 miles east of Vieques—I was considered neither part of the Puerto Rican press nor part of the national media. Navy spokesmen and protest leaders alike occasionally questioned my reasons for so aggressively covering events on Vieques. Knowing my reports might not reach all of Puerto Rico or the mainland, they sometimes resisted giving me information or access, although there are as many Viequenses living in the U.S. Virgin Islands as on Vieques itself.

When the first Navy patrol boat appeared out of nowhere and began its high-speed pursuit, I realized I was fully committed to the story with no way to stand back and observe from afar. At that point, I couldn't be neutral. I was on a fisherman's boat trespassing in Navy waters, and my fate was inextricably linked to theirs.

Prior to debarking that morning, I had dogged the

Navy for its perspective on the protests. I repeatedly asked permission to ride along on one of the Navy patrols—either on land, sea, or air—to tell the story through the experiences and words of the sailors who were just doing their jobs by keeping the protesters off of the range.

Navy officials denied me permission every time, citing liability as the reason. After the dangerous chase, however, I realized that if the Navy had allowed a witness, its spokesmen would not have been able to tell the lies that the Navy later told that day.

When I returned from the sea that morning, I had not yet heard the Navy's version, and I had a clear story in my head and notes. I got to work immediately while my adrenaline was still pumping and while I could still smell the smoke from the overworked motors and feel the sting of salt in my eyes.

A Latin America correspondent for a major Florida daily who was staying at my hotel was the first to report the Navy's version. I was floored when he told me that the Navy was reporting that fishermen had viciously attacked sailors.

At first I was worried that I had missed the real story somewhere else, and that my story about two Navy vessels grounding on shallow reefs would fade quietly behind a story about fishermen attacking sailors with metal bars. I immediately drove to the northern port to check out my theory, but after asking around and finding that no boats from the Isabel Segunda docks had ventured into Navy waters that morning, I realized that I had not missed the story; instead, the Navy spokesmen were making up one of their own. I called back to my editors and told them what I was up against: that it was going to be my word against the U.S. Navy.

I then called the Navy spokesman myself. Before I played my hand, I asked him what happened in waters near the bombing zone on Vieques earlier that morning. He described exactly what he had already told local reporters and would later tell the national media. The spokesman even denied that any boats had run aground, not knowing that photos of the wrecks had been taken.

When I then revealed that I had been on one of the boats, the spokesman immediately threatened me with legal action, saying that I was involved in criminal acts including an attack against U.S. servicemen in the line of duty. He said that the Navy turned over a videotape of the events to the FBI and that the evidence would be used against me and the fishermen in federal court. The FBI acknowledged that it received the tape and also warned me that I was a witness to a federal crime and that I should not talk about it.

That was out of the question, however. As news spread that I was on one of the boats and had a very different story to tell, editors from several Puerto Rican and national media organizations began ringing my hotel to verify it. One especially important call was from the Caribbean desk editor of a national wire service. After I recounted the events, she made it clear she intended to report only the Navy's version. That is what the nation read the next day, and that is what audiences around the world heard after the wire story was picked up by national networks.

While I worked on my story on Vieques, my editors and fellow reporters back on St. Thomas were scrambling to make sure we had the story nailed down from every angle. They looked at every word, every line of my story to extract me from the story as much as possible. Their biggest fear was not that I had gotten it wrong, but that we were onto a big story that would die silently right there in the Virgin Islands, never making it to the mainland audiences and policy-makers. Since the wire service obviously was not going to pick it up, *The Daily News* staff devised a last-minute plan to get our paper delivered to Puerto Rico the next morning. A group of Puerto Rican university students translated the story into Spanish and distributed it along with digital photos taken of the grounded Navy boats, gradually giving the story a larger audience in Puerto Rico and the U.S. mainland.

Although the Navy continues to stick to its version of the story, the videotape has never been used against the fishermen and no charges were ever brought against my paper or any of the boats' other occupants.

Many Puerto Ricans point to the story as a record of what really happened and as proof of the Navy's long history of controlling information about Vieques. The truth made it into print by the slimmest of chances only because one reporter out of dozens was there to bear witness and tell the story.

BEST NEWSPAPER WRITING 2001
PHOTOJOURNALISM
C O M M U N I T Y   S E R V I C E

Poynter.

Promoting better journalism through community focus

The move to honor photojournalists in the annual American Society of Newspaper Editors competition was several years in the making and had many champions. Led by *Austin American-Statesman* editor Rich Oppel, ASNE's president in 2000-2001, the Community Service Photojournalism Award became a reality this year.

Poynter's Kenny Irby, one of the early advocates for recognizing the storytellers who carry cameras, joined an advisory group of seven high-powered photojournalism leaders in early 2000. That group included Sonya Doctorian, then with the *St. Petersburg Times*, Steve Rice of the Minneapolis *Star-Tribune*, Marcia Prouse of *The Register* (Orange County, Calif.), Mike Smith of *The New York Times*, and Patty Reksten of *The Oregonian* (Portland, Ore.). Oppel appointed Zach Ryall, the *American-Statesman*'s director of photography, and AME Sharon Roberts to lead the way in defining the new award category.

Newspapers of the 21st century face many challenges as journalists strive to produce content that is relevant to readers' lives. The Community Service Photojournalism Award, fully presented on the CD-ROM included with this edition of *Best Newspaper Writing,* honors photographic reporting that offers compelling visual content and has had such an impact on the community that changes came about as a result.

ASNE has chosen to make the advancement of community service photography one of its primary goals, acknowledging the fact that words and pictures go hand in hand as newspapers work to inform, educate, and strengthen their communities.

John Beale
Community Photojournalism

John Beale, 43, joined the *Pittsburgh Post-Gazette* as a staff photographer in 1984. He graduated from Indiana University of Pennsylvania with a bachelor's degree in journalism.

Beale's community journalism has been recognized nationally with awards from Sigma Delta Chi, National Press Photographers Association Pictures of the Year, Society of News Design, National Headliners, Clarion Awards, and the Inland Press Association. In 2000 he was awarded the Pennsylvania Newspaper Association's Distinguished Visual Award, the organization's highest honor for photojournalists, artists, and illustrators. His last project, which he also wrote, chronicled his 23-year friendship with a reclusive woodsman.

John Beale and his wife, Janis, a child-care consultant for the Head Start program in suburban Pittsburgh, have two children and reside in Plum Boro, Pa.

Beale's photo storytelling in "Our Community of Faith" takes readers into intimate, meaningful moments of prayer, meditation, and ordinary life. His photos rise well above simple voyeurism and provide a new angle on Pittsburgh's racial, ethnic, and spiritual diversity.

Our Community of Faith

A river of spirituality flows through Western Pennsylvania. A current of every hue, it courses through the pew, the pulpit, the sanctuary, the temple, the mosque, and the synagogue.

Staff photographer John Beale spent more than a year documenting the faithful as they gathered in groups large and small, rich and poor, to pay homage to Jehovah, Allah, the Creator, Jesus, the Supreme Being, and God (or gods). The resulting pictures show how faith—and the moral compass it provides—unites our community in a surprisingly diverse display of ritual, prayer, and celebration.

The region owes its religious diversity in large part to the state it sits in. Founded by William Penn as a haven for Quakers and others persecuted because of their beliefs, Pennsylvania has a long, proud legacy of religious tolerance.

Documented here are images that illuminate Beale's discoveries. The project was an eye-opener in the newsroom, and judging from the strong positive response from readers, in the community as well.

—Adapted from the Pittsburgh Post-
Gazette ASNE contest entry

A conversation with
John Beale

KENNY IRBY: Why faith, and what was the genesis of the story?

JOHN BEALE: On my commute to work each day, I passed several temples and a half-dozen other churches. The ride serves as a reminder of the diversity of religions in this area. It also has prompted me to make some observations: We think we know a lot about the people who make up our community. We probably know what our neighbors do for a living. We likely know their preferences in sports and music, and we may even be able to predict what their kids will order on a visit to the local McDonald's. But how much do we know about the religion that forms the basis of their moral compass?

How did you get your arms around such a huge project?

There were a couple of things that I knew. We had talked about religion a lot in the newsroom, and with my 17 years of experience at the paper, I knew that faith was important in the community. I took some photos in December 1999 focused on Hanukkah and Christmas expressions of faith and worked on the project off and on for a little over a year. Then there were the two shootings: one at two fast-food restaurants and the other that included shots fired in a Jewish temple, another temple being defaced, shots fired at an Indian grocery store, an African American wounded at a karate school, and shots fired into a Chinese restaurant. I was involved in the news coverage of both shootings. The combination of these events reaffirmed the value of the story I wanted to report. Religion is the fabric of the community, and the shootings increased the news value.

Was the newspaper receptive to your original idea?

I always wanted to communicate just how diverse our

community was. I find it effective and easier if you come up with some images. It's stronger than trying to describe the images. When (director of photography) Curt Chandler asked me to write something down, it was just a huge list of picture possibilities. Curt's reaction to the list was that "this would look like a book," and not a newspaper project. I never envisioned it as a book, but rather as a section of the paper. My vision initially was to focus intimately on a year in faith, with holidays and celebrations.

Once you had your focus, how did you research your subject and make contacts?

I started searching phone books and the Internet to find out what faiths are represented in our circulation area. I met with Ann Rodgers-Melnick, the *Post-Gazette*'s religion writer, in early 2000 and got information about demographics. She was very helpful and had a huge Rolodex that we started with. The photo story was proposed to editors as an overview of religion and religious worship in western Pennsylvania and beyond. For a few months, I attended church services and events, searching for photographs that were representative of those religions. I asked picture editors to steer any religion photo assignments in my direction.

What were your reporting and editing relationships like?

The most defining moment in the concept came after the second shooting. I met with Lynn Johnson, who serves as a part-time photo coach for the *Post-Gazette*, and turned over the body of my work to her for review. Her first reaction was for me to quit gathering photos. Instead, she encouraged me to get past the obvious; to make more meaningful images that show the lives of the people, not just the services and ceremonies they attend.

From that point on, I moved to a level of emotional images and not just surface, literal images. Then Ervin Dyer, my writing colleague, started to work with me. I had a great relationship with him. His work really enhanced the photos. His pull-quote work was excellent.

What was it like to deal with so many forms of worship?

All along, I didn't know what to expect. As with politics, people have strong feelings about their beliefs. From May to October, I visited at least one church, synagogue, mosque, or temple each weekend. Before visiting a faith, I did research online and in a booklet about world religions. Sometimes I called in advance, but most often I showed up unannounced.

It seemed that when people knew I was coming, they

would try to steer me to a specific person or encourage me to come on a specific day. I tried to arrive early and stay until well after the service. On some occasions I was invited to stay for a luncheon or dinner, which I always did.

What was the greatest challenge you faced while covering this story?

One thing I learned is that if you show up at somebody's church on Sunday morning and you want to talk about their faith, you had better be prepared to talk about your own. But I did not want this story to be about me. I liked the Hindu group's spring festival. They felt that the emphasis should be on God and not the people. I tried to focus not only on deities and religious articles, but more on the people.

One of the most challenging things about this assignment was that they did not know me and I was making cold calls. While working on this project I made more than 70 visits, going to as many as four services on a Sunday. At times, people were skeptical of what I was doing. On several occasions I was asked to address the congregations about my intentions. If people didn't want to be photographed, I honored their requests.

What surprised you about this project as you journeyed from faith to faith?

Most of all, the openness was overwhelming. For me, several surprising things took place, from experiencing the Korean Assembly of God service, to visiting the Amish father trying to live by the graven image command of Deuteronomy, who said to me, "You can go about your business." In the end, I think that the mission of most of these churches and ministries is to welcome people and strangers like me.

It's rare to have this type of opportunity. What were some of the lessons you learned?

■ Contacts are the key to great access and making connections. A chat with the director of a Presbyterian camp got me the name of a Mennonite woman in another county. The e-mails to the Mennonite woman put me in touch with an Amish family in Northern Maryland (two hours away) who agreed to be photographed. A Methodist minister introduced me to the leader of a Sikh temple, and a call to a local charismatic church offered information on a prison ministry a few counties away.

■ Don't cling to early expectations and preconceived ideas. Remain open to possibilities. I was really struck by the range of opinions. I asked people to refer me, and most of the time they referred me to people who worship and praised the way they did. But they did lead me to other valuable subjects.

■ I was concerned about invading people's privacy. I tried to use lenses that made me an observer of—and not a part of—the service. There were times to be a fly on the wall and a conscious observer.

Looking back, how has the project affected you and your paper?

We intended for this project to promote understanding and not to offend. We went out of our way to be fair and to represent the community. Within our newsroom, some felt that there should be a more proportionate number of images reflecting the Catholics and Protestants, thus a better representation of the paper's demographics.

I hoped that the photographs were able to promote understanding about just how diverse Pittsburgh's "Yunzers" (the local slang for "folks") are. Most photographers would like to believe their craft can help make a difference, if only in a small way. I was not looking to change the world. But I do hope that my photographs have the power to promote understanding. When we offer readers images that make them think and feel, we prompt them to see their community in a whole new way.

The Beacon News

Leigh Daughtridge

Finalist, Photojournalism

Leigh Daughtridge is a free-lance photo-journalist based in North Carolina. She attended the University of North Carolina at Chapel Hill, receiving her bachelor's degree in journalism and mass communications in 1994. Daughtridge won the prestigious New York Festivals and International CINDY Competition in 1997 for co-producing the multimedia documentary "Into Africa."

Daughtridge is a consummate photojournalist who is passionate about documenting the stories of the people in her community with intimacy and dignity. Her work documenting Northern Illinois senior citizens' struggles to pay for prescription medication was recognized in the 2000 Pictures of the Year competition in which she won or shared in six awards.

Daughtridge was a staff photographer at *The Beacon News* in Aurora, Ill., when she did this project.

Paying the Price: Seniors and Prescription Drugs

Many older Americans who take prescription drugs are increasingly in terrible shape, both financially and physically. Drug prices keep rising and Medicare, the health safety net for the elderly, often won't pay.

So what do these seniors do to survive? Some risk damaging their health by cutting their dosages to stretch the medicine. Others skimp on nourishment or even live without heat in order to pay for their prescriptions.

Staff photographer Leigh Daughtridge initiated this story, did long hours of research to give it focus, and found all of the subjects who opened their lives to readers.

The three-day series garnered an empathetic response from newly educated readers. Several generous monetary donations and even donations of medicine came in to help the people who were profiled. In one case, the story of a heart transplant patient and the trials she faced with the medical bureaucracy was sent on to the Mended Hearts organization for national distribution.

—Adapted from The Beacon News ASNE contest entry

Photographers' Workshop

BY KENNY IRBY

A fresh eye can illuminate a subject and make it more real and compelling. Leigh Daughtridge brought that eye, a dedication to teamwork, and a probing journalistic spirit to the story of how rising medical prices were affecting some of those who couldn't afford to pay.

The result was "Paying the Price: Seniors and Prescription Drugs," a three-part series that helped Chicago-area readers see the faces of people whose issue was the talk of the presidential campaign.

"It was a project that I always wanted to do," said Daughtridge. She conceived of the idea after *The Beacon News* published a project at the end of 1999 on local centurions, a body of work that Daughtridge says "received the most positive feedback in Copley history."

To prepare for covering the complex system of healthcare confronting senior citizens, Daughtridge studied up on health insurance, Medicaid, and Social Security. In January 2000 she attended a conference on aging in St. Charles, Ill. Then she identified her "unit," the team of people with whom she'd partner for the project. The team included Loup Langton, then director of photography for Copley Chicago Newspapers; Mike Davis, who was director of photography for Sun Publications; and Denise Crosby, Sunday editor and reporter for *The Beacon News*.

"I took most of my own quotes," and Crosby confirmed them and used them in the stories, Daughtridge says. The resulting photographic work, delivered powerfully with reporter Nell Smith's stories, raised awareness, which is the essence of community service photojournalism.

Almost immediately, the newsroom felt the series' impact on its readers. Letters, money, and calls came in large numbers. Daughtridge was most touched by the words of Jackie Gates, one of the story subjects. After people sent her money to handle her medical needs, Gates told Daughtridge, "Thanks a million for putting

God in my hands. I cannot see, but I could hear the kindness in your heart."

Daughtridge came away with six tips for those hoping to accomplish what she's done:

■ **The photographer's voice should be heeded in newsrooms.** Daughtridge thoroughly researched this project idea and created a huge community resource list.

■ **Be open to change and tight editing.** Initially, the project was conceived as a smaller undertaking. Daughtridge said she was struck by the size of the problem and realized that the story couldn't be told using just one person. "How people adapted was so varied that we had to tell several people's stories," she said.

■ **Look for feeling and emotion in the photographic storytelling.** "In talking with my editors, I needed to focus on fewer people who covered a wide enough range. We were trying to capture a feeling, rather than a literal image of someone taking medication. These people were alone, and I wanted to capture that feeling. And I wanted to be true and honest to the subject."

■ **There is no replacement for research.** "Do your homework, I'm still learning, and no one is going to help you with it," Daughtridge said. "You need to do the research and make those first phone calls, get out of your car, and be proactive. Check your idea out. Start the ball rolling. This will also build self-confidence."

■ **Don't get caught up in the "black-and-white vs. color" debate.** "I would have liked to have had black and white on the cover for continuity, but readers were not debating that issue," Daughtridge said. "Journalists get too caught up in the aesthetics."

■ **Honest relationships make the most compelling images.** "I took the time to be with the people and not take pictures," Daughtridge said. "I was just being with them. Working for the people in the community, you must make a human connection first. I feel that openness and fair reporting allowed me to reveal the true situation."

Thom Scott

Finalist, Photojournalism

Thom Scott has been a staff photographer for *The Times-Picayune* since 1994. He lives in LaPlace, La., and works in the newspaper's River Parishes Bureau, covering the communities of the Mississippi River corridor.

Scott studied photojournalism at Loyola University and was photo editor of the *Loyola Maroon* in 1989. He was an intern at *Tulsa World* in 1989 and *The Times-Picayune* in 1990. He worked as a contract photographer for Agence-France-Presse from 1990 to 1994, covering David Duke's 1991 bid for governor of Louisiana and the aftermath of Hurricane Andrew in 1992.

As a staff photographer for *The Times-Picayune,* Scott has documented the daily life of the River Parishes and its vanishing Cajun culture. He has also documented coastal restoration efforts along Louisiana's shorelines, historic preservation of African-American structures, and the 1997 volcano eruption on the island of Montserrat.

Scott and *Times-Picayune* staff writer John McQuaid worked on the "Unwelcome Neighbors" series for a year and a half, examining the issue of environmental justice and the disproportionate share of pollution, declining property values, and diminishing quality of life suffered by poor and minority communities living near polluting industries.

Unwelcome Neighbors

Across Louisiana, small communities sit uneasily in the shadows of sprawling refineries, chemical plants, incinerators, dumps, and rail cars carrying hazardous waste. The toxic substances they emit don't have to travel far to reach their neighbors. The danger of an industrial accident is as close as their back yards.

Many of these communities are poor and their populations almost entirely African American, founded by former slaves who worked the sugar plantations that once lined the Mississippi River. At a time when black citizens were shut out of government, heavy industry moved in and bought up the agricultural lands that lay fallow.

Today, most residents aren't employed by industry, yet they bear the brunt of industry's downside: pollution, health risks, odors, noise, falling property values, and a declining quality of life. "Unwelcome Neighbors" documents the long-ignored problems of these historic neighborhoods. Their plight also represents a new eruption of the divisions of race and class in American society. The series set out to explore what that means.

—Adapted from The Times-Picayune ASNE contest entry

Photographers' Workshop

BY KENNY IRBY

Thom Scott lives and works in the River Parishes, a collection of small municipalities between New Orleans and Baton Rouge that are home to marshland and Cajuns. The area is also home to a number of industrial plants that pump so many pollutants into the air and water that the region is known as "cancer alley."

Scott used his connections in the community to get started on the project.

"I live in a neighborhood where everyone else is a factory worker," he said. "I gained the trust of people. Much of my life while assigned to this project felt a lot like Erin Brockovich," the crusading legal assistant made famous in Hollywood by Julia Roberts.

In the "Unwelcome Neighbors" package, strong photojournalism made difficult-to-tell stories soar. Scott's photographs, in concert with reporter John McQuaid's stories, illustrated the price of being poor and living next to industrial and chemical plants, refineries, and dumps. It was a story many didn't know—or didn't want to know. But Scott helped drive it home by digging deep to deliver an understanding of both the people and the peril.

For the photojournalist, Scott's work provides a number of opportunities to think, learn, and practice:

■ This was an abstract and complicated project that lasted two years. How do you think the photojournalist developed his relationships with the subjects? When do you think he began visual documentation? How long do you think it would take?

■ The degree of difficulty is heightened by the lack of cooperation by the factory ownership and potential reluctance of the workers and citizens. What can the photographer do to gain access and capture more natural, authentic moments?

■ Visual variety is a very critical concept when creating a master narrative of this size. By the nature of the story there are lots of distance issues to be addressed and, thus, many juxtaposition scenarios being photographed. How could the newspaper better visually report such events?

■ Lens choices, camera location, and lighting are key elements of photographic presentation. What observations can you make about those elements from this project?

■ *The Times-Picayune* is a large organization with lots of editors. What role should editors play in making the final selection of photographs?

■ Re-edit the package of six selected images on the CD-ROM to tighten the visual narrative of the story. How are the storytelling qualities of tone, impact, and pacing affected by your choices?

■ Consider any crops that you might make to the images to maximize their impact.

■ So many of the story subjects have been photographed in isolation, rather than in relation to other subjects or the industrial plants, which are crucial to the story. What do you suggest as a strategy to increase the intimacy of the overall story?

Annual Bibliography

BY DAVID SHEDDEN

WRITING AND REPORTING BOOKS 2000

Bragg, Rick. *Somebody Told Me*. Tuscaloosa, Ala.: University of Alabama Press, 2000.

Brooks, Brian S., George Kennedy, Daryl R. Moen, and Don Ranly. *Telling the Story: Writing for Print, Broadcast and Online Media*. New York: Bedford/St. Martins, 2000.

Brooks, Brian S., James Pinson, and Jean Gaddy Wilson. *Working with Words: A Handbook for Media Writers and Editors*. New York: Bedford/St. Martins, 2000.

Bunton, Kristie, et al. *Writing Across the Media*. New York: Bedford/St. Martins, 2000.

Chance, Jean, and William McKeen, eds. *Literary Journalism: A Reader*. Belmont, Calif.: Wadsworth Publishing, 2000.

Clark, Roy Peter, and Christopher Scanlan, eds. *America's Best Newspaper Writing*. New York: Bedford/St. Martins, 2000.

Davis, Foster, and Karen F. Dunlap. *The Effective Editor: How to Lead Your Staff to Better Writing and Better Teamwork*. St. Petersburg, Fla.: The Poynter Institute, 2000.

Friedlander, Edward Jay, and John Lee. *Feature Writing for Newspapers and Magazines*. New York: Longman, 2000.

Friend, Cecilia, Don Challenger, and Katherine McAdams. *Contemporary Editing*. Lincolnwood, Ill.: NTC/Contemporary Publishing Group, 2000.

Goldstein, Norm, ed. *The Associated Press Stylebook and Briefing on Media Law.* Cambridge, Mass.: Perseus Publishing, 2000.

Greenwald, Marilyn, and Joseph Bernt, eds. *The Big Chill: Investigative Reporting in the Current Media Environment.* Ames, Iowa: Iowa State University Press, 2000.

Hartsock, John C. *A History of American Literary Journalism.* Amherst, Mass.: University of Massachusetts Press, 2000.

Itule, Bruce D., and Douglas A. Anderson. *News Writing and Reporting for Today's Media*, 5th ed. Boston: McGraw-Hill, 2000.

LaRocque, Paula. *Championship Writing.* Oak Park, Ill.: Marion Street Press, 2000.

Leiter, Kelly, Julian Harriss, and Stanley Johnson. *The Complete Reporter.* Boston: Allyn and Bacon, 2000.

Murray, Donald M. *Writing to Deadline: The Journalist at Work.* Portsmouth, N.H.: Heinemann, 2000.

Rich, Carole. *Writing and Reporting the News: A Coaching Method.* Belmont, Calif.: Wadsworth Publishing, 2000.

Scanlan, Christopher, ed. *Best Newspaper Writing 2000.* St. Petersburg, Fla.: The Poynter Institute, 2000.

Stepp, Carl Sessions. *Writing as Craft and Magic.* Lincolnwood, Ill.: NTC/Contemporary Publishing Group, 2000.

Thompson, Terri, ed. *Writing About Business.* New York: Columbia University Press, 2000.

Williams, Eesha. *Grassroots Journalism.* New York: Apex Press, 2000.

CLASSICS

Atchity, Kenneth. *A Writer's Time: A Guide to the Creative Process, From Vision Through Revision.* New York: W.W. Norton & Co., 1996.

Bell, Madison Smartt. *Narrative Design: A Writer's Guide to Structure.* New York: W.W. Norton & Co., 1997.

Berg, A. Scott. *Max Perkins: Editor of Genius.* New York: Berkley Publishing Group, 1997.

Bernstein, Theodore M. *The Careful Writer: A Modern Guide to English Usage.* New York: Atheneum Books for Young Readers, 1977.

Blundell, William E. *The Art and Craft of Feature Writing: The Wall Street Journal Guide.* New York: Dutton/Plume, 1988.

Brady, John. *The Craft of Interviewing.* New York: Knopf, 1977.

Brande, Dorothea. *Becoming a Writer.* Los Angeles: J.P. Tarcher; Boston: distributed by Putnam Publishing, reprint of 1934 edition, 1981.

Brown, Karen, Roy Peter Clark, Don Fry, and Christopher Scanlan, eds. *Best Newspaper Writing.* St. Petersburg, Fla.: The Poynter Institute. Published annually since 1979.

Cappon, Rene J. *The Associated Press Guide to News Writing.* Paramus, N.J.: Prentice Hall, 1991.

Clark, Roy Peter. *Free to Write: A Journalist Teaches Young Writers.* Westport, Conn.: Heinemann, 1995.

Clark, Roy Peter, and Don Fry. *Coaching Writers: The Essential Guide for Editors and Reporters.* New York: St. Martin's Press, 1992.

Dillard, Annie. *The Writing Life.* New York: Harper-Collins, 1999.

Elbow, Peter. *Writing With Power: Techniques for*

Mastering the Writing Process. 2nd ed. New York: Oxford University Press, 1998.

Follett, Wilson. *Modern American Usage: A Guide.* Revised by Erik Wensberg. New York: Hill & Wang, 1998.

Franklin, Jon. *Writing for Story: Craft Secrets of Dramatic Nonfiction by a Two-Time Pulitzer Prize Winner.* New York: Dutton/Plume, 1994.

Garlock, David. *Pulitzer Prize Feature Stories.* Ames, Iowa: Iowa State University Press, 1998.

Goldstein, Norm, ed. *AP Stylebook.* Cambridge, Mass.: Perseus Publishing, 2000.

Gross, Gerald, ed. *Editors on Editing: What Writers Should Know About What Editors Do.* New York: Grove/Atlantic, 1993.

Harrington, Walt. *Intimate Journalism: The Art and Craft of Reporting Everyday Life.* Thousand Oaks, Calif.: Sage, 1997.

Hugo, Richard. *The Triggering Town: Lectures & Essays on Poetry & Writing.* New York: Norton, 1992.

Kerrane, Kevin, and Ben Yagoda. *The Art of Fact.* New York: Scribner, 1997.

Klement, Alice, and Carolyn Matalene, eds. *Telling Stories, Taking Risks. Journalism Writing at the Century's Edge.* Belmont, Calif.: Wadsworth Publishing, 1998.

McPhee, John. *The John McPhee Reader.* William L. Howard, ed. New York: Farrar, Straus & Giroux, 1990.

Mencher, Melvin. *News Reporting and Writing.* 8th ed. New York: McGraw-Hill, 1999.

Metzler, Ken. *Creative Interviewing: The Writer's Guide to Gathering Information by Asking Questions.* 3rd ed. Needham Heights, Mass.: Allyn & Bacon, 1996.

Mitford, Jessica. *Poison Penmanship: The Gentle Art of Muckraking*. New York: Farrar, Straus & Giroux, 1988.

Murray, Donald. *Shoptalk: Learning to Write With Writers*. Portsmouth, N.H.: Boynton/Cook, 1990.

Perry, Susan K. *Writing in Flow: Keys to Enhanced Creativity*. Cincinnati: Writer's Digest Books, 1999.

Plimpton, George, ed. *Writers at Work: The Paris Review Interviews*. Series. New York: Viking, 1992.

Ross, Lillian. *Reporting*. New York: Simon & Schuster Trade, 1984.

Scanlan, Christopher, ed. *How I Wrote the Story*. Providence Journal Company, 1986.

Sims, Norman, ed. *Literary Journalism in the Twentieth Century*. New York: Oxford University Press, 1990.

Stafford, William, and Donald Hall, eds. *Writing the Australian Crawl: View on the Writer's Vocation*. Ann Arbor, Mich.: University of Michigan Press, 1978.

Stewart, James B. *Follow the Story: How to Write Successful Nonfiction*. New York: Simon and Schuster, 1998.

Strunk, William, Jr., and E.B. White. *The Elements of Style*. 4th ed. Needham Heights, Mass.: Allyn & Bacon, 1999.

Talese, Gay. *Fame & Obscurity*. New York: Ivy Books, 1971.

Wardlow, Elwood M., ed. *Effective Writing and Editing: A Guidebook for Newspapers*. Reston, Va.: American Press Institute, 1985.

White, E.B. *Essays of E.B. White*. New York: HarperCollins, 1999.

Zinsser, William. *On Writing Well: An Informal Guide to Writing Nonfiction*. 6th ed. New York: Harper Collins, 1998.

— *Writing to Learn*. Reading, Mass.: Addison-Wesley Educational Publishers, 1997.

— *Speaking of Journalism: 12 Writers and Editors Talk About Their Work*. New York: HarperCollins, 1994.

ARTICLES 2000

Bugeja, Michael. "Bust a Plagiarist in 30 Minutes or Less." *Quill* (April 2000): 44.

Bunton, Kristie, Stacey Frank Kanihan, and Mark Neuzil. "Improving Media Writing with Ability Groups." *Journalism & Mass Communication Educator* (Summer 2000): 60-72.

Clark, Roy Peter, and Tom Rosenstiel. "Do Not Add. Do Not Deceive." *Columbia Journalism Review* (January/February 2000): 36.

Freedman, Wayne. "Keep It Simple." *Communicator* (June 2000): 42.

Fry, Don. "Aiming for Better Instead of 'Not Bad.'" *The American Editor* (October 2000): 23.

Henriques, Diana B. "Business Reporting: Behind the Curve." *Columbia Journalism Review* (November/December 2000): 18-21.

Izard, Ralph. "Gotcha Journalism." *The IRE Journal* (September/October 2000): 6-7, 33.

Kallan, Richard A. "Teaching Journalistic Cogency with 55-Word Short Stories." *Journalism & Mass Communication Educator* (Autumn 2000): 81-88.

Kirtz, Bill. "Narrative Writing." *Presstime* (February 2000): 38-40.

Larocque, Paula. "Doing Right By Your Writers." *Quill* (April 2000): 45.

McGrath, Kevin. "Try Taking a Walk in Your Writers'

Shoes." *The American Editor* (July 2000): 19.

Mitchell, Amy, and Tom Rosenstiel. "Don't Touch That Quote." *Columbia Journalism Review* (January/February 2000): 34-36.

Reagan, Brad. "Details, Details." *American Journalism Review* (January/February 2000): 50-55.

Schultz, Ellen. "Interview Both Sides of Mouth." *The IRE Journal* (May/June 2000) 10-11.

Spear, Michael. "Lingually Challenged." *Editor & Publisher* (July 10, 2000): 17.

Strupp, Joe. "Policing Plagiarism." *Editor & Publisher* (August 7, 2000): 18-22.

Weinberg, Steve. "Making the Writing Golden." *The IRE Journal* (September/October 2000): 16-17.

Wissner-Gross, Elizabeth. "Writing with Wings Won't Fly." *Quill* (March 2000): 36.

The Journalist's Toolbox

Here is a selective index that loosely follows the writing process developed by longtime columnist and author Don Murray. It will take you to the places in this book where journalists shine a light on the tools and techniques that helped make their work stand out.

Left to right: Dr. Roy Peter Clark, the Institute's senior scholar; *Best Newspaper Writing* editor Keith Woods of the ethics faculty; Christopher Scanlan, writing programs group leader; Aly Colón, editor of the *Poynter Report* and a member of the ethics faculty; Institute Dean Dr. Karen Dunlap; and Kenny Irby, visual journalism group leader.

The Poynter Experience

The Poynter Institute, which opened in 1975 as the Modern Media Institute, is a school dedicated to improving the quality of journalism in the United States and wherever the press is free. Each year, the Institute hosts more than 50 professional development seminars, three programs for college students, seminars for college professors, a year-round journalism program for Tampa Bay high school students, and summer writing camps for the area's elementary and middle-school children and their teachers.

The Institute coordinates and supports the National Writers' Workshops each spring, joining more than 5,000 writers in a celebration of the craft. Poynter also has established connections around the globe with training institutes and the journalists they serve.

Through its publications and website, Poynter.org, the Institute connects journalists to their peers and promotes the notion that ethics is synonymous with excellence in all areas of the craft. Poynter faculty speak at journalism conventions, advise working journalists, consult in news organizations, and provide commentary on the everyday issues arising in the industry. Six members of the faculty, pictured above, played a part in producing this book.

Poynter.

About the CD-ROM

Included with this volume is a CD-ROM containing all the images in the winner's and finalists' entry packages. Each package is presented with the photo captions and stories that accompanied the images. In addition, we have included full-screen images that are printable at low resolution for classroom projects and an interactive cropping tool that allows for re-editing of selected photos.

The CD project was created by Poynter design intern Jen Ogborn using Macromedia Flash. Designer/producer Larry Larsen of Poynter's publications department created the interactive cropping tool and assisted with technological aspects of the project. Kenny Irby of the Poynter faculty worked closely with editor Keith Woods and publications director Billie M. Keirstead on the presentation of the Community Service Photojournalism category.

The CD will run on both Windows and Macintosh platforms. It is designed to open at full-screen size. The Flash Player and Adobe Acrobat Reader applications are included on the CD.

We hope you find this CD useful and enjoyable.